Synesthesia

SYNESTHESIA

Perspectives from Cognitive Neuroscience

Edited by
Lynn C. Robertson and Noam Sagiv

2005

OXFORD
UNIVERSITY PRESS

Oxford   New York
Auckland   Bangkok   Buenos Aires   Cape Town   Chennai
Dar es Salaam   Delhi   Hong Kong   Istanbul   Karachi   Kolkata
Kuala Lumpur   Madrid   Melbourne   Mexico City   Mumbai   Nairobi
São Paulo   Shanghai   Taipei   Tokyo   Toronto

Copyright © 2005 by Oxford University Press, Inc.

Published by Oxford University Press, Inc.
198 Madison Avenue, New York, New York, 10016

www.oup.com

Oxford is a registered trademark of Oxford University Press

Library of Congress Cataloging-in-Publication Data
Synesthesia : perspectives from cognitive neuroscience /
edited by Lynn C. Robertson and Noam Sagiv.
p.   cm.
Includes bibliographical references and index.
ISBN 0-19-516623-X
1. Synesthesia.   2. Senses and sensation.   3. Cognitive neuroscience.
I. Robertson, Lynn C.   II. Sagiv, Noam.
QP435 .S96 2004
152'.1'89—dc22   2003019496

9   8   7   6   5   4   3   2   1

Printed in the United States of America
on acid-free paper

Dedicated to the memory of Jeffrey Alan Gray

Preface

S ynesthesia is not a new phenomenon. It has appeared in the written literature for centuries and has piqued the interests of many critical thinkers, including philosophers, psychologists, psychiatrists, and theologians. It has now entered a different scope with new interest in the phenomenon by scientists who study vision, cognition, and the brain. Unlike color generated from light waves or odors by chemical compounds, the color, smell, sound, taste, or touch that is experienced by synesthetes is generated by a physical stimulus that for most of us is entirely unconnected to its induced sensation (e.g., middle C invokes the sight of red; the shape of a ball invokes the taste of chocolate). For instance, while wavelength induces color perception in both synesthetes and nonsynesthetes alike, additional inducers such as particular shapes or sounds can also evoke color perception for synesthetes.

The varied manifestations of synesthesia and its phenomenological nature have made it difficult to verify and study, and skeptics abound. However, recent scientific evidence, as indicated by the contributions to this volume, demonstrates that the question of its existence as a "real" phenomenon is no longer in doubt (although its prevalence remains debatable). Neuroscientific evidence using functional imaging techniques have shown brain activation in predicted areas that corresponds to synesthetes reported experiences (e.g., synesthetic color activates areas that normally respond to color). Behavioral data have also substantiated the perceptual reality of synesthesia, and cognitive scientists have moved on to questions such as how synesthesia might be related to perceptual learning, perceptual organization, and attention and to what degree the mechanisms that support synesthesia operate similarly to or differently from mechanisms underlying non-synesthetic experience.

This volume reflects the diversity, yet relative normality, of synesthesia. The seeds for this book were planted when one of us (N.S.) and Edward Hubbard (then graduate students at the University of California, Berkeley, and the University of California, San Diego, respectively) organized a symposium entitled "The Cognitive Neuroscience of Synesthesia" for a meeting of the Cognitive Neuroscience Society held in San Francisco in the spring of 2002. Some of the authors in the current volume presented papers at this symposium (Merikle, Ramachandran, Rich, Robertson), and the response suggested that the time was right for an edited book on the subject. We added chapters by synesthetes themselves as well as by others who have studied the cognitive and/or neural basis of synesthesia. Since synesthesia is so often induced by letters, words, or sounds that we learn to identify during childhood, we added contributions from researchers who have considered how synesthesia develops. Other contributors have studied how closely synesthesia resembles subjective experience we typically call normal and how awareness might contribute to the synesthetic experience.

Synesthesia may have even wider implications. It might represent a basic mechanism for the development of metaphors, but in a more vivid form, and it may even question fundamental assumptions about the nature of biological systems. The chapters in this volume were solicited to stimulate thought across a wide spectrum, from computations that could produce such phenomenon to philosophical questions of functionalism that the existence of synesthesia may question. Synesthesia has become more than a curiosity. It is a phenomenon for a larger part of the population than we originally thought. It is a real perceptual experience induced by stimulation that does not induce a similar experience for most individuals. It is a scientific puzzle, and it raises fundamental issues about how it may relate to "normal" perception and how brains must work such that they can generate such phenomena.

We have far too many people to thank than can be listed here, including synesthetes themselves for making this fascinating topic one that has attracted the public interest. This volume would not have been possible without the extensive help provided by the people at Oxford University Press. A special thanks goes to Catharine Carlin, who embraced the idea for this volume with enthusiasm.

Contents

Contributors

Randolph Blake
Department of Psychology/Vanderbilt
    Vision Research Center
Vanderbilt University
Nashville, TN 37203

Sean Day
Department of English and
    Journalism
Trident Technical College
Charleston, SC 29406

Mike J. Dixon
Department of Psychology
University of Waterloo
200 University Ave.
West Waterloo, Ontario N2L 3G1
Canada

Jeffrey Gray
PO Box 78, Department of Psychology
Institute of Psychiatry
De Crespigny Park
London SE5 8AF, UK

Edward M. Hubbard
Center for Brain and Cognition 0109
University of California–San Diego
La Jolla, CA 92093-0109

Chai-Youn Kim
Department of Psychology/Vanderbilt
    Vision Research Center
Vanderbilt University
Nashville, TN 37203

Lawrence E. Marks
John B. Pierce Laboratory
290 Congress Avenue
New Haven, CT 06519
    and
Department of Epidemiology and
    Public Health and Department of
    Psychology
Yale University School of Medicine
New Haven, CT 06520

René Marois
Department of Psychology/Vanderbilt
    Vision Research Center
Vanderbilt University
Nashville, TN 37203

Jason B. Mattingley
Cognitive Neuroscience Laboratory
School of Behavioural Science
University of Melbourne
Victoria 3010, Australia

Daphne Maurer
Department of Psychology
McMaster University
128 Main St. West
Hamilton, Ontario L8S 4L8, Canada

Philip M. Merikle
Department of Psychology
University of Waterloo
Waterloo, Ontario N2L 3G1, Canada

Catherine J. Mondloch
Department of Psychology
McMaster University
128 Main St. West
Hamilton, Ontario L8S 4L8, Canada

Thomas J. Palmeri
Department of Psychology
Vanderbilt University
Nashville, TN 37203

Eric C. Odgaard
John B. Pierce Laboratory
290 Congress Avenue
New Haven, CT 06519
  and
Department of Epidemiology and
  Public Health, and Department of
  Psychology
Yale University School of Medicine
New Haven, CT 06520

V. S. Ramachandran
Center for Brain and Cognition 0109
University of California–San Diego
La Jolla, CA 92093-0109

Anina N. Rich
Cognitive Neuroscience Laboratory
School of Behavioural Science
University of Melbourne
Victoria 3010, Australia

Lynn C. Robertson
Medical Research Service 151
Veterans Administration
150 Muir Road
Martinez, CA 94553
  and
Department of Psychology
University of California
Berkeley, CA 94720

Noam Sagiv
Department of Psychology
University of California
Berkeley, CA 94720

Daniel Smilek
Department of Psychology
University of Waterloo
Waterloo, Ontario N2L 3G1, Canada

Anne Treisman
Department of Psychology
Princeton University
Princeton, NJ 08544-1010

Christopher W. Tyler
Smith-Kettlewell Eye Research
  Institute
2318 Fillmore St.
San Francisco, CA 94115

Part I

General Overview

1

Synesthesia in Perspective

Noam Sagiv

What Is Synesthesia?

The term synesthesia (Greek; syn = together, aesthesia = sensation) has been used to describe a wide variety of phenomena. Most commonly, it is used to denote a condition in which stimulation in one sensory modality also gives rise to an experience in a different modality. However, conditions involving different qualities within one modality (e.g., when the sight of letter shapes evokes color) are labeled synesthesia as well. Phenomena of this sort have also been reported in patients with eye disease, brain damage, and migraines (e.g., Armel & Ramachandran, 1999; Jacobs, Karpik, Bozian & Gothgen, 1981; Podoll & Robinson, 2002). Similar experiences have been reported in healthy individuals using mescaline and LSD (e.g., Hartman & Hollister, 1963) or drinking psychoactive brews such as Ayahuasca (Shanon, 2002). Divine intervention has also been invoked as a possible trigger of synesthesia.[1]

Yet some otherwise normal, healthy individuals experience synesthesia regularly under normal conditions.[2] This is known as developmental synesthesia (for discussion, see Harrison & Baron Cohen, 1997; for synesthetes' perspectives, see Duffy, 2001). Developmental synesthesia is the focus of this and most other chapters in this book, and I shall simply refer to it as synesthesia. An attempt to estimate the proportion of synesthetes in the general population suggests that synesthesia is experienced by at least 0.05% of the population (Baron-Cohen, 1996). Given that this value was based on responses to a newspaper ad (that some synesthete readers may have chosen not to respond to), many suspect that the condition may be much more common.[3] In these cases, synesthetic perception has been experienced as early as individuals can remember, although some forms, such as

3

chromatic-graphemic synesthesia, may only be formed upon acquisition of certain skills—in this case, reading.

Synesthesia-producing stimuli ("inducers") do not appear to be restricted to simple sensory input. In fact, typically inducers are meaningful units such as letters, digits, words, or the tonality of a piece of music. In some cases, however, more abstract concepts may serve as inducers. These include time units, personalities, and more.

The resulting synesthetic experience ("concurrent" as it has been labeled by Grossenbacher & Lovelace, 2001) is not limited to color. In visual synesthesia, these often also include textures and shapes, either moving or stationary, and may have spatial or topographic qualities. Other senses may be involved (e.g., Ward & Simner, 2003) as well as affective properties and a variety of non-sensory experiences. Letters or objects may have a gender (that may or may not match the grammatical gender). Alternatively, digits may have moods or otherwise come to life in forms such as: "4 is gloomy," "7 is rambunctious." In sum, both inducers and concurrents span a wide range of qualities. For more detailed discussion of specific types of synesthesia, see Day (this volume). Cytowic (2002), who adheres to a limbic theory of synesthesia, places great emphasis on the affective qualities that accompany synesthesia. These include conviction and a sense of certitude, such as an "ah-ha" experience when seeing A, for example, in the "right" shade of red. The synesthetic experience can be very satisfying at times or induce disgust when there is a mismatch. Quite a few synesthetes have strong feelings about color choices or other choices involving inducers (e.g., spelling of names; Day, this volume). However, it would be fair to say that this is one of the least explored aspects of synesthesia, and we should probably expect considerable variability here too.

Nonsynesthetes may show some consistent patterns of certain cross-sensory associations (e.g., brightness and pitch; Marks 1974) or use synesthetic metaphors such as "sharp cheese" (Ramachandran & Hubbard, 2001). Such phenomena are sometimes viewed as pseudo-synesthesia (Harrison & Baron-Cohen, 1997) and indeed they lack the hallmark of synesthesia—a concrete experience. Nevertheless, as Ramachandran and Hubbard recently suggested (2001), the study of synesthesia may be instrumental in understanding the neural basis of metaphors. We have yet to explore whether similar mechanisms underlie developmental synesthesia and related phenomena, from metaphors and cross-sensory correspondences to synesthesia resulting from nerve injury or psychoactive substances.

Diagnosing Synesthesia

Although it has been described for decades, synesthesia has only recently gained a legitimate status among scientists, and since it not life threatening, it is unlikely to receive attention from most clinicians any time soon. Being the diverse collection of phenomena that it is, it may not come as a shock that there is no standardized test that determines whether one is a synesthete or not. Furthermore, as a private, subjective experience, it simply cannot be shared with an independent observer. This does not put synesthesia research in much worse position than perception research in general, as perception is, after all, a private, subjective experience.

Fortunately, we are able to obtain indirect, objective measures of synesthesia in many cases by looking at a subject's performance, typically involving a congruency manipulation between certain stimulus quality and a similar synesthetic quality evoked by another stimulus. For example, synesthetes may be slower to judge the color of a green square if preceded by a letter that they experience as red than by another letter experienced as green (e.g., Mattingley et al., 2001).

Beyond this, a number of criteria are generally expected to be met in synesthesia (Cytowic, 1997). First, the report must be consistent across time. For example, when prompted months or even years later, without warning, a true chromatic-graphemic synesthete will report the same letter–color correspondence. We must also rule out that the report is neither due to a delusional state or drug use nor simply metaphorical speech. It must be present from childhood, involuntary, and vividly experienced, although not necessarily projected externally (Smilek & Dixon, 2002).

Recently, several studies emphasized the perceptual reality of synesthesia (Palmeri et al., 2002; Ramachandran & Hubbard, 2001), with the rationale of addressing skepticism dismissing synesthesia as "crazy talk" or metaphorical speech. However, if perceptual reality is taken as a requirement for synesthesia, some variants of synesthesia may fall between the cracks. It may become harder to defend these as real, although they resemble perceptual synesthesia in many respects and are very real for the person experiencing them.

Synesthesia and Its Place in Cognitive Science

In the context of cognitive science, understanding synesthesia involves not only documenting the phenomenon but also asking what it tells us about normal cognition. It should be clear by now that synesthesia touches many major aspects of human cognition: perception and attention, consciousness, memory and learning, language and thought, and, finally, development.

We often try to learn about normal cognition or brain function by examining flaws and deficits. This approach has taught us a great deal. However, there is much to be learned from positive phenomena like synesthesia, possession of exceptional talents and skills, as well as less desirable conditions such as hallucinatory syndromes.

How we view synesthesia is a rather different question. Is synesthesia good? Is it normal? These are some of the easy questions: Most of those who have synesthesia would not give it up and consider it a gift. Furthermore, synesthesia is normal for synesthetes. Not having synesthesia is as perplexing for synesthetes as synesthesia is for the rest of us. However, there is a more fundamental sense in which we may consider synesthesia to be normal or not. Cytowic (2002, p. 2) believes that synesthesia is "a normal brain process that is prematurely displayed to consciousness in a minority of individuals." Similarly, Shanon (2002, p. 338) sees synesthesia as a mode of operation that is "very basic to human cognition, but under normal conditions is not very apparent." Merleau-Ponty (1962) made similar statements half a century earlier. Marks' findings (e.g., 1974, 1987) suggest that at least some synesthetic correspondences do indeed manifest in non-synesthetes' performance, consistent with such views.

However, different views are prevalent. Synesthesia is often seen as representing a sort of dysfunction and described in terms such as "breakdown of modularity" (Baron-Cohen et al., 1993). There have been different ideas on what forms this breakdown of modularity might take. With the exception of dedifferentiation, these ideas assume cross-activation between otherwise normally developed modules, either via disinhibition of normally present connections or through abnormal connectivity (via horizontal connection or pathway convergence; Grossenbacher & Lovelace, 2001). Recent neuroimaging findings do support the idea that at least functional brain organization in synesthetes may be abnormal in yet another manner: the color module may have been split such that one submodule (left V4) subserves color perception derived from wavelength, while the other (right V4) subserves synesthetic color experience (Nunn et al., 2002). Although, to date, there is no direct demonstration of abnormal connectivity in synesthetes, it is widely accepted.

How do we reconcile such different views of synesthesia? For the most part, dysfunction theories have been concerned with identifying where the link is in the brain or what is different in synesthetes at the physiological levels, while remaining agnostic about the possibility that considerable cross-modal interaction goes on anyway. Some developmental theories of synesthesia posit that we may all have been synesthetes in the first few months of life (e.g., Maurer, 1997; Maurer & Mondloch, this volume). It remains to be seen whether most of us truly grow out of this mode of operation or whether it is still there, under the surface. One of the greater challenges remaining is to understand what determines synesthetic correspondences in predisposed individuals and to account for the apparently arbitrary nature of such correspondences.

Synesthesia also brings a message of diversity; reminding us that we do not all see the world the same way. Most people rarely stop to think about it. Communication between human beings depends on the assumption that there is somebody out there that is capable of thinking, feeling, and perceiving as we do (Meltzoff & Decety, 2003). But we really have no guaranty that our experiences are identical, and indeed they appear not to be. Furthermore, the markedly variable nature of different synesthetes' experiences (even for those whose synesthesia involves the same two senses) suggests that synesthesia may expose not only common cognitive processes but also individual differences (such as the extent to which one relies on verbal or spatial information).

Another central issue in cognitive science is the nature of mental representations. The idea that features, objects, concepts, events, goals, and actions are represented in the mind or brain is widely accepted. Such beliefs (in particular, assuming a medium of representations or viewing representations as entities) have been criticized even before the cognitive revolution (Wittgenstein, 1953; for a more recent synthesis of antirepresentationalist views, see Shanon, 1993). Synesthesia provides a basic demonstration of the problem. It reminds us that whatever is represented cannot merely be a copy of the corresponding object, event, and so on. In other words, the world as it is perceived should not be mistaken for a copy of the world as it is described by physics or biology (e.g., Merleau-Ponty, 1962).

Challenges in the Study of Synesthesia

We are almost ready to begin exploring recent advances and ideas in synesthesia research. But before we continue, let us consider some of the challenges and pitfalls we face.

As noted earlier, even when studying normal perception, we often seek to obtain objective measures of experience. What makes the study of synesthesia more challenging is the idiosyncratic nature of synesthetic experiences, including not only multiple types of synesthesia but also individual differences in both the specific mapping between the senses involved (e.g., color–letter correspondences in color-graphemic synesthesia) as well as remarkable variability of the nature of the experience (e.g., vividness, spatial extent, affective components). We must therefore apply caution before collapsing together data from different synesthetes (Smilek & Dixon, 2002).

It would be fair to say that we have only begun to chart the phenomenology of synesthesia, and much remains to be done. It should be obvious that this would be a crucial aspect of the study of synesthesia, but a detailed report of the phenomenology has not always been pursued. We should also bear in mind that commonly used labels may be ambiguous or not consistently applied, may fail to capture all aspects of the experience, or may otherwise be inadequate.[4]

Finally, Cytowic (e.g., 1997) observed that synesthetes, as a group, may have more than their share of left-handedness, mathematical deficiencies, spatial disorientation, right–left confusion, family history of dyslexia, and more. These observations, in addition to individual differences between synesthetes, have important implications for experimental design. Primarily, this calls for the use of within-subject designs to ensure that we can tell apart the effects of synesthesia per se from comorbid factors.

The study of the cognitive and neural bases of synesthesia is only in its infancy. We have very few answers and many more questions at this point. Application of converging methods—behavioral, electrophysiological, neuroimaging, developmental, and genetic—will undoubtedly increase our understanding of synesthesia. Finally, increased public awareness to synesthesia will help promote an open discussion on the varieties of this fascinating phenomenon.

Acknowledgments   I thank Guy Mayraz, who asked me in 1995 if I had heard about synesthesia, Lynn Robertson for encouraging me to pursue this line of research and for commenting on an earlier draft of this chapter, and Hubert Dreyfus and David Tsabar for helpful discussions.

Notes

1. "And all the people saw the thunderings, and the lightnings, and the noise of the trumpet, and the mountain smoking" (Exodus 20:18).

2. As a non-synesthete I feel a need to apologize here. Not having synesthesia will be referred to as "normal" throughout this book. It is normal at least in the sense that it is more common not to have synesthesia (or, as some might claim, not having realized you are a synesthete yet).

3. For example, synethesia may be more common among painters and musicians (Cytowic, 2002). Additionally, researchers in several laboratories also suspect that synesthetes tend to aggregate in universities. Anecdotally, we found 3 synesthetes among 170 students who recently took a cognitive neuroscience class at Berkeley.

4. For example, the term "chromatic-graphemic" was used by Baron-Cohen et al. (1993) to describe colored word synesthesia where color is largely determined by graphemic content (rather than phonemic content or a unique lexical parallel). Others have not always looked at the word level. The term has been used to describe the condition in which letters have individual colors, either when presented visually or regardless of the modality in which the stimulus was presented. Additionally, some have emphasized the fact that colors were largely determined by grapheme shape (e.g., 5 and S have similar colors), but this has not been found in all graphemic synesthetes. Further, not all chromatic-graphemic synesthetes

are alike. The spatial extent of the perceived color varies. Some project the colors externally, others do not. Additionally, the color may be projected on the letter surface or elsewhere.

References

Armel, K.C., & Ramachandran, V.S. (1999). Acquired synesthesia in retinitis pigmentosa. *Neurocase, 5(4)*, 293–296.

Baron-Cohen, S., Harrison, J., Goldstein, L.H., & Wyke, M. (1993). Coloured speech perception: Is synaesthesia what happens when modularity breaks down? *Perception, 22*, 419–426.

Cytowic, R. (1997). Synaesthesia: Phenomenology and neuropsychology. In S. Baron-Cohen & J.E. Harrison (Eds.), *Synaesthesia: Classic and contemporary readings* (pp. 17–39). Oxford: Blackwell.

Cytowic, R.E. (2002). *Synesthesia: A Union of the Senses.* (2nd ed.). New York: MIT Press.

Duffy, P.L. (2001). *Blue cats and chartreuse kittens: How synaesthetes color their world.* New York: Times Books.

Grossenbacher, P., & Lovelace, G. (2001). Mechanisms of synesthesia: Cognitive and physiological constraints. *Trends in Cognitive Sciences, 5*, 36–41.

Harrison, J.E., & Baron-Cohen, S. (1997). Synaesthesia: An introduction. In S. Baron-Cohen & J. Harrison (Eds.), *Synaesthesia: Classic and Contemporary Readings* (pp. 3–16). Oxford: Blackwell.

Hartman, A.M., & Hollister, L.E. (1963). Effect of mescaline, lysergic acid diethylamide and psilocybin on color perception. *Psychopharmacolgia, 4*, 441–451.

Jacobs, L., Karpik, A., Bozian, D., & Gothgen, S. (1981). Auditory-visual synesthesia: sound induced photisms. *Archives of Neurology, 38*, 211–216.

Marks, L.E. (1974). On associations of light and sound: The mediation of brightness, pitch, and loudness. *American Journal of Psychology, 87*, 173–188.

Marks, L.E. (1987). On cross-modal similarity: Auditory-visual interactions in speeded discrimination. *Journal of Experimental Psychology: Human Perception and Performance, 13*, 384–394.

Mattingley, J.B., Rich, A.N., Yelland, G., & Bradshaw, J.L. (2001). Unconscious priming eliminates automatic binding of colour and alphanumeric form in synaesthesia. *Nature, 410*, 580–582.

Maurer, D. (1997). Neonatal synaesthesia: Implications for the processing of speech and faces. In S. Baron-Cohen & J.E. Harrison (Eds.), *Synaesthesia: Classic and contemporary readings* (pp. 182–207). Oxford: Blackwell.

Meltzoff, A.N., & Decety, J. (2003). What imitation tells us about social cognition: A rapprochement between developmental psychology and cognitive neuroscience. *Philosophical Transactions of the Royal Society of London B, Biological Science, 358(1431)*, 491–500.

Merleau-Ponty, M. (1962). *Phenomenology of perception.* New York: Routledge & Kegan Paul.

Nunn, J.A., Gregory, L.J., Brammer, M., Williams, S.C.R., Parslow, D.M., Morgan, M.J., Morris, R.G., Bullmore, E.T., Baron-Cohen, S., & Gray, J.A. (2002).

Functional magnetic resonance imaging of synesthesia: Activation of V4/V8 by spoken words. *Nature Neuroscience, 5*, 371–375.

Palmeri, T.J., Blake, R., Marois, R., Flanery, M.A., & Whetsell, W. Jr. (2002). The perceptual reality of synesthetic colors. *Proceedings of the National Academy of Sciences USA 99(6)*, 4127–4131.

Podoll, K., & Robinson, D. (2002). Auditory-visual synaesthesia in a patient with basilar migraine. *Journal of Neurology, 249(4)*, 476–477.

Ramachandran, V.S., & Hubbard, E.M. (2001). Synaesthesia—A window into perception, thought and language. *Journal of Consciousness Studies, 8*, 3–34.

Shanon, B. (1982). Colour associates to semantic linear orders. *Psychological Research, 44*, 75–83.

Shanon, B. (1993). *The representational and the presentational: An essay on cognition and the study of mind.* London: Harvester-Wheatsheaf.

Shanon, B. (2002). *The antipodes of the mind: Charting the phenomenology of the ayahuasca experience.* Oxford: Oxford University Press.

Shanon, B. (2003). Three stories concerning synaesthesia: A commentary on the paper by Ramachandran and Hubbard. *Journal of Consciousness Studies, 10(3)*, 69–74.

Smilek, D., & Dixon, M.J. (2002). Towards a synergistic understanding of synaesthesia: Combining current experimental findings with synaesthetes' subjective descriptions. *Psyche* [on-line], *8*. Available: http://psyche.cs.monash.edu.au

Ward, J., & Simner, J. (2003). Lexical-gustatory synaesthesia: linguistic and conceptual factors. *Cognition, 89*, 237–261.

2

Some Demographic and Socio-cultural Aspects of Synesthesia

Sean Day

To me, the taste of beef is dark blue. The smell of almonds is pale orange. And when tenor saxophones play, the music looks like a floating, suspended coiling snake-ball of lit-up purple neon tubes.

I am a synesthete, and I study synesthesia. Synesthesia is not a disease, nor is it a deficit in most cases. So, from a synesthete's point of view, why would the study of synesthesia be important? In this chapter, I address this question from both my own experience and from what I have learned from communicating with well over 800 other synesthetes, over the course of more than 25 years, via e-mail, telephone, handwritten letters, and face-to-face conversations.

Over the years that I have been investigating synesthesia, I have heard others frequently refer to what benefits the study of synesthesia might throw upon other, serious and life-threatening disorders. Synesthesia appears to have some aspects in common with—and thus helps us to understand—such conditions as phantom limbs (see, e.g., Ramachandran & Blakeslee, 1998; Ramachandran & Hubbard, 2001b; Ramachandran & Rogers-Ramachandran, 1996). Correspondences I have received over the past 10 years also indicate that synesthesia may have some possible connections or associations with some forms of autism (Temple Grandin, for example, asserted this in personal communication to me on December 9, 1998), some types of epilepsy (see Cytowic, 2002), and migraines (see, e.g., Podoll & Robinson, 2002). These are unquestionably worthwhile causes to pursue for further research. However, I feel that one major reason for studying synesthesia frequently and persistently seems to be overlooked: There are a lot of synesthetes out there in the world who live with synesthesia—and with being a synesthete—all of their lives. It is a real phenomenon to them, as much as hearing ringing in one's ears is a real phenomenon for those who have tinnitus or as much as color vision is a real phenomenon for trichromats. The fact that a large number of individuals join sensations in a different way should not distract from its value as an area of scientific investigation.

Overview and Prevalence of Synesthesia

Synesthesia is the general name for two related sets (or "complexes") of cognitive states (see Baron-Cohen & Harrison, 1997; Cytowic, 1993, 2002; Day, 2001, 2003; Grossenbacher & Lovelace, 2001; Ramachandran & Hubbard, 2001a, 2001b). In the first set, "synesthesia proper," stimuli to one sense, such as smell, are involuntarily and simultaneously perceived as if by one or more other, additional senses, such as sight and/or hearing. For example, I have three types from this set of synesthesia: The sounds of musical instruments will make me see certain colors, each color specific and consistent with the particular instrument playing. I also have colored taste and smell sensations; for example, the taste of espresso coffee can make me see a pool of dark green, oily fluid about four feet away from me.

With the second form of synesthesia, which I call "cognitive" or "category synesthesia," certain sets of things which individual cultures teach us to put together and categorize in some specific way (like letters, numbers, or people's names) also get some kind of sensory addition, such as a smell, color, or flavor. The most common forms of cognitive synesthesia involve such things as colored written letter characters (graphemes), numbers, time units, and musical notes or keys. For example, the synesthete might see, about a foot or two before her (the majority of synesthetes, approximately 72%, are female), different colors for different spoken vowel and consonant sounds, or perceive numbers and letters, whether conceptualized or before her in print, as colored. A friend of mine always perceives the letter "a" as pink, "b" as blue, and "c" as green, no matter what color of ink they are printed with.

Synesthesia apparently has neurological aspects in regard to its causation, and it seems to be heritable, with one component (possibly a "trigger factor") perhaps passed down genetically as autosomal dominant. However, Bailey and Johnson (1997) propose X-linked dominance, with male lethality (see also Cytowic 2002, pp. 51–59, which lends support to this proposition). The percentage of the general human population which has synesthesia varies with the type involved; estimates run from 1 in 500 for basic types of cognitive synesthesia (colored graphemes or musical pitches), to 1 in 3,000 for more common forms of synesthesia proper (colored musical sounds or colored taste sensations), to 1 in 25,000 or more (1 in a couple million?) for people with rare (such as one synesthete I know of who synesthetically tastes things she touches) or multiple forms of synesthesia proper.

All forms of synesthesia are known for being quite idiosyncratic. No two people's sets of synesthetic associations are the same. However, there are a few trends among synesthetes; discovering such trends has been the focus of one of my major lines of research over the past 11 years. In 1991, I created an international e-mail forum for synesthetes, researchers of synesthesia, and all interested other parties, called The Synesthesia List (I have since come to regret the choice of name, but it has been around too long now to easily change). Over the past 10 years, I have studied cases of colored grapheme synesthesia in attempt to discern whether there are any trends. Approximately 27% of my current data comes from publications tracing all the way back to accounts such as that of Sachs (1812) and up to recent reports such as those mentioned by Cytowic (2002); the other 73% stems from my use of The Synesthesia List, personal letters and phone calls, and face-to-face interviews.

Establishing criteria for color selection was somewhat difficult. In the end, from trial and error with various methods attempted during interviews and correspondences, as well as from the influence of my background in an-thropology and ethnography, I settled upon Kay's (see Berlin and Kay, 1969; Kay, 1975; Kay and McDaniel, 1978) designation of 11 basic irreducible color terms for English (black, white, red, green, yellow, blue, brown, gray, orange, pink, and purple), and Crayola Crayons (those crayons having the exact same prementioned names/designations) for best example or focus of each of these colors. Ready worldwide availability of the crayons, their ease in transport and use, and the fact that most subjects were very familiar with them, often proved extremely useful in facilitating matters. (Besides that, what crayons lack in scientific rigor, they more than make up for in being fun—which is usually far more essential to most subjects, particularly adolescents—and certainly helps in assuring future participation in addi-tional interviews.)

For cases mentioned in the literature, most all listings of colors associated with letter graphemes given by the synesthetes used these 11 color desig-nations. For those cases I gathered myself, I asked the synesthete to try to classify things within the 11 categories, usually suggesting (and often using, in face-to-face interviews) Crayola Crayons as a guide. When a different color designation was used, it was usually fairly easy to place it as a subtype of one of the 11 given: for example, "tangerine" is a type of orange; "mint green" a type of green; and "cherry" a type of red. I used my own judgment on this, but based my judgment heavily on what category the synesthetes I worked with felt was most proper (e.g., while many used the term "navy," virtually all who did so then allowed that this was a type of blue). Some synesthetes mentioned more than one color for a particular letter; if two colors were mentioned, I scored each as 1/2 (0.5); if more than two colors were mentioned, I listed this as "extended" and excluded such from appropriate later calculations.

With 11 colors, if things were evenly distributed, that means that any particular letter (A, for example) would have one of these colors (red, for example) about 9.1% of the time. In my study, of 172 "colored letter" synesthetes, 43% perceive the letter A as red ($\chi^2 = 134.93$); of 123 synesthetes, 57% perceive the letter O as white ($\chi^2 = 277.37$). The letter I holds interest: of 119, 38% perceive this letter as white, 28% as black, and 12% as gray; that is, 78% perceive it as non-hued; likewise, 75% perceive the letter O as non-hued. Of 93 synesthetes, 44% perceive Y as yellow. Actually, working with the assumption of even distribution across all 11 colors, only one letter, Q, falls within parameters ($\chi^2 = 14.38$), and this might just be serendipitous.

One could raise the argument, as per Kay's (1975) studies, that certain color names, such as black, white, red, and green, are more common than others, such as orange, pink, or purple. However, this would imply that, as samplings increase, all letter colors would progress towards black, white, red, or green being the mode. Such does not occur. In addition, the synesthete is attempting to describe specifically what color is seen or associated with each letter, not just rapidly picking out a random convenient color name. Plate 2.1 presents my findings for the most common synesthetic colors for each alphabet letter and numerical digit, based on my research sample of synesthetes—thus, a "typical" synesthete's set.

You might notice that the letters, as a whole, are not very colorful, and feature a fair amount of grays, browns, and dull tones, while the digits are far more colorful and brilliant. This is typical for the majority of colored grapheme synesthetes. We might instead investigate this phenomenon by asking whether certain synesthetic colors are more likely to be connected with certain geometric shapes (e.g., white with circles, such as with O and Q; red with triangles, such as with A, black with crosses, such as with X). Further, far more extensive research is needed to resolve such questions.

Table 2.1 lists which types of synesthesia are more frequent, less so, or yet unseen among 572 reported cases I have come across. As with the previous data, approximately 27% of the case studies come from previous publications. Of these published accounts, approximately 47% are of women, 36% of men, and 17% of undisclosed sex. Again, the remaining approximately 73% of the cases I looked at have come to me over the past 11 years via e-mail to The Synesthesia List, personal phone calls, handwritten letters, and face-to-face interviews. For this group, approximately 75% are female, 24% are male, and 1% has remained anonymous and of undisclosed sex.

Note that some of these cases are people with multiple synesthesiae. Table 2.1 is not meant to be an exhaustive list of every type of synesthesia there might possibly be. Messages on The Synesthesia List, for example, have led me and others to consider the possibility that some reports of "colored auras" being seen around people might be the results of synesthetic interactions between facial recognition (perhaps at that part [parts?] of the brain affected

Table 2.1. Types of synesthesia.

Type	No. synesthetes[a]	%
Colored graphemes	394	68.8
Colored time units	134	23.4
Colored musical sounds	106	18.5
Colored general sounds	82	14.3
Colored musical notes	62	10.8
Colored phonemes	60	10.5
Colored tastes	43	7.5
Colored odors	40	6.9
Colored pain	36	6.3
Colored personalities	26	4.5
Colored touch	25	4.0
Colored temperatures	15	2.6
Colored orgasms	7	1.2
Smell–synesthetic sound	4	0.6
Smell–synesthetic taste	1	0.1
Smell–synesthetic temperature	1	0.1
Smell–synesthetic touch	4	0.6
Sound–synesthetic smell	9	1.5
Sound–synesthetic taste	29	5.0
Sound–synesthetic temperature	4	0.6
Sound–synesthetic touch	25	4.3
Taste–synesthetic sound	1	0.1
Taste–synesthetic temperature	1	0.1
Taste–synesthetic touch	4	0.6
Temperature–synesthetic sound	1	0.1
Touch–synesthetic smell	2	0.3
Touch–synesthetic sound	2	0.3
Touch–synesthetic taste	3	0.5
Touch–synesthetic temperature	1	0.1
Vision–synesthetic smell	6	1.0
Vision–synesthetic sound	6	1.0
Vision–synesthetic taste	11	1.9
Vision–synesthetic temperature	2	0.3
Vision–synesthetic touch	5	0.8
Personality–synesthetic smell	1	0.1

[a] Total of 572 surveyed. Other possible combinations I have not yet found in 572 cases: taste–synesthetic smell ("smelling flavors"); temperature–synesthetic smell ("smelling temperature gradients"); temperature–synesthetic taste ("tasting temperature gradients"); temperature–synesthetic touch ("feeling temperature gradients").

in cases of prosopagnosia) and color processing centers of the brain, or perhaps between those portions of the brain that recognize overall human body form and those parts that see color.

In current literature (see, e.g., articles in Baron-Cohen & Harrison, 1997, but see also Cytowic, 2002), there is a claim that the current ratio of male to female synesthetes is about 1:6. My own studies indicate that, for those cases in published literature, 47% are female, 36% are male, and 17% are of undisclosed sex. Assuming a 1:6 M:F ratio, if we also divide the 17% into a 1:6

ratio, this results in $\chi^2 = 47.60$. Likewise, for my collection of nonpublished cases, I have rates of 75% female, 24% male, and 1% of undisclosed sex. Again, assuming a 1:6 male to female ratio and dividing the 1% accordingly, this results in $\chi^2 = 8.30$. However, there have also been proposals, put forth previously by myself and others, that the ratio of male to female synesthetes is more correctly approximately 1:3. If we assume this 1:3 ratio, the percentages of male and female cases in my total data collection results in $\chi^2 = 0.48 < 3.84$. If Baron-Cohen et al.'s 1:6 ratio is more accurate, this still leaves the question of how this ratio can easily be explained in terms of what many currently assume regarding the genetics of synesthesia based on various collections of case reports: to wit, that it has characteristics of being autosomal dominant, yet it also seems to be passed down solely or at least overwhelmingly only via the mother's side of the family, and has a significantly high rate of females to males. However, ratios just off of but approaching 1:3 can readily be explained with the proposal that the genetics of synesthesia involve an X-linked dominant gene and male lethality (a proposal previously suggested by Bailey & Johnson, 1997 and Cytowic, personal communication, May 18, 2002). As Bailey and Johnson, Cytowic, and others have pointed out, if the aspect of male lethality is involved, this would imply that, in families with synesthetes, we would see a higher than normal rate of spontaneous miscarriage. I can only offer anecdotal information at this time, but it does indeed seem to be the case that, over the past 10 years, female members of The Synesthesia List have reported a higher than normal rate of miscarriage for themselves; likewise, both male and female synesthete members have indicated the same regarding their mothers (I have little information regarding daughters in this regard). A joint project by researchers at the University of Waterloo (Ontario, Canada), the University of California–San Diego, the Laboratory of Human Neurogenetics at Rockefeller University, and other U.S. institutions is underway to more precisely pin down the genetics of colored grapheme synesthesia; additional institutes, such as University College London, the University of Melbourne (Australia), and the University of Hannover (Germany) may soon join in to broaden the scope.

It should be pointed out that synesthesia can also result from certain types of brain injury or seizures. Jacobs, Karpik, Bozian, and Gøthgen (1981) wrote about nine cases of visual synesthesia induced by auditory stimuli, resulting from lesions of the anterior portion of the optic nerve and/or chiasm. The synesthetic visions always appeared within a defective portion of the visual field; the sound stimuli producing the synesthesia were always heard in the ear ipsilateral to the eye in which the photisms were seen. Vike, Jabbari, and Maitland (1984) wrote of visual synesthesia to auditory stimuli resulting ipsilateral to a tumor in the left medial temporal lobe and adjacent midbrain. The synesthesia disappeared with removal of the tumor mass. One of the more recent subscribers to The Synesthesia List was a teenaged girl who was involved in a car accident when she was 14. It is uncertain as to whether she suffered a concussion in the accident; there was nerve damage, she lost her sense of taste and smell, but apparently there was no noticeable brain injury, from radiological evidence. However, since that time, she has also experienced synesthetic smell perceptions induced by auditory stimuli (that is, she "smells" music). I should add that it is not unusual for someone who is without a particular sensory input mechanism to nevertheless experience synesthesia in that sense. There are also other examples of anosmatic synesthetes who "smell" color, and blind synesthetes who "see" colors. These synesthetes, however, were not born with these conditions. To my knowledge, all of these cases of synesthesia induced through injury are of the "pure" synesthesia form. There are no such cases resulting in, for example, colored letters, numbers, or days of the week.

Sacks (1995) writes of the loss of developmental synesthesia due to injury, in the case of "Mr. I" (the colorblind painter), who suffered a concussion in an automobile accident. Before the accident, Mr. I experienced visual synesthesia to music stimuli (colored musical notes); after the accident, music was deadened. Mr. I suffered achromatopsia (loss of color perception) and temporary alexia (reading difficulty) as well. Unfortunately, the location of the brain damage in Mr. I remains unknown.

It appears that synesthesia is in no way limited by geography, nationality, or race. Over the past 10 years, I have interacted with Chinese, Brazilian, and Nigerian synesthetes, as well as synesthetes from Japan, Chile, and India, to name but a few. Odgaard, Flowers, and Bradman (1999) reported on a synesthete of Choctaw (Native American, USA) descent.

Although synesthesia is now generally considered to have genetic-based, biological causes, these are influenced by cultural factors. Synesthesia is, to some extent, also learned; or, rather, we might say that one learns how to be a synesthete. My research strongly suggests to me that most if not all correspondences which a given synesthete experiences are not via learned associations; however, I have encountered rare cases in which a handful of the correspondences (particularly the first four or five items in a sequence, such as the alphabet) are very evidently through childhood association.

Is Synesthesia a Problem?

Synesthesia is currently quite unknown among the general population of medical practitioners worldwide. It is recognized by the American Medical Association and the American Psychological Association, and an acknowledged American Synesthesia Association now exists. Nevertheless, an adolescent of, say, 13 years old, reporting aspects of synesthesia to her parents, teachers, and, perhaps eventually, her family doctor, is often greeted with disbelief or outright scorn. In some of the most damaging cases, synesthetes have been sent to "specialists" who have sometimes misdiagnosed them as schizophrenic or just crazy. This has happened not just in non-Western countries, but also in the United States and Canada.

Knowing that they may be socially rebuked, many synesthetes keep their synesthesia a secret. This, in essence, basically means (perhaps especially in regard to the synesthesia "proper") denying how they have perceived the world all of their lives (or, from what my correspondence files and studies suggest, at least since about age four or five, when developmental synesthesia most frequently begins to firmly manifest itself) and pretending that one or more of their modes of perception work differently.

Let us put this into a kind of perspective: imagine being sighted, with "normal" visual abilities and perceptions of sensations, including typical full color vision, and being forced and pressured by those people and situations around you to deny all existence of colors and to try to pass for being wholly colorblind. Or having full, normal hearing and being pressured to pass as being profoundly deaf—including having to learn sign language in order to communicate. Some synesthetes use phrases derived from the gay and lesbian community, adopting such expressions as "closet synesthete" and "coming out to my family" in regard to their synesthesia. Although the rate of full-scale "coming out" is currently not increasing much, the rate of use of such phrases is growing quite rapidly and becoming common among synesthetes "still mostly in the closet." However, at least as many also describe their situation as being akin to being an extraterrestrial, nonhuman alien, or, perhaps, an animal such as a bat, trying to pass for human. Frequently, synesthetes fear ridicule by "normals." Far worse for some is the fear of being misdiagnosed and in one way or another trapped by professionals and parents who wish to attempt a diagnosis or cure.

One of my synesthete friends wrote to me the following:

> In his book *The Man Who Tasted Shapes* [Cytowic 1993], Dr. Cytowic talks about the tendency of the medical community (in the U.S., at least) to reject patients' claims related to synesthesia. I read it about 5 years ago, but as I recall it, the training that medical students receive (esp. since the 1940s or so) gives credence only to symptoms which can be objectively observed by the physician. Fundamentally subjective experiences (such as self-reporting of cross-sense experiences by synesthetes) tend to be discounted or rejected.
>
> I can say that almost no one in the psychology/psychiatry profession with whom I have spoken has ever heard of synesthesia—until recently, since synesthesia has received more attention in the press. One psychiatrist (quite young, I might add) had never heard of it before, and recommended that I have an MRI done to be sure there wasn't some kind of injury to my brain! I had to explain (emphatically) that synesthesia

wasn't just some delusion I was experiencing, but rather a documented phenomenon.

It's kind of ironic that, of all people, doctors (and psychiatrists and psychologists in particular) should be the most incredulous.

Another synesthete friend, whose adolescent daughter is also a synesthete, wrote to me,

I've always been pretty open about sharing syn[esthesia] with others. Maybe because I find it so fascinating and feel it is a gift rather than a disorder. Most people have been interested and non-judgmental. Only two occasions have been met with hesitation and those were both by professionals who I assumed would be more open to variations from the norm than the general public. One was a professional counselor who gave me a look like I should be locked up and that ended the conversation. The second was my daughter's school teacher. My daughter is a syn[esthete] and I thought her teacher would find it interesting to learn about a different way that students may process information. She was open to the discussion but indicated she thought it was a very isolated instance and referred to it as a dysfunction rather than a gift. Even though my daughter is a gifted student. She told me later that she had spoken with her sister—a psychologist—who had heard of it but suggested that it would need to be "diagnosed." That word scares me. We haven't discussed it since.

Yet another synesthete, who works in a laboratory with researchers studying perception, wrote,

Mostly, I am just curious, but I'm considering being a little more open about my synesthesia. For the record, I've told my immediate family (my mother is a synesthete), about 4 close friends, and my coworkers at my summer job, since I work in a perception lab and my synesthesia could impact how I perform on certain perceptual tests. I've told a couple of professors (in the fields of psychology and neurology) and have to admit that I've gotten the strangest reactions from them. One thought I was a savant, and the other tried to offer his condolences for "my condition." (I got a laugh out of that one later.) It's this type of reaction that keeps me silent.

In the past 6 years, I have also received urgent e-mail messages from synesthetes in Chile, Peru, and Italy. In each of these cases, the synesthete had sought out doctors to get more information about their synesthesia, only to get caught in a complex web where one or more doctors, plus various family members, wanted to institutionalize them, or at least perform a series of quite potentially harmful tests involving drugs. With the Peruvian and Italian cases, the synesthetes eventually got away from the doctors and family members, and, last I heard, are no longer being pressured (or threatened) regarding institutionalization. I do not know what happened with the Chilean; I fear the worst.

Beginning about 3 years ago, I corresponded for almost a year via e-mail with a Canadian teenage girl, whose parents (I am assuming) had immigrated from India a few years prior to that time, and who was, at the time, a runaway living in the United States. Throughout the course of our correspondences, she kept herself anonymous, and moved from town to town about every three weeks. More than once, she told me that a main reason she had run away was that her father used to beat her severely every time she had mentioned any type of synesthetic experience (she only had the most common type, colored letters and numbers, but to an extremely strong degree). She claimed that her parents had taken her to numerous doctors in Canada and the United States, virtually all of whom had suggested major psychiatric treatment, and many of whom had suggested institutionalization. She also told me that she was strictly forbidden to mention her colored letters in any way to any other people besides doctors, and was often locked up in her room and denied contact with any other people besides her immediate family. When I last heard from her, she was still roaming the southern United States, had determined never to return to her parents, and had gotten a job (she would not reveal where) as an artist, she based her artwork on various things she "saw" synesthetically.

Is Synesthesia a Benefit?

This is not to say, however, that all or even most synesthetes have had severe problems with their conditions, nor that synesthesia is a drawback for everyone. Take, for example, the situation with Ian (a pseudonym), a 12-year-old synesthete I am currently assisting. Ian has colored-grapheme synesthesia, and is currently having trouble with algebra in school. Both he and his parents, as well as some of his teachers and administrators at his school, were worried that this form of synesthesia might, in itself, somehow create an insurmountable drawback for Ian in a number of academic areas. It gave them comfort to hear that not only did people use colored letters and numbers to advantage, but that Richard Feynman used his to memorize formulae that gained him a Nobel Prize (the fact that synesthete Vladimir Nabokov [figure 2.1] was the author of Lolita and Ada gave some of the teachers a little less comfort, but this can perhaps be countered by the amazingly strong piousness of Olivier Messiaen and Amy Beach [figure 2.2], both also synesthetes). Ian's problems in mathematics are similar to that of a couple of other young synesthetes whom I am also assisting. To give a basic example of these types of problems, see Plate 2.2.

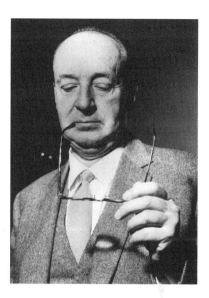

Figure 2.1. Vladimir Nabokov. (Reproduced with permission of Getty Images.)

Taking complications a step further, it is not infrequent that such colored-grapheme synesthetes will also perceive numbers (and, less often, letters) as having gender and personality, such as 2 being a shy, wimpy boy and 9 being a vain, elitist girl. Thus, extending our example from plate 2.2, Bob might really dislike certain things (such as 7 × 7, or office number 294) that result in putting 4 (a plain but decent, hard-working older woman) and 9 together,

Figure 2.2. Amy Beach. (Reproduced with permission from the Milne Special Collections, University of New Hampshire Library.)

as they greatly dislike each other and do not get along at all. Plate 2.3 is the set of letters and numbers, with their gender and personality descriptions, of one of my previous Synesthesia List members.

A recent subscriber to The Synesthesia List wrote,

> I have an intense association between colours and numbers. I migrated to Australia from the UK in the 1970s with my parents and remember having to do a maths test at primary school to determine what grade I should be put in. I think I was around 5 or 6 years old. I drew blocks of colour for my answers. Some of them just one colour—others two colours merging together. I remember the sum three plus five. Three is yellow for me and five is blue so I drew a merging of blue and yellow (a nice kind of green) as my answer. The teacher was appalled and held the sheet up in front of the class saying something like, "This might be how they do maths in England but it certainly isn't how we do it here." Much laughter and humiliation. At this point, I realised other people didn't see it this way and I tried to filter it out, which worked—to a degree.

However, I do not wish to convey that these types of synesthesia always present a problem for the synesthete, nor that they cannot be overcome—often in amusing and enjoyable manners. Plate 2.4 presents an example from one of my Synesthesia List members.

Then there is the story of a synesthete I know who replaced all of the keys on his laptop computer. Rather than displaying the graphemes, the new keys displayed only the colors which corresponded with each grapheme, creating a rainbow across the keyboard. After having done this, my friend reported that it was so much easier for him to recognize the various keys that his typing at least doubled in speed!

There have been many major figures who have not kept their synesthesia hidden, and have even used their synesthesia to advantage in their work. In the musical world, we have composers such as Franz Liszt (1811–1886): "When Liszt first began as Kapellmeister in Weimar (1842), it astonished the orchestra that he said: 'O please, gentlemen, a little bluer, if you please! This tone type requires it!' Or: 'That is a deep violet, please, depend on it! Not so rose!' First the orchestra believed Liszt just joked; later on, they got accustomed to the fact that the great musician seemed to see colors there, where there were only tones" (quoted from an anonymous article in the Neuen Berliner Musikzeitung, August 29, 1895; quoted in Mahling 1926, p. 230; trans. by author).

Nikolai Rimsky-Korsakov (1844–1908) had synesthetically colored musical keys:

C major	white
G major	brownish-gold, light

D major	daylight, yellowish, royal
A major	clear, pink
E major	blue, sapphire, bright
B major	gloomy, dark blue with steel shine
F♯ major	grayish-green
D♭ major	darkish, warm
A♭ major	grayish-violet
E♭ major	dark, gloomy, gray-bluish
B♭ major	darkish
F major	green, clear (color of greenery)

This is according to an article in the Russian press (Yastrebtsev, 1908).

Amy Beach (1867–1944) used her colored hearing as a basis for some of her compositions:

> Other interesting stories about Amy's musical personality and her astounding abilities as a prodigy are recounted in almost all previous biographical writings. One such story is Amy's association of certain colors with certain keys. For instance, Amy might ask her mother to play the 'purple music' or the 'green music'. The most popular story, however, seems to be the one about Amy's going on a trip to California and notating on staff paper the exact pitches of bird calls she heard. (Brown, 1994, p. 16; references are to letters in the Crawford Collection, Library of Congress)
>
> Amy's mother encouraged her to relate melodies to the colors blue, pink, or purple, but before long Amy had a wider range of colors, which she associated with certain major keys. Thus C was white, F-sharp black, E yellow, G red, A green, A-flat blue, D-flat violet or purple, and E-flat pink. Until the end of her life she associated these colors with those keys. (Jenkins, 1994, pp. 5–6; reference is an interview of Beach by George Y. Loveridge in the *Providence Journal*, December 4, 1937, p. 5)

Another synesthete composer and musician was Jean Sibelius (1865–1957; figure 2.3):

> For him there existed a strange, mysterious connection between sound and color, between the most secret perceptions of the eye and ear. Everything he saw produced a corresponding impression on his ear—every impression of sound was transferred and fixed as color on the retina of his eye and thence to his memory. And this he thought as natural, with as good reason as those who did not possess this faculty called him crazy or affectedly original.
>
> For this reason he only spoke of this in the strictest confidence and under a pledge of silence. "For otherwise they will make fun of me!" (Adolf Paul, 1890, as quoted in Ekman, 1938, pp. 41–42)

Figure 2.3. Jean Sibelius. (Reproduced with permission of Atelier Apollo, Helsinki [Music pic nr8879].)

Olivier Messiaen (1908–1992) was self-admittedly a synesthete, as is quite well detailed in his own writings and in interviews (see Samuel 1986/1994). Many of his compositions, such as "Oiseaux Exotiques," "L'ascension," and "Couleurs de la cite celeste," are directly based on trying to "produce pictures" via sound, writing specific notes to produce specific color sequences and blends.

Synesthete composers and musicians now living include the Hungarian György Ligeti (born 1923). Ligeti is probably best known to the wider world for his early works, some of which were used by Stanley Kubrick for the soundtrack of *2001*.

> I am inclined to synaesthetic perception. I associate sounds with colours and shapes. Like Rimbaud [Rimbaud was most likely not a true synesthete], I feel that all letters have a colour.
>
> Major chords are red or pink, minor chords are somewhere between green and brown. I do not have perfect pitch, so when I say that C minor has a rusty red-brown colour and D minor is brown this does not come from the pitch but from the letters C and D. I think it must go back to my childhood. I find, for instance, that numbers also have colours; 1 is steely grey, 2 is orange, 5 is green. At some point these associations must have got fixed, perhaps I saw the green number 5 on a stamp or on a shop sign. But there must be some collective associations too. For most people the sound of a trumpet is probably yellow although I find it red because of its shrillness. (Ligeti, 1978/1983, p. 58)

A strange twist: Ligeti studied and taught (1950–1956) at the Franz Liszt Academy in Budapest.

There is also the contemporary composer Michael Torke, definitely a synesthete, reporting that one of his types is colored time units (days of the week, years, and such). Torke has composed pieces with titles such as "Ecstatic Orange" and "Bright Blue Music." Other contemporaries include jazz-rock drummer Manu Katchè, jazz guitarist Tony de Caprio, the American composer Harley Gittleman, and violinist Itzhak Perlman.

In the realm of creative fiction writers, there have also been more than a few synesthetes. Perhaps the most famous was Vladimir Nabokov (1899–1977). In his autobiography, *Speak Memory* (1966), Nabokov tells us of his

> fine case of colored hearing. Perhaps "hearing" is not quite accurate, since the color sensation seems to be produced by the very act of my orally forming a given letter while I imagine its outline. The long a of the English alphabet (and it is this alphabet I have in mind farther on unless otherwise stated) has for me the tint of weathered wood, but a French a evokes polished ebony. This black group also includes hard g (vulcanized rubber) and r (a sooty rag bag being ripped). Oatmeal n, noodle-limp l, and the ivory-backed hand mirror of o take care of the whites. I am puzzled by my French on which I see as the brimming tension-surface of alcohol in a small glass. Passing on to the blue group, there is steely x, thundercloud z, and huckleberry k. Since a subtle interaction exists between sound and shape, I see q as browner than k, while s is not the light blue of c, but a curious mixture of azure and mother-of-pearl. Adjacent tints do not merge, and diphthongs do not have special colors of their own, unless represented by a single character in some other language (thus the fluffy-gray, three-stemmed Russian letter that stands for sh [Ш], a letter as old as the rushes of the Nile, influences its English representation).
>
> . . . In the green group, there are alder-leaf f, the unripe apple of p, and pistachio t. Dull green, combined somehow with violet, is the best I can do for w. The yellows comprise various e's and i's, creamy d, bright-golden y, and u, whose alphabetical value I can express only by "brassy with an olive sheen." In the brown group, there are the rich rubbery tone of soft g, paler j, and the drab shoelace of h. Finally, among the reds, b has the tone called burnt sienna by painters, m is a fold of pink flannel, and today I have at last perfectly matched v with "Rose Quartz" in Maerz and Paul's *Dictionary of Color*. The word for rainbow, a primary, but decidedly muddy, rainbow, is in my private language the hardly pronounceable: kzspygv. (pp. 34–35).

It should be mentioned that Nabokov's mother was a synesthete, as was his wife and his son Dmitri. Contemporary synesthete authors include Brits Julie Myerson and Jane Yardley.

As for other famous synesthetes, there is the artist David Hockney (see Cytowic, 2002). He sees synesthetic colors to musical stimuli. In general, this does not show up in his painting or photography artwork too much. However, it is a common underlying principle in his construction of stage sets for various ballets and operas, where he bases the background colors and lighting upon his own seen colors while listening to the music of the theater piece he is working on. Richard Feynman (1918–1988), winner of the 1965 Nobel Prize in Physics, was a synesthete. Feynman had colored letters and numbers: "When I see equations, I see the letters in colors—I don't know why. As I'm talking, I see vague pictures of Bessel functions from Jahnke and Emde's book, with light-tan j's, slightly violet-bluish n's, and dark brown x's flying around [see plate 2.5]. And I wonder what the hell it must look like to the students" (Feynman, 1988, p. 59). There are strong indications and good reasons for believing that the Serbian-born American physicist and inventor Nikola Tesla (1856–1943) was also a synesthete (see, e.g., Tesla, 1982).

I do not mention these famous synesthetes merely for curiosity's sake or to disperse trivia. These types of "heroes" can play essential roles both for young synesthetes and for their non-synesthete parents.

How then do we help students like Ian? This is a genuine concern; and I do not really have a good answer yet. However, one of the counselors at Ian's school points out to me that, whereas Ian has problems with math and also, upon occasion, with spelling, he seems to be coping quite fine. His parents, on the other hand, seem to be far more the problem at the moment. They want specific answers, in layman's terms that they can understand, as to whether something is wrong with their son, what the problem is, why he cannot do math the same as others, whether he will ever be able to do math at an adequate level, whether he needs medications or therapy, and so on. In other words, while Ian's synesthesia is a minor but still present problem for Ian, lack of information about synesthesia to give his parents is a major problem for Ian's school system.

Is Synesthesia a Special Gift?

One of the recurring themes on The Synesthesia List is the matter of whether synesthesia is, in some way, a "sixth sense" or a type of extrasensory perception (ESP), or a gift or blessing. I do not believe there is a synesthetic sixth sense. There is, rather, an atypical joining of the existing senses. Most normal perceivers have multiple senses within each of the traditional senses anyway. What we call touch might actually be broken down into at least five different senses (consider, for example, the difference between feeling a tickle on your arm and a sensation inside your stomach). Also, pain could probably be broken down into at least two if not three or more separate senses. And temperature could be broken down into two separate components—heat detection is separate from cold detection. And then there is also proprioception, balance, vomeronasal perception of pheromones, and others.

Beyond this, synesthesia does not add to the range of sensory perception. That is, for example, whereas a normal perceiver cannot see into the ultraviolet spectrum, neither can a synesthete. Whereas a normal person cannot hear ultra-high frequencies that a bat hears, neither can a synesthete. The ranges are not different, nor are they increased. Instead, synesthesia combines sensory experiences. Normal perceivers, for example, see colors; they also hear music. I see colors. I hear music. I also see colors when I hear music. There is no additional, sixth sense here. People with normal perception also taste things. I see colors when I taste things. Again, no sixth sense.

A question then emerges: What does the synesthete who is aware that, for example, the rest of the world does not see colors when hearing music think about the reality of synesthetic perceptions? Most synesthetes that I correspond with tell me that they basically work along lines of "two (simultaneous) realities": "other people's reality" and "my reality." The concept of having multiple realities does not seem to bother them. Similarly, Ramachandran and Blakeslee (1998) report that amputees with phantom limbs tend to eventually start operating with two simultaneous realities, "the phantom limb does exist and is still there," and "the limb does not exist and is not there." However, unlike with synesthetes, most amputees with phantom limbs cannot reconcile their two realities.

Humans take for granted that what each of us sees, hears, tastes, smells, and otherwise perceives is very much like that of the next person. Especially at a sensory level, most of us believe that our realities are pretty much the same. A person with synesthesia is, of course, no different in this sense. It might, however, be of interest to normal perceivers to hear that the quite larger majority of "colored-music" synesthetes I have corresponded with over the years were firmly convinced that everybody perceived music as colored; most of them were not shaken from this belief until well over the age of 20.

I personally do not feel that my own synesthesia is some kind of gift from someone or something. I am not somehow mystically blessed in that I somehow see a hidden truth that others do not. I believe I perceive music and flavors differently because my brain is sending signals to places different and/or in a different fashion than how it does in the average brain. To say that I "take in so much more of the world than normal people do" (to paraphrase a claim regarding synesthetes frequently expounded upon on The Synesthesia List and elsewhere) would imply that there is something actually out there to take in that others are not getting. I really do not think there is something extra out there. Rather, odd wiring and/or neuronal feedback is creating something in here—inside my head. It may be perceptually real in one way, but it is not real (and I know very well it is not real) in another, more generally applicable, way.

Nevertheless, for the past few months, I have been dealing (fairly unsuccessfully) with trying to burst the bubbles of more than one non-synesthete colleague who seem quite seriously convinced that I have some form of mystic, spiritual connection to alternate dimensions or astral realms. From about October 2002 through February 2003, I served as a consultant to a commercial chemical laboratory which makes food additives, training and working as a taste-tester and "nose." Researchers at the company are interested in whether the synesthetic colors I "see" for various tastes and odors might help them in more accurately discerning fine-scale differences in products. However, these researchers have also frequently presented me with speculations regarding "auras," based, I deduce, on ideas extracted indirectly from Besant and Leadbeater's theosophy (see, e.g., Besant and Leadbeater, 1901/1978; Leadbeater, 1902/1925), with perhaps a touch of Kandinsky's interpretations. I have been hearing a lot about Zen philosophy and "astral seeing," too. During the course of various experiments and conversations, I have been asked, "Can you do this for us?" or "Can you do that?" and I am left once again trying to explain to them that synesthesia—not only mine but all that of all other synesthetes I have encountered and read about—does not work that way. Despite my presenting team members with scientific journal articles regarding synesthesia (such as those by Ramachandran and Hubbard), after 5 months, I am still basically considered by them as having "special insight" into "hidden truths" and that my "gift" is not via a neurological difference but from having a "more developed connection" with . . . something.

This is by no means the first time I have had to deal with such matters. Nor is it by any means a trivial concern: For example, recently, on an unmonitored synesthesia discussion chat-room web page, I noted one person who declared herself to be a synesthete explaining to another (self-declared) synesthete, who had come hoping for expert advice from trained medical professionals, how his touch–sound synesthesia perceptions were based upon "lines" and "vibrations" as per Californian variations on concepts of Buddhism, mysticism, and chakras. During the last year that I lived in Taiwan (2000–2001), I was interviewed by an associated group of television stations and newspapers for an evening news and newspaper feature regarding my synesthesia. When the features came out (all in Chinese), they were titled with a Chinese phrase which may be generally translated as "super-powers"; the same phrase is used in describing mythological demons, demigods, and cartoon and comic book superheroes. Rather than being informative pieces about a rare neurological condition, the features became an embarrassing joke that I then had to deal with for the next month.

I have been asked by various people over the years, "So what? Why should you care about other people's opinions and views regarding synesthesia?

What difference does it make if they want to see synesthesia that way?" I am not really too concerned about the religious beliefs of others. I am far more concerned about those who distract synesthetes and other concerned parties (such as worried parents of synesthete children) from scientifically based information and conclusions, providing them instead with misinformation and concepts based upon belief and faith which have no scientific foundation or supporting solid evidence to back them up. Many subscribers to The Synesthesia List, for example, have come to me after having waded through numerous web sites providing gross misinformation and unfounded conclusions regarding synesthesia; these people are often extremely confused, but they also come holding incorrect assumptions, which it is then very difficult to dissuade them from. Pseudoscience, mysticism and such are not mere trivial concerns here; the spreading of misinformation, and lack of concern about the spread of misinformation, can directly hurt and impede synesthetes, just like it can hurt epileptics, autistic people, homosexuals, or others. As I write this paragraph, my most recent request for consultation on a project came from a person who hoped to find and employ synesthetes to help him detect ghosts.

After all of the horror stories I have mentioned about misdiagnosis, ridicule, scorn, and bad science, do I have anything positive to say regarding any doctors, psychiatrists, and other types of researchers? I most certainly do! There have been many who have definitely advanced our knowledge of synesthesia and thus lent a helping hand. A few of those recent workers are described below.

Baron-Cohen, Wyke, and Binnie (1987) established a set of tests that are now deemed to show that synesthesia is a real phenomenon, based upon its consistency; variants of this test are used to determine whether subjects may be shown to have certain forms of synesthesia before then proceeding to further experiments. In 1989, Cytowic produced his volume on synesthesia, reintroducing the topic to the neuroscience and medical community. He followed through in 1993 with a "pop reader" book on synesthesia which went on to gain international attention, including bestseller status, and was translated into additional languages. In 1995, Paulesu and his colleagues (1995) (which included Baron-Cohen) did positron emission tomography scan studies of colored-word synesthetes, revealing that there were sections of the brains of synesthetes that "lit up" differently than those of non-synesthetes performing the same word-recognition tasks, indicating that there were, indeed, neurological differences between synesthete and non-synesthete brains. Such studies have now been followed up using functional magnetic resonance imaging, magnetoencephalography, and event related potential technologies; Paulesu et al.'s basic findings hold up quite well, and are now supported by a rapidly growing body of data revealing neurological differences between synesthetes and non-synesthetes. Duffy, a synesthete, has produced a volume that is a combination of autobiography, biography of other synesthetes, and general reader information regarding synesthesia (2001); this book has gone into paperback editions and is gaining widespread recognition, leading many to seek additional information regarding synesthesia. In separate, simultaneous studies, Mattingly, Rich, Yelland, and Bradshaw (2001) in Melbourne, Australia, Ramachandran and Hubbard (2001a, 2001b) in La Jolla, California, and Smilek, Dixon, Cudahy, and Merikle (2001a, 2001b, 2002) at Waterloo, Ontario, Canada, developed sets of tests to show conclusively that colored-grapheme synesthesia is a perceptual phenomenon, not a visual aberration, and, once again, to show that synesthetes could not possibly be making it up. And we now have these researchers and others joining together each year to share their work with each other and with synesthete and non-synesthete audience members at conventions such as those held by the American Synesthesia Association.

Revealing Synesthesia

On May 19, 2000, the first annual meeting of the American Synesthesia Association was held at Princeton University. Unfortunately, I was unable to attend. However, I received quite a lot of e-mail directly after the event. Perhaps not surprisingly, one of the things that most attendees mentioned was the coffee breaks between the paper and presentation sessions. Virtually every message I received, from synesthete and non-synesthete alike, mentioned how the synesthetes around the coffee and cookies were happily proclaiming, "Finally, I feel justified! After all these years, I finally feel like my way of seeing the world is just as good—is also real!"

One of the subscribers to The Synesthesia List wrote the following in 1997:

> About 3 days ago, I discovered that synesthesia is the name for the way I have been thinking my whole life. My mother clipped an article from the *Washington Jewish Week* about perfect pitch for me (I also have perfect pitch) and the article mentioned that an even smaller subset of people are "synesthetes" and see colors for every musical tone. Well, it was like a thousand Hallelujah choruses in my head at once. It has a name!
>
> Though I know that only one in so many people have synesthesia, I honestly can't imagine what it must be like NOT to see the world in a series of colors. Everything in my mind is color-coded. For me, what I now know to be synesthesia is not just a cute or freakish "talent," it is the manner in which I organize my thoughts and understand the world around me.
>
> I don't know why I see the colors that I do. I don't know why Biology is green, Chemistry is red, and Physics is yellow. They just are.

As mentioned above, synesthesia is not considered a problem in most cases. However, lack of knowledge about synesthesia—within the medical and scientific community, and, more broadly, among the general public—is considered a major problem by the synesthete community. Synesthetes do not need a cure for synesthesia. Rather, we need and want non-synesthete experts, family members, and concerned others to be informed about the occurrence and nature of our experiences so that it stops being thought of as an aberration, but rather as a normal variant of perception. Together, we all need to work at finding ways to get rid of biases, misconceptions, pseudoscientific misinformation, dogmatism, and intolerance, so that far many more synesthetes can finally feel a sense of relief and acceptance.

That is why I study synesthesia, and, for me, this is what this book is for. And that is why I sincerely applaud the other contributors to this book: You are of the small, but I hope growing, crowd of people who are making an extremely significant difference!

References

Bailey, M.E.S., & Johnson, K.J. (1997). Synaesthesia: Is a genetic analysis feasible? In S. Baron-Cohen & J.E. Harrison (Eds.), *Synaesthesia: Classic and contemporary readings* (pp. 182–207) Cambridge, MA: Blackwell.

Baron-Cohen, S., & Harrison, J.E. (Eds.). (1997). *Synaesthesia: Classic and contemporary readings.* Cambridge, MA: Blackwell.

Baron-Cohen, S., Wyke, M.A., & Binnie, C. (1987). Hearing words and seeing colours: An experimental investigation of a case of synaesthesia. *Perception, 16,* 761–767.

Berlin, B., & Kay, P. (1969). Basic color terms: Their universality and evolution. Berkeley: University of California Press.

Besant, A., & Leadbeater, C.W. (1901/1978). *Thought-forms.* Adyar, India: Theosophical Publishing.

Brown, J.W. (1994). *Amy Beach and her chamber music: Biography, documents, style.* Metuchen, NJ: Scarecrow Press.

Cytowic, R.E. (1993). *The man who tasted shapes.* New York: Putnam.

Cytowic, R.E. (1989). *Synesthesia: A union of the senses.* New York: Springer-Verlag.

Cytowic, R.E. (2002). *Synesthesia: A union of the senses* (2nd ed.). New York: Springer Verlag.

Day, S.A. (2001). Semi-reflection of types of synaesthesia. In C.W. Spinks (Ed.), *Trickster and ambivalence: The dance of differentiation* (pp. 111–117). Madison, WI: Atwood.

Day, S.A. (2003). Types of synaesthesiae [on-line]. Available: http://www.users.muohio.edu/daysa/types.htm

Duffy, P.L. (2001). *Blue cats and chartreuse kittens: How synesthetes color their worlds.* New York: Henry Holt.

Ekman, K. (1938). *Jean Sibelius: His life and personality.* (E. Birse, Trans.). New York: Alfred A. Knopf.

Feynman, R.P. (1988). *What do you care what other people think?* New York: Norton.

Grossenbacher, P.G., & Lovelace, C.T. (2001). Mechanisms of synesthesia: cognitive and physiological constraints. *Trends in Cognitive Sciences, 5(1),* 36–41.

Jacobs, L., Karpik, A., Bozian, D., & Gøthgen, S. (1981). Auditory-visual synesthesia: sound-induced photisms. *Archives of Neurology, 38,* 211–216.

Jenkins, W.S. (1994). *The remarkable Mrs. Beach, American composer.* Warren, MI: Harmonie Park Press.

Kay, P. (1975). Synchronic variability and diachronic change in basic color terms. *Language in Society, 4,* 257–270.

Kay, P., and McDaniel, C.K. (1978). The linguistic significance of the meanings of basic color terms. *Language, 54(3),* 610–646.

Leadbeater, C.W. (1902/1925). *Man visible and invisible.* Wheaton, IL: Theosophical Publishing.

Ligeti, G. (1981/1983). *Ligeti in conversation.* London: Eulenburg Books.

Mahling, F. (1926). Das Problem der "Audition colorée": Eine historische-kritische Untersuchung. *Archiv für die Gesamte Psychologie, 57;* 165–301.

Mattingley, J.B., Rich, A.N., Yelland, G., & Bradshaw, J.L. (2001). Unconscious priming eliminates automatic binding of colour and alphanumeric form in synaesthesia. *Nature, 410,* 580–582.

Nabokov, V. (1966). *Speak, memory: an autobiography revisited.* New York: Putnam.

Odgaard, E.C., Flowers, J.H., and Bradman, H.L. (1999). An investigation of the cognitive and perceptual dynamics of a color-digit synesthete. *Perception, 28,* 651–664.

Paulesu, E., Harrison, J., Baron-Cohen, S., Watson, J.D.G., Goldstein, L, Heather, J., Frackowiak, R.S.J., & Frith, C.D. (1995). The physiology of coloured hearing: A PET activation study of colour-word synaesthesia. *Brain, 118,* 661–676.

Podoll, K., & Robinson, D. (2002). Auditory-visual synaesthesia in a patient with basilar migraine. *Journal of Neurology, 249,* 476–477.

Ramachandran, V.S., & Blakeslee, S. (1998). *Phantoms in the brain.* New York: Quill.

Ramachandran, V.S., & Hubbard, E.M. (2001a). Psychophysical investigations into the neural basis of synaesthesia. *Proceedings of the Royal Society of London, B, 268,* 979–983.

Ramachandran, V.S., & Hubbard, E.M. (2001b). Synaesthesia—A window into perception, thought and language. *Journal of Consciousness Studies, 8(12),* 3–34.

Ramachandran, V., & Rogers-Ramachandran, D. (1996). Synaesthesia in phantom limb induced with mirrors. *Proceedings of the Royal Society of London, 263,* 377–386.

Sachs, G.T.L. (1812). *Historia naturalis Duorum Leucaethopium Auctoris Ipsius et Sororis eius.* Thesis presented at the Friedrich-Alexander University, Erlangen, Germany.

Sacks, O. (1995). *An anthropologist on Mars*. New York: Vintage Books.

Samuel, Claude. (1986/1994). *Olivier Messiaen: music and color. Conversations with Claude Samuel* (Trans. E. Thomas Glasow). Portland, OR: Amadeus Press.

Smilek, D., Dixon, M.J., Cudahy, C., & Merikle, P.M. (2002). Concept driven color experiences in digit-color synesthesia. *Brain and Cognition, 48,* 570–573.

Smilek, D., Dixon, M.J., Cudahy, C., & Merikle, P.M. (2001a). Digit-colour synaesthesia: An investigation of extraordinary conscious experiences. *Consciousness and Cognition, 9(2),* 39.

Smilek, D., Dixon, M.J., Cudahy, C., & Merikle, P.M. (2001b). Synaesthetic photisms influence visual perception. *Journal of Cognitive Neuroscience, 13(7),* 930–936.

Tesla, N. (1982). *My inventions: The autobiography of Nikola Tesla* (Ed. Ben Johnson). n.p.: Hart Brothers.

Vike, J., Jabbari, B., & Maitland, C.G. (1984). Auditory-visual synesthesia: Report of a case with intact visual pathways. *Archive of Neurology, 41,* 680–681.

Yastrebtsev, V. (1908). On N.A.Rimsky-Korsakov's color sound contemplation. *Russkaya muzykalnaya gazeta, 39–40,* 842–845.

3

Varieties of Synesthetic Experience

Christopher W. Tyler

S ynesthesia is often associated with a limited subset of sensory associations, particularly colors with music, colors with numbers, and sounds with shapes. But as a concept it embraces any cross-sensory association and even cross-modality association within specific senses, such as color with shape, for example. Indeed, the commonly reported association between color and number is itself an association between a sensory attribute and the conceptual attribute of number, which is not associated with any specific sense. For this article, I was asked to offer comments about synesthesia from a personal perspective, since I experience a limited degree of synesthesia. In fact, consideration of the variety of possible synesthetic relations revealed many of them actually in operation in the realm of my own experience when attention was brought to bear on the issue.

Visual Color Experiences

My primary synesthetic association is the well-studied one of colors with numbers. Although I am not a vivid synesthete in the sense of those individuals studied by Mattingly et al. (2001) and Ramachandran and Hubbard (2001), the color–number associations are quite explicit, consistent, and stable. That is, when I see the number 3, for example, it does not appear in color on the page. But when I think of the number three, I image the Arabic digit projected into dark space with an explicit golden-yellow color spread around it, as though projected by a spotlight. There is an internal projective space in which numbers, images, equations, and so on are projected, just as described by Kosslyn (1994). It is the space that is accessed by closing my eyes (although the first impression on closing my eyes is of an array of

34

afterimages from the scene that I have just been seeing, so those need to be allowed to fade first). The image space is a colored space, so that the image of a rose, for example, is a deep red flower with a thorny green stem in this image space.

I do not see the synesthetic image at the same time as the visual array from the outside world, but I can switch voluntarily between seeing and thinking of the image of something. It is almost as though I can look through the page or the wall to see the dark field of the imagination behind it. I imagine that this is what vivid synesthetes mean when they say that printed numbers have the color in which they are printed as well as the synesthetic color, although this interpretation does not seem to have been fully evaluated. This view implies that the numbers have simultaneously both their printed color and their synesthetic color, but that attention can be switched between the two characteristics, just as non-synesthetes can switch between thinking about the font and thinking about the meaning of a word, while it is hard to consider the two attributes simultaneously. Consider, for example, the font and the meaning of the word "treacle." One cannot think about one attribute without losing mental grip on the other.

However, there is still a difference between my synesthesia and the synesthesia of the most vivid cases described in the literature, which one might call "obligate synesthesia." In those cases, the colors seem to be always present and even to act as cues to indiscriminable characters (Mattingly et al., 2001; Ramachandran & Hubbard, 2001). In my case, the colors never appear attached to the physical numbers, but only at the level of nonstimulus, or internal, imagery rather than a direct stimulus-bound evocation. It is important to emphasize that this experience is not metaphorical, in the sense that one may talk of "purple prose" or "yellow journalism" without implying an image of the page actually printed in that color. The synesthetic image called to mind actually appears perceptually colored, although identifiably in a different perceptual space than the physical image. This level of access is also available to obligate synesthetes, as exemplified by Joanne Innis, a synesthete studied by Carol Mills. Mills reported that Innis has access to color impressions that do not normally manifest themselves as being in the sensory image: She associates words with the color of the first letter but could also turn on the individual colors of every letter in a word, an especially useful trait when she was learning languages in high school (Mills, Viguers, Edelson, Thomas, Simon-Dack & Innis 2002).

For the record, the colors of my numbers are: 1 – black, 2 – blue-white, 3 – golden yellow, 4 – forest green, 5 – lemon yellow, 6 – red, 7 – leaf green, 8 – electric blue, 9 – dark brown, and 0 – white. As for many synesthetes, the colors of the compound numbers are influenced by the digit components. Thus, the teens are basically the same color as their last digit, while the twenties are lighter versions of the same sequence. The higher numbers tend to be strongly influenced by their first digit, with the second digit as a modulating influence, or a mottling of the base color. For larger numbers of digits, the colors fade as less attention is paid to the individual digits. The numbers have had these colors for as long as I can remember. The particularity of the choices, with some light and others dark, and two of them white, makes it unlikely that they derive from the coloring of the first numbers that I learned, but I cannot exclude this possibility since I do not remember back to when I learned numbers.

One of my experiences on attending talks about synesthesia is that, while I may not be aware of the colors of the numbers explicitly, I react strongly against lists of someone else's color associations, thinking, "How can you possibly imagine 6 as blue?" It may thus be that a latent synesthesia is brought out by exposure to a list of the associations of another synesthete, the negative reaction revealing one's own preferences. It is thus worthwhile to peruse the list of my associations slowly, to see if they evoke any negative reaction and reveal an unsuspected level of synesthesia if the right sort of attention is brought to bear on the mental processing. I presume that this was the kind of thing that Kandinsky was targeting when he was searching for means to train his own synesthesia and that of others. Plate 3.1 is a Kandinsky painting that seems to particularly evoke the synesthetic experience. Kandinsky frequently spoke of how an understanding of art and music can expand the value of using associative techniques aimed at enhancing sensory exchange, and the idea that he developed his innate capabilities is supported indirectly by our knowledge of how he worked as well as the circumstantial evidence contained in his writings (Kandinsky, 1913). He also desired to bring the essence of cross-modal experience to a wider audience. Kandinsky explored cross-modal sensory experience on the assumption "that one can feel the multi-sensory consonances and dissonances in simultaneously performed color movements, musical movements and dance movements" (quoted in van Campen, 1997). One well-known collaborative work that conveys this was his musical play, *The Yellow Clang*. Conceived with the composer Thomas de Hartmann and the dancer Alexander Sacharoff, this production was one of the springboards of the modern dance movement, from Isadora Duncan to Serge Diaghilev.

On perusing the literature, I came across reference to synesthetes who associated colors with the alphabet in addition to numbers. My first thought was that my own synesthesia was limited to numbers, but then I started running through the letters of the alphabet and realized that, indeed, they did evoke particular colors when I paid attention to this modality. These letter colors seem fainter than the number colors, but dwelling on each letter allows its color to emerge in my image space, again as though a spotlight is on an image of the letter. The colors of the letters are: A – dark gray, B – persimmon, C – blue-white, D – buff, E – light brown, F – light gray, G – chestnut, H – sky blue, I – mid gray, J – violet, K – dark brown, L – aquamarine, M – dark blue, N – dark green, O – white, P – blue, Q – white, R – maroon, S – lemon yellow, T – orange, U – gray, V - moss green, W – primary yellow, X – apricot, Y – (blank), and Z – orange tiger stripes. It is noteworthy that there are missing colors from both the number and letter lists: primary (grass) green, pink, purple, and cyan.

The persimmon of B is that orange-yellow characteristic of the fruit, a little more orange than apricot. The aquamarine of the letter L is a blue near the border with green, but not in the narrow band of exact green-blue that is denoted by cyan. The specificity of these designations raises the question of how the synesthete identifies the color of the letter. In my case, the process of defining these colors is an interplay with the verbal description. I focus attention on the letter and realize that a color is evoked, then try to name that color. The color name itself evokes a perceived color that is either felt consonant with or different from the color evoked by the letter. I try different color names until I find one that does not evoke a dissonance reaction. For some reason, no color was evoked by attending to the letter Y.

Auditory Color Experiences

Color–sound associations are also a common form of synesthesia (Baron-Cohen, Harrison, Goldstein & Wyke, 1993; Marks, 1978; Myers, 1916), although they may occur predominantly among musicians and relate to the associations between letters and notes or numbers and the intervals between notes, rather than directly to the sounds themselves. For example, I do not have absolute pitch, although I have a very accurate sense of relative pitch. (It is excruciating for me to listen to violinists such as Yehudi Menuhin, because his sense of pitch seemed to be loose enough that he often played slightly out of tune. Similarly with many opera singers, whose voice tonalities are so complex that it may be difficult for them to identify the exact pitch, or match the pitch of their voice to that of the orchestra.) However, unless I have recently heard a specified note, I cannot tell the pitches of notes with any accuracy, so they do not have specific colors associated with them. Indeed, it would be interesting to look for individuals with the same sense of relative pitch as mine, but who can generate absolute pitch based on a synesthetic association with color or other sensory experience (e.g., "that must be A because it is green").

The whole issue of absolute pitch is an intersensory question akin to synesthesia. In fact, it is hard for me to fully conceptualize absolute pitch in the abstract. A music teacher once got very excited because she thought that my 7-year-old son had absolute pitch and should go to the music conservatory to become a musician. When I tried to test him myself, it became clear that I could not really do so because he did not have a clear association between the letter designation of a note and its sound in order to report which note had been played. It is not until this arbitrary convention is firmly established that one can even ask the question about absolute pitch. In the absence of this convention, testing for absolute pitch would require playing one note first and then another at a later time, and asking whether the two were the same or different. But doing this task is described as having relative pitch, while absolute pitch requires naming the note when played only once. I suppose that one could play a note one day and then play a single note the next day and ask the relation between the two notes. Perhaps remembering the note overnight would qualify as establishing absolute pitch, in the form of long-term memory for a note in those listeners unfamiliar with musical notation.

In terms of pitch synesthesia, the closest my own sensations would come is a visual association of a rather monochrome gradient of shades from dark gray or brown for the low notes through a pearlescent white in the mid-range of the keyboard to a bright silver for the high notes. These associations seem too "obvious" to me to really qualify as synesthesia. It is just a general tendency from low to high notes to correspond to the low to high dimension of brightness. On the other hand, even the terminology of low frequencies being considered spatially low, and high ones spatially high, is a kind of synesthesia. I was amazed to find that my young son could often start playing the piano by reading the music upside down - playing the left hand (low notes) from the upper stave and the right hand (high notes) from the lower stave. He would say "Why does this sound wrong?" and then happily resolve the problem by switching hands for the high and low staves. This error seems to illustrate that there is nothing inherently high about "high" notes, since at least some individuals need to learn the association of up on the page with high-note sounds as an arbitrary convention. So perhaps this is a kind of synesthesia, but one in the form of a rather broad association of the two dimensions (height and pitch) rather than a one-to-one mapping of one set of discrete features to another, like letters and colors.

The upshot of the issue is that I do not have synesthesia for individual notes except to the extent that I think of their letter names, which I would regard as color–letter synesthesia rather than color–pitch synesthesia. I do, however, have color associations with the chord types. In one sense, the chords are their own auditory colors, and musicians use the term "chromatic" in a sense close to this. Chords and the transitions between them seem highly chromatic, in the sense of evoking strong sensations that seem very different from each other along many perceptual dimensions. My predominant sense is that chords are very enjoyable in their own right, without necessarily evoking specific associations, either with color, meaning, or any other modality. Just as green is qualitatively different from purple, without the difference being describable to a blind person, so the dominant seventh chord is vividly different from the diminished chord or the augmented chord, without necessarily evoking color associations.

However, if I pay attention to the chromatic quality of chords, I do have noticeable color associations with them. Of course, these will only be meaningful to those with a musical background, but table 3.1 describes those synesthetic associations. Once again, these are not verbal associations, but experienced colors in the image space accessible when I close my eyes or switch attention away from the current visual scene at which I am looking.

The yellow of the major chord is descriptive of the sense that the sun has come out when it is played—a bright, cheerful, positive sound. (This is true whatever key the chord is played in.) The blue of the minor chord may be influenced by the common use of the term "blue" and "blues" for the minor chord and its use in songs. It might be closer to violet for me (and even deeper for Duke Ellington, as implied by his tune "Mood Indigo"). I have never come across the verbal association of violet with the minor chord, so the shift in that direction would appear to be my own synesthetic connection. The diminished 3rd is characteristic of the epiphany in the first movement of Beethoven's "Moonlight Sonata" a familiar piece for many amateur musicians. It has many chromatic transitions, dominantly among the minor keys, but the climax consists of a sequence of diminished thirds that plumb the depths of the water over which the moon is reflecting, gaining what for me is a purplish hue. Again, this association seems to be synesthetic rather than experiential because the moon's physical reflection has a greenish rather than violet tinge.

Further exploration of musical experience reveals that I have strong associations of color with Beethoven's symphonies, in the sense that the color swirls around as I listen to, or imagine, characteristic themes from symphonies. His Third Symphony, "Eroica," is golden yellow, particularly its luscious slow movement; the famous Fifth Symphony is light yellow, although the opening drumbeats of the first movement are black; the Sixth, "Pastoral," is predominantly scarlet, the Seventh is grass green (for the textural growth of the themes in the second movement), the Eighth is a classical blue, and the Ninth is a rich brown, associated strongly with those powerful cellos

Table 3.1. The perceived colors of chords

Chord type	Example	Color
Major	C, E, G	Yellow
Minor	C, E♭, G	Blue
Dominant 7th	C, E, G, B♭	Orange
Diminished 3rd	C, E♭, F♯	Purple
Augmented 4th	C, E♯, G♯	Mauve
Seventh	C, E, G, B	Lime green

that carry the "Ode to Joy" theme. There are thus clear associations of these extended pieces with particular colors. Comparison with the colors of my numbers reveals that these colors are tightly coupled to those of my digits, although I first thought of the colors in relation to the music and only later realized the connection to the numbers.

However, many of my color associations extend to pieces well beyond the Beethoven numbering system. Wagner's "Tristan und Isolde" idyll is again a golden yellow; Berlioz's "Symphonie Fantastique" is crimson, Mahler's First Symphony evokes a chartreuse green, Rachmaninov's Second Piano Concerto is a concatenation of purple hues, and so on. The color may not characterize all passages of these pieces, but it suffuses my memory of them and represents the dominant impression. Evidently, the number–color association is not the whole story. My sense was that these associations are widely shared, at least among music lovers, despite the claims of only 1 in 2,000 being synesthetes, but I have not done any systematic survey.

Auditory Replay and Epileptic Auras

In the present context, it may be relevant to bring up the concept of auditory replay of well-known tunes or music in one's head. This phenomenon is widely experienced as an annoying repetition that cannot be suppressed. There is nothing that we see that impresses itself on the visual system in this way (except for highly-charged emotional experiences, such as a dagger plunging towards one's face during an attempted robbery). But almost everyone seems to experience a catchy tune "going around in their head," to the point of annoyance if it is a tawdry jingle. While not a cross-modal synesthesia, this auditory replay is a vivid experience of a sensory quality that is not physically present, evoked by a relatively brief exposure to the tune. It gives a sense of the internal experience that may be evoked in synesthetic evocations.

Auditory replay is reminiscent of the ground-breaking experiments of Penfield and Rasmussen (1950), who found that electrical stimulation in the temporal lobes of epileptic patients undergoing brain surgery evoked long sequences of visual, auditory, or generic intersensory memories of specific past events long forgotten. This research revealed that memories can be stored in time-sequential fashion, like a videotape of the events as they unfolded. The auditory replay exhibits the same characteristic—not just a sound but an ordered music sequence. Evidently these sequences are stored in, or accessible through, the temporal lobe.

The epilepsy of these patients is also germane to the issue of synesthesia. Many epileptics experience 'auras' as a precursor to a seizure event. The aura is a sensory experience specific to the neural location of the seizure. Epileptics have reported feeling a wind rushing through their stomach, seeing visual motion, or hearing bells pealing before a seizure, for example. Another kind of neural seizure is the fortification migraine that passes through the visual field in many people, with a duration almost universally of 18 min. The 'fortification' is a boundary criss-cross pattern of colored scintillations that progresses across the visual field from fovea to periphery, leaving a region of temporary blindness behind it. I have experienced several such events over the past decade.

Recently, one such event was triggered by a synesthetic activation. When I stepped into the shower one morning and turned my face to the spray, the water drops drumming on my forehead elicited the visual experience of intense red sparks with yellow highlights in the image space before my face. This activation made me feel slightly overwhelmed, but I completed the shower and soon realized that a fortification migraine had begun its course across my visual field. It was unusual in that it progressed downward through the inferior field rather than the usual superior direction that I experience. Evidently, the visuotactile synesthesia of the water droplets had been strong enough to trigger the neural migraine attack. This experience suggests a new twist on the concept of synesthesia—the synesthetic migraine. My visual migraines are then triggered by seeing bright reflections or patterns, but in this case the visual trigger was evidently the synesthetic experience of the bright droplets.

The Visual Consequences of Meditation

While not strictly a form of synesthesia, it seems germane to discuss the visuotactile experience that can be evoked by particular forms of meditation. There are many forms of meditation, from chanting to yoga to self-hypnosis. One form that interested me in the 1960s (when the Beatles went to an Indian ashram), was the idea of meditating by trying to look out through the third eye, conceptualized as being in the center of the forehead. The aim was to explore the experience of meditation per se, rather than with any religious goal in mind. I sat cross-legged on a bed to try this, in the amateur lotus position with eyes closed. As I elevated my attention in the attempt to direct my gaze out through my forehead, I began to see a strong golden glow appear in the distance of my dark image space. This glow grew brighter and gradually approached, filling my visual field. Over a period of about 15 min, the light seemed to spread over my face, down my neck and shoulders, and to envelope my whole body. It engendered a feeling of great calm and serenity, as though the light was evaporating my body in the classic Zen sense, making my spirit one with the universe, as it is often described.

It should be emphasized that I am reporting these observations as a purely experiential occurrence. I did not, and do not, draw any implications as to the existence of an external spiritual realm, or a higher being beyond. It seems that I had discovered the trigger for the core mystical experience by this simple imaging strategy of attempting to look through the third eye. I had no prior practice with meditation, or other religious interests. My view is that anyone should be able to duplicate the experience if they follow the same strategy. I interpret the effect as a physiological result of elevating and converging the eyes in their sockets (which I verified by palpation to be the physical consequence of the strategy).

It is not widely appreciated, but EEG practitioners are generally aware that elevating the eyes has the almost universal effect of generating a large increase in the alpha rhythms recorded from the occipital lobe (Mulholland and Evans, 1965). The mechanism of this alpha enhancement has not been established, but it is a powerful phenomenon. Since alpha is closely associated with both meditation and biofeedback relaxation, I assume that the effect of the image of looking through the third eye is to elevate the eyes in their sockets and cause an immediate increase in the cortical alpha activity, leading to the luminous experience that I describe. Moreover, it is well known to professional hypnotists that the most hypnotizable subjects typically have the whites of their eyes visible below the iris (above the lower eyelid), implying an unusual elevation of the eyes in their sockets. While the mechanism of the link between eye elevation and alpha activation remains mysterious, there seem to be too many connections to dismiss it as coincidence.

The visual and emotional experience of being enveloped by an approaching light is well-known in another context—near-death experiences (Kübler-Ross, 1992). Many have drawn the implication that the universality of these experiences implies that they are, in fact, tapping into an external reality that represents a view of existence after death. In fact, similar images of a holy light can be found in classical art and accounts of Christian heaven, both verbal and visual. The ease with which similar experiences of an approaching light bringing calm and a sense of loss of self may be evoked simply by elevating the eyes in their sockets suggests an alternative view: that the patients who have become deeply anesthetized (either artificially or by the ravages of disease or starvation) have elevated their eyes and triggered the luminous experience by the same alpha-enhancement circuit that my meditation achieved. The universality of the experience is not, then, a reflection of an external reality but of a neurophysiological curiosity whose activation has similar effects in all brains, whether near death or fully healthy. I have not followed up on this hypothesis to determine what proportion of people are susceptible to the visuotactile experience of submersion in light, but anyone who doubts it is welcome to try the technique for themselves.

Variety and Frequency

The final issue I will address is that of the frequency of occurrence of varieties of synesthesia. It is well established that scientific surveys find synesthesia to be as rare as 1 in 2,000 individuals (Baron-Cohen et al., 1993). It is not clear, however, whether such surveys would have found a level of synesthesia such as I describe. Is it really possible that a sensory effect that is so readily evoked by a small dose of hallucinogen would be so sparsely represented in the population?

In this context, I report a conversation among a group of attendees of a conference on vision, at which there had been a talk about synesthesia. I canvassed the group as to who had any kind of synesthetic experience. Although not many reported color–number synesthesia, one volunteered that the seasons of the year had strong coloration, while a second described vivid coloration of the months around an oval shape.

One participant also described an elaborate number-based spatial organization. The numbers progressed around an imaginary clock face in traditional fashion until 10 o'clock, then began to spiral backwards onto a second clock face above and behind the first up to number 20, with successive loops of the helix fading into the distance for each decade beyond that. One can see how such an arrangement would be derived from exposure to learning to tell time, but the point is that the arrangement was projected visually into physical space, with the explainer indicating the vividness of the visual representation by helical gestures.

In a group of eight people, more than 50% reported some form of synesthesia, a vastly different rate from the 1/2,000 in the literature. In fact, on further questioning, most of the group agreed that music evoked a sense of movement in a visual space before them. (In the context, the term "volume" for the strength of sound has interesting synesthetic connotation, since it implies that the sound fills a three-dimensional image space.) Typically, the strength of the sound connoted its distance, just as intended by many composers, with loud sounds being close and soft ones far away. This is, of course, a natural interpretation given our experience of the distance of a particular sound source. The point here is that the sounds were experienced in a spatial manner, not just conceptualized in that way, qualifying the experience as a synesthetic one. Music was reported to evoke a wide variety of rotating, soaring, and dancing motions through space.

Thus, we have gone from synesthesias of predominantly color associations with sounds, letters, and numbers to a wide range of intersensory links and spatial experiences in the internal image space. Once synesthesia is cast in this form, it may be found to be a rather more common occurrence than is commonly appreciated.

Acknowledgments   My thanks to Amy Ione for critical comments.

References

Baron-Cohen, S., Harrison, J., Goldstein, L., & Wyke, M. (1993). Coloured speech perception: Is synaesthesia what happens when modularity breaks down? *Perception, 22,* 419–426.

Kandinsky, V. (1913/1982). Reminiscences. In K.C.L. Lindsay & P. Vergo (Eds. and Trans.), *Kandinsky: Complete writings on art* (p. 364). London: Faber & Faber.

Kosslyn, S.M. (1994). *Image and brain: The resolution of the imagery debate.* Cambridge, MA: MIT Press.

Kübler-Ross, E. (1992). *On life after death.* Berkeley, CA: Celestial Arts Publishing.

Marks, L.E. (1978). *The unity of the senses: Interrelations among the modalities.* New York: Academic Press.

Mattingley, J.B., Rich, A.N., Yelland, G., & Bradshaw, J.L. (2001). Unconscious priming eliminates automatic binding of colour and alphanumeric form in synaesthesia. *Nature, 410,* 580–582.

Mills, C.B., Viguers, M.L., Edelson, S.K., Thomas, A.T., Simon-Dack, S.L., & Innis, J.A. (2002). The color of two alphabets for a multilingual synesthete. *Perception, 31(11),* 1371–1394.

Mulholland, T., & Evans, C.R. (1965). An unexpected artefact in the human electroencephalogram concering alpha rhythm and the orientation of the eyes. *Nature, 206,* 746.

Myers, C. (1914). A case of synaesthesia. *British Journal of Psychology, 6,* 228–232.

Penfield W., & Rasmussen T. (1950). *The cerebral cortex of man. A clinical study of localization of function.* New York: Macmillan.

Ramachandran, V.S., & Hubbard, E.M. (2001). Synaesthesia—A window into perception, thought and language. *Journal of Consciousness Studies, 8(12),* 3–34.

van Campen, C. (1997). Synesthesia and artistic experimentation. *Psyche, 3(6).*

Part II

Perception and Attention

4

On the Perceptual Reality
of Synesthetic Color

*Randolph Blake, Thomas J. Palmeri, René Marois,
and Chai-Youn Kim*

Synesthesia, the mental mixture of real and illusory sensory experiences, is incredibly fascinating to read or hear about but frustratingly complex to study. Those of us who are not synesthetes are spellbound by the accounts of those who are, but at the same time we are mystified by why these mixtures would occur. As the chapters in this volume document, scientific investigation of synesthesia has rapidly developed into an area of great interest and debate within cognitive neuroscience, and our group at Vanderbilt University is among those seeking to understand this fascinating phenomenon.

In our work, we have focused on color-graphemic synesthesia: the perception of color when viewing achromatic alphanumeric characters (in this chapter, we use the term "achromatic" to refer to figures printed in black ink against a white background). Judging from the existing literature on synesthesia, as well as from the tremendous volume of unsolicited, anecdotal accounts we have received from synesthetes, color-graphemic synesthesia appears to be the most common form of the condition. Certainly this variety of synesthesia provides for some of the most memorable and amusing accounts. Thus, for example, one individual who sees digits vividly colored volunteered to us that she performed arithmetic using her colors and was surprised upon first learning that others did not: "I thought everyone did math with colors—that yellow plus yellow was red for everyone." Another individual complained that she often confused appointments scheduled for Tuesday or for Thursday, because both days are "red." Still another confessed to an unfounded dislike of the city of Houston "just because the word was a ugly shade of brown" and another acknowledged that "my husband knows that I couldn't have married him if his name had been the 'wrong' color for me . . . we are, color-wise, perfectly compatible." These and the many other transcriptions we have compiled from synesthetic volunteers lead us to accept that their graphemic colors are vivid and, in some sense, real.

The great challenge in learning about synesthesia, of course, is to develop objective experimental strategies for going beyond these colorful verbal accounts. To be honest, our interest in synesthesia grew entirely out of the fortuitous identification of a few individuals within our academic community who experience color-graphemic synesthesia. Although none in our research group was expert in color vision, we were all intrigued by the initial descriptions offered by these individuals, and we were gratified by their motivation to explore their synesthetic experiences in more detail. The overarching theme to our work with these two people (L.R. and W.O.) has been an exploration of the perceptual reality of their synesthetic colors.

In this chapter we address three important issues concerning synesthesia: (1) the extent to which synesthesia is genuinely perceptual in nature, (2) the degree to which attention and awareness are necessary to the synesthesic experience, and (3) possible neural substrates for this most unusual perceptual experience.

An Introduction to W.O. and L.R.

Both of our adult synesthetes (one male and one female) have perfectly normal vision, including excellent trichromatic color perception as assessed by the modified version of the Munsell 100-Hue test and the Ichihara color plates. W.O. describes seeing "colored" numbers and letters as far back as he can remember, but L.R. actually dates her color associations to a set of colored letters and numbers affixed to her refrigerator door (and, indeed, her color associations correspond exactly to the color sequence of those magnets). On multiple occasions we have asked these two individuals to match their synesthetic colors using one of the color palettes from Adobe Photoshop, and their color matches are remarkably reliable. When performing their matches, W.O. and L.R. typically spend considerable time getting each color just right, implying that their experiences are subtle and not simply categorical in nature. Incidentally, W.O. and L.R. both take great pleasure in their colors and refuse to perform any exercise that might eliminate or alter their colors. W.O. in particular relies on his colors for remembering technical terms (he is a neuroanatomist) as well as for recalling telephone numbers. We have not yet documented the extent to which W.O.'s memory performance indeed benefits from his colors, but based on the results of others (Smilek, Dixon, Cudahy & Merikle, 2002) we have no reason to doubt his claims.

Both synesthetes describe seeing their colors upon the achromatic letters themselves, not simply in their mind's eye; this description would place them in the category of "projective" synesthetes as opposed to "associative" synesthetes (e.g., see Dixon, Myles, Smilek & Merikle, 2002). When viewing alphanumeric characters printed in colored ink, W.O. and L.R. readily perceive the real colors of the characters but, at the same time, can perceive their synesthetic colors in the characters. This simultaneous existence of two colors in a single figure is one of the most baffling aspects of their descriptions. We have tried presenting a given letter against a background whose color exactly matches the individual's synesthetic color (e.g., a P, which is synesthetically yellow for W.O., against a yellow background), but the letter remains synesthetically visible. We have employed a speeded reaction time task on which W.O. and L.R. must make a vowel/consonant judgment for achromatic characters presented against colored backgrounds (some matched to the synesthetic color of the character presented on a given trial). Here, too, we find no differences in speed or in accuracy regardless of the relation between the synesthetic color of the character and the real color of the background (but see Smilek, Dixon, Cudahy & Merikle, 2001).

L.R. and W.O. both consistently describe seeing synesthetic colors when shown characters defined solely by retinal disparity (random-dot stereograms) and in characters defined solely by differential motion (random-dot cinematograms). These observations point to cortical processes in the induction of color-graphemic synesthesia, for the figural information specifying the character's identity must be extracted by neural mechanisms sensitive to binocular disparity and mechanisms sensitive to structured motion. This does not necessarily mean, however, that the synesthetic experience itself is expressed within these areas; we return to this issue of interactions between induction and expression of the actual synesthetic experience in a later section of this chapter.

Concerning the stimulus conditions eliciting synesthetic experiences, there is one enigmatic way in which W.O. and L.R. differ. We have induced afterimages of alphanumeric characters by having W.O. and L.R. stare for 1 min at achromatic induction figures, after which they stare at a white background. Not surprisingly, both W.O. and L.R. experience a clear afterimage of the induction character. L.R. perceives the synesthetic color appropriate for that character (e.g., her afterimage of the letter A is perceived as red, her synesthetic color for A), but to his surprise and our's, W.O. experiences no color whatsoever for his afterimages. Indeed, the first time we performed this test on him, W.O. spontaneously exclaimed that he had never seen letters without colors and he continues to puzzle over his missing colors for characters viewed as afterimages. We have convinced ourselves that the "problem" has nothing to do with the clarity of W.O.'s afterimages, for he does see colors in real characters blurred and reduced in contrast to a degree mimicking his afterimages. Moreover, we have confirmed that the absence of colors in his afterimages is not attributable to the synesthetic color he invariably experiences during the induction period. And, finally, we have verified that W.O. experiences normal colored afterimages when exposed to colored inducing figures. To date, W.O.'s failure to perceive synesthetic colors in achromatic afterimages remains a mystery.

For both W.O. and L.R., semantic context can modulate the perceived color of an alphanumeric character. Looking at figure 4.1a, you may experience the middle "character" either as the number 13 or as the capital letter B, depending on the context in which the character appears. W.O. and L.R. both describe the character as one color when it is seen as a number and an entirely different color when it is seen as a letter. Both individuals report that the color competes between these two alternatives when both contexts are present simultaneously, and they claim to be able to influence this competition by attending to one context or the other. In a similar vein, both W.O. and L.R. can see either of two colors when viewing Navon-type figures (Navon, 1977) such as the one shown in figure 4.1b; the entire figure takes on one color when attending to the global form and another color when attending to the local elements composing that form (see also Ramachandran & Hubbard, 2001b; Rich & Mattingley, 2001). In a subsequent section, we return to this question of the possible role of attention in the perception of synesthetic colors.

W.O. and L.R.'s verbal descriptions make it very tempting to conclude that color-graphemic synesthetes genuinely perceive colors when viewing achromatic characters, colors that are as perceptually real as those the rest of

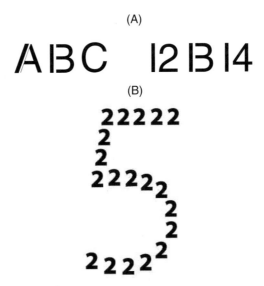

Figure 4.1. Two examples of ambiguous characters. (A) The middle character may be seen as the number 13 or the letter B. (B) A Navon-type figure in which a global digit is composed of many local digits.

us experience when viewing characters printed in colored ink. Based on the observations described so far, however, we cannot rule out the possibility that these descriptions are conceptually based, arising from strongly overlearned associations between colors and alphanumeric characters. Most of us associate "green" with "envy" because we have heard or read this metaphor over and over, but we do not actually experience the color green when we see the word envy. Perhaps graphemic synesthetes have a richer catalog of these same kinds of conceptually grounded associations, so deeply ingrained that viewing a given character automatically brings to mind a given color. To rule out this conceptual account of color-graphemic synesthesia requires going beyond verbal description and relying on more indirect techniques for assessing the perceptual reality of synesthetic colors. Toward that end, we have developed variants of several well-known visual tasks, our aim being to learn whether synesthetic colors behave like real colors.

Do Synesthetic Colors Behave Like Real Colors?

Consider first the Stroop task (Stroop, 1935), on which color names interfere with the speed and accuracy of naming the colors of ink in which those words are written (thus, for example, it takes longer to respond "red" when presented with the word BLUE printed in red ink than it does when presented with the word BOAT printed in red ink). Several research groups, ours included, have created variants of the classic Stroop task on which non–color-related words are printed in ink colors that are congruent and incongruent with the color associations of a synesthetic observer. For example, when W.O. is asked to name the colors of ink in which successively exposed words are printed, he is especially fast if those words are printed in colors that match his synesthetic colors for those words (e.g., BANK printed in pink). But when words are printed in ink colors that do not match his synesthetic colors (e.g., BANK printed in blue), W.O. takes longer to name the ink colors and stumbles over many words. His speed and accuracy at naming the colors of inks in which arbitrary characters are printed fall in between his congruent and incongruent performance levels. Comparable synesthetic Stroop effects have been reported by others (Dixon, Smilek, Cudahy & Merikle, 2000; Mills, Boteler & Oliver, 1999; Mattingly, Rich, Yelland & Bradshaw, 2001; Odgaard, Flowers & Mradman, 1999), pointing to an inability to ignore the synesthetic colors associated with words (in the same way that nonsynesthetic observers cannot ignore the real colors of the ink in which color names are printed). Still, these results do not definitively rule out conceptual processing as the basis of the synesthetic Stroop effect. After all, normal observers can show Stroop interference when tested with geometric figures and color names that have been repeatedly associated to the point where the associations are highly automatized (MacLeod & Dunbar, 1988; see also MacLeod, 1991). If conceptual association leads to Stroop interference for normal observers, it could certainly do the same thing in the case of synesthesia. For this reason, we were motivated to try another task—visual search—where color plays a potent role that is generally believed to be genuinely perceptual in nature.

It is well known that a target of one color can easily be picked out from an array of background distractors differing in color from the target (Treisman & Gelade, 1980). Do synesthetically colored targets and distractors behave in a same fashion? In one of our first interviews with W.O., we showed him an array of letters like that depicted in plate 4.1a and simply asked him what he saw. Without hesitation, he exclaimed that the 2 stood out conspicuously from the 5s because it was a different color as in plate 4.1b. When shown different variants of these kinds of arrays, he continued to respond quickly and with confidence based on the color disparity between the oddball digit and the background of distractors. This "pop-out" effect encouraged us to perform a more systematic study of W.O.'s ability to find a target digit among a background of distractor digits using the classic visual search paradigm.

In this visual search task, the targets and distractors always appeared as white numerals against a black background, but, of course, W.O. always described these numerals with their characteristic colors. On half the presentations, the target digit was present among distractors and on the other half the target was absent; from trial to trial the number of elements in an array (set size) varied from 16 to 36. Observers (W.O. and seven nonsynesthetic control observers) were instructed to press one of two keys as quickly as possible to indicate whether or not the target was present. We devised two categories of search arrays, "color-similar" trials in which target and background elements were highly similar in synesthetic color (e.g., a 8 amongst 6s, which are both blue for W.O.) and "color-different" trials in which target and background elements differed in synesthetic color (e.g., a 2 among 5s, which are orange and green for W.O., respectively).

Results from this study are shown in plate 4.1c,d. For nonsynesthetic observers, response times (RT) on target-present trials increased with set size for both categories of search arrays. For W.O., RTs on color-similar trials (i.e., 8 among 6s) were comparable to those for nonsynesthetes, increasing markedly with set size. But for color-different trials (2 among 5s) W.O. showed considerably faster RTs, especially for the largest set size. Moreover, these extraordinarily fast RTs were not achieved at the expense of accuracy; W.O.'s error rate in the color-different condition was equivalent to that for the color-same condition, and both matched the error rates of nonsynesthetic observers. These RT results substantiate W.O.'s subjective report that the oddball "colored" item "pops out" in much the same way that a real orange item would pop out among an array of green distractor items. However, as can be seen in plate 4.1d, it did take W.O. a little longer to find the target among a large set of distractors, implying that search was not performed in a strictly parallel fashion. We return to the implications of this finding in a subsequent section.

Our visual search results dovetail nicely with experiments by Ramachandran and Hubbard (2001a) showing that color-graphemic synesthetes are more accurate than nonsynesthetic controls at judging the shape formed by a cluster of letters whose "color" differs from that of the background letters. Presumably the common color of the elements defining the shape promotes perceptual grouping, which, in turn, causes the shape to emerge from among the background letters. Of course, the skeptic could develop an alternative account for this observation in which semantically related features (e.g., digits previously associated with a given color) automatically form salient groupings that readily segregate from groupings formed by other semantically related features. For that matter, this kind of explanation, which downplays the visual potency of synesthetic colors, could perhaps be extended to our visual search results as well.

To test definitively whether synesthetic colors are perceptually equivalent to real colors, we devised another, more foolproof test of the perceptual reality of synesthetic colors: We determined whether synesthetically experienced colors can produce an orientation contingent color after effect—the McCollough effect (McCollough, 1965). Ordinarily, to induce such an after-effect, observers alternately view, say, red vertical contours and green horizontal contours, with this alternating adaptation continuing for many minutes. Thereafter, an achromatic test figure composed of horizontal and vertical gratings appears faintly colored but in the reversed pairing of color and form, with the vertical bars appearing greenish and the horizontal bars appearing pinkish. In the pilot experiment of work soon to be reported (Kim, Blake, Palmeri, Marois & Whetsell, 2003), we devised tailor-made inducing figures for W.O. and for L.R., figures in which vertical contours were defined by letters generating the experience of red and horizontal contours were defined by letters generating the experience of green (see figure 4.2). It is important to keep in mind that the letters themselves were achromatic—it was the synesthetic experience that "colored" the horizontal and vertical gratings. The observer was exposed to one of these synesthetic gratings and then the other for 5 sec at a time, for a total of 5 min of adaptation. Next, the observer was shown a test figure composed of horizontal and vertical contours defined by nonalphabetic characters that elicited no synesthetic sensation on their own.

Upon viewing this test figure, L.R. described the vertical contours as having a faint green appearance and the horizontal ones as being faint pink. It should be stressed that L.R. has never seen nor heard of the McCollough effect, and she expressed puzzlement at the color appearance of the forms in

Inducing Figures

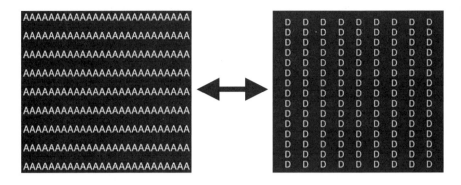

Test Figure

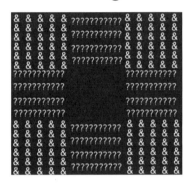

Figure 4.2. Gratings used to induce a synesthetic McCollough effect. For L.R. the horizontal grating appears green and the vertical grating appears red.

the test figure, forms that never before had appeared colored. W.O.'s experience was somewhat different, but in a very intriguing way. He too saw the horizontal contours as pinkish, but he experienced no color whatsoever on the vertical contours. While he had not heard of the McCollough effect, W.O. was aware of colored afterimages. We next tested W.O. using vertical and horizontal induction gratings that were really colored red and green, once again alternately adapting him for a total of 5 min. At the end of this period, he again experienced horizontal contours as pinkish and vertical contours as colorless. We have no idea why W.O. gets only half of the McCollough effect, but it is noteworthy that this pattern of results obtains for contours that are really colored as well as those that are synesthetically colored.

These remarkable after-effects defy explanation in terms of overlearned associations between color names and alphanumeric characters. If W.O. and L.R. were merely "thinking" about their colors during adaptation, not actually seeing them, why would they subsequently report seeing complementary colors in portions of a test figure that ordinarily appear achromatic? We believe W.O. and L.R. were reporting what they saw in the achromatic test figure—genuine orientation-selective color after-effects, not synesthetic associations—and those color experiences were generated by the colors of the inducing figures, not the names of the inducing colors. These results thus provide compelling evidence for the perceptual reality of synesthetic colors.

But if synesthetic colors are indeed comparable to "real" colors, we are once again confronted with the paradox mentioned earlier: W.O. and L.R. experience both real and synesthetic colors in the same figure at the same time. How can the letter A printed in blue ink look at once both "blue" and "red"? Does the synesthetic "redness" of the A alter its genuine blueness? What, in other words, is the nature of the interaction between synesthetic colors and real colors? The following section summarizes some of our efforts to answer this question.

Do Synesthetic Colors Interact with Real Colors?

We began by having W.O. carefully and repeatedly match the perceived synesthetic color of digits printed in different colored inks. W.O. reliably sets a point within the Adobe Photoshop color palette map to essentially the same hue/brightness value upon repeated testing of a given character printed in a variety of different colored inks. His synesthetic color matches, in other words, are not affected by the actual color of the inducing figures. This conclusion stands up to forced-choice testing in which W.O. must select the best synesthetic match from among an array of eight color chips differing slightly from one another in hue and brightness. Despite random variations in the position and values of the chips, W.O. always selects the chip displaying the same color/brightness value.

Similarly, we have asked W.O. to match the color of a circular patch composed of one group of identical digits (e.g., a circular patch of 9s which, for WO, appear yellow) surrounded by a large annulus of many repetitions of a non-alphanumeric character printed in ink of a given color (e.g., an annular patch of &s printed in blue). We were careful to select synesthetic color and real color combinations that, under ordinary circumstances yield reliable color contrast effects (e.g., the central "yellow" patch would appear slightly brighter and more orangish compared to its appearance in the absence of the surrounding blue annulus). Again, the real colored surround did not influence W.O.'s matches, implying that his synesthetic colors are immune to an effect from real colors. This observation stands in contrast to the results described by Smilek et al. (2001), who reported that a digit-color synesthete made more errors locating a digit presented against a colored background when the synesthetic color of the digit matched the real color of the background (the statistically significant difference in percent-correct performance for congruent vs. incongruent trials was 8%). Smilek et al. employed a speeded decision task, whereas we have allowed W.O. extended viewing when making color matches; conceivably, exposure duration is critical in determining the strength of the interaction between real and synesthetic colors, although our vowel/consonant RT experiments with W.O. and L.R., described earlier, were designed to encourage speeded decisions, and we did not find differences in RT between background congruent and background incongruent conditions. We have no ready explanation for this seeming discrepancy between our findings and those of Smilek et al.

While our simple color-matching experiments do not hint at any systematic influences between synesthetic and real colors, more recent studies from our lab have revealed situations where these two forms of color perceptions interact (Kim, Blake, Palmeri, Marois & Whetsell, 2003). Although our results are still preliminary, we are confident reporting several interesting results. First, perception of bistable apparent motion (AM) sequences can be strongly influenced by the color relations among the AM tokens, even when one pair of tokens is colored in virtue of synesthesia and the other pair is actually colored. In plate 4.2, notice that frame 1 of this simple AM sequence consists of two achromatic letters and frame 2 consists of two colored figures. Nonsynesthetic observers viewing these two frames shown in rapid succession can see the tokens moving in either of the two possible directions, clockwise or counterclockwise, and over trials the likelihood of either motion path is approximately equal. Both W.O. and L.R., however, consistently see the path of motion for which their synesthetic colors in frame 1 correspond to the real colors in frame 2 (e.g., clockwise in the example shown in plate 4.2). Now, it is well established that normal observers readily resolve ambiguous motion when real colors are available to solve the correspondence problem (Kolers & von Grünau, 1976). The behavior of W.O. and L.R. imply that motion correspondence also can be established between real colors and synesthetic colors. Incidentally, both W.O. and L.R. reliably perceive a given path of motion when real colored tokens are presented in frame 1 and synesthetically colored letters are presented in frame 2 and, for that matter, when different achromatic letters generating the same synesthetic color are presented in both frames of the AM sequence.

In a second project, we are finding that a synesthetically colored letter readily groups with an actually colored, non-alphanumeric form during binocular rivalry, the result being an increased incidence of combined predominance of the achromatic letter and colored form. In fact, the magnitude of this grouping tendency is the same as that found in nonsynesthetic observers viewing pairs of real colored figures. This tendency for synesthetically comparable digits to perceptually group is reminiscent of an observation reported by Hubbard and Ramachandran (2001a); they found that strings of numerals tended to group into extended contours when their synesthetic colors were similar.

In summary, we do find conditions where synesthetic colors interact with real colors to influence performance on visual tasks. Given these reliable, robust interactions, it is all the more mysterious to us why real colors and synesthetic colors do not interact in the determination of color appearance. Resolution of this paradox awaits further work.

Are Attention and Awareness Necessary for Synesthesia?

Granting the perceptual reality of synesthesia, an independent issue concerns the role of attention to the achromatic figure that induces a color experience. In other words, must the synesthete attend to and be aware of the identity of the inducing stimulus before that stimulus can trigger a synesthetic experience? According to Mattingley et al. (2001), synesthetic interactions arise after overt recognition of inducing stimuli: "synaesthesia is elicited by selectively attended stimuli that are available for conscious report" (p. 582). In a similar vein, Rich and Mattingley (2002) conclude that "activation of the colour module might not occur before the letter or digit is fully processed and available for overt report" (p. 51). These two related conclusions imply the operation of a serial process, by which an alphanumeric form must first be explicitly recognized ("that figure is an A . . ."), after which the synesthetic concurrent can be elicited (" . . . and it's blue").

Obviously, some recognition of the inducing stimulus must precede any elicitation of the concurrent synesthetic experience, but it is arguable whether inducer recognition and conscious awareness of its identity must both precede synesthetic experience. Maybe form recognition, and hence synesthetic elicitation, occurs in the absence of conscious awareness. In addition, it is not obvious why inducer recognition and synesthetic experience must proceed in a strictly serial fashion. Perhaps form recognition and synesthetic elicitation proceed in a cascaded fashion, with incremental evidence in favor of a particular form giving rise to incremental elicitation of synesthetic color. Although form processing would begin before synesthetic color was triggered, the representations of form and color could emerge concurrently. In the following paragraphs we critique the one study that points to the need for attention and awareness of the inducer.

Mattingley et al. (2001) conducted a series of experiments to determine whether binding of synesthetic color to alphanumeric form can occur in the absence of conscious awareness of the inducer stimulus. Mattingley et al. essentially used a modified version of the Stroop task by which the inducer letter was first presented for 500 ms followed by a colored target patch. As quickly as possible, the synesthetic observers named the color of the target patch, which could be congruent or incongruent with the synesthetic color of the prime. Just as in the standard synesthetic Stroop task, the synesthetic color of the inducer slowed naming the color of the target patch when the colors were incongruent. Having established a Stroop interference effect, Mattingly et al. next presented the inducer letter for a sufficiently brief duration and accompanied by a pattern mask so as to preclude visual awareness of that letter. Would "unconscious" identification of the inducer still lead to significant interference when its synesthetic color differed from the actual color of the target patch? In two different variants of this task, no significant Stroop interference was observed when the exposure duration of the inducer was 56 ms or 28 ms. At these brief durations, participants reported being unaware of the presence of the inducer.

Most critically, to demonstrate that some degree of processing of the prime did occur at these short presentation durations, Mattingley et al. (2001) conducted a control experiment involving letter naming. In this task, the primes were again letters, but the targets were now letters as well. The task was to name the identity of the target letter. The primes and the targets had different cases, with congruent trials having the same identity (a → A) and incongruent trials having a different identity (b → A). For prime durations of 56 ms and 28 ms, the magnitudes of the statistically significant interference effects on incongruent trials (relative to congruent trials) were 21ms and 7 ms, respectively (although that difference could just as well reflect a facilitation effect for congruent trials).

Although the results of Mattingly et al. (2001) could imply that conscious identification of the inducer stimulus is necessary for the elicitation of synesthetic color, there are some issues that must be considered before accepting this conclusion. Their critical finding was that at both 28 ms and 56 ms prime durations, a letter prime had significant influence on letter identification, but the synesthetic color of a letter prime did not have significant influence on color naming. The influence of the prime on letter identification in the control task was rather small (21 ms in the 56 ms prime condition and only 7 ms in the 28 ms prime condition), but that is not necessarily uncommon in priming experiments of this kind. Unfortunately, Mattingley et al. did not report absolute identification times in the letter identification control task, but we might expect letter identification to be somewhat faster and somewhat less variable than color naming. Statistically, with a relatively small number of observations (48 trials per observer per condition), a 21 ms or 7 ms interference effect can only be detected in a task with sufficiently low variability, such as letter identification. Even if a 21 ms or 7 ms interference effect were present in the color naming task, it would be difficult to detect such a small difference in a task with higher variability. Indeed, in the synesthetic color-priming version of the task, the 28 ms prime duration produced about a 5 ms interference effect, and the 56 ms prime produced approximately a 29 ms interference effect (as estimated from their figures); these differences, although statistically nonsignficant, are quite comparable to the 7 ms and 21 ms significant effects observed in the letter priming version of the task. Mattingley et al. did not report a power analysis on the sensitivity of their color-naming task to reveal a priming effect of the magnitude observed in the letter identification task. For these reasons, we are not entirely persuaded that these findings constitute evidence against unconscious realization of synesthetic colors.

Moreover, there are other recent results suggesting that concurrent synesthetic color can influence the detection and identification of the inducer, implying that induction of synesthetic color does not require the explicit conscious recognition of a form. The essential strategy of those studies was to assess identification of the inducer, not its real or synesthetic color. Thus, if synesthetic color nonetheless influences identification, we can conclude that synesthetic color is available before the explicit identification of the inducer. If the inducer has already been consciously identified before the color emerges, how could synesthetic color further enhance its identification?

One piece of evidence showing the influence of synesthetic color on inducer identification is provided by our visual search study, the results from which appear in plate 4.1b. Recall that search times for nonsynesthetic observers increased linearly with set size regardless of target-distractor pairing, and this was true regardless of whether nonsynesthetes were searching for a 2 among 5s or an 8 among 6s. W.O. also experienced difficulty searching for an 8 among 6s, which both appear bluish to him. In contrast, W.O. was significantly faster searching for a 2 among 5s. Also, W.O. described his search strategy as sometimes first seeing a patch of orange and then verifying that there was a 2 located at that position.

Although W.O. described his experience as a pop out of the synesthetic color of the 2, the slope of W.O.'s search function for a 2 among 5s was not completely flat, as would be expected of true pop-out produced by searching for a real orange 2 among real green 5s. We conjectured that W.O. performs a serial-like search through the visual display, just like nonsynesthetic individuals, but that he was able to reject distractors more quickly using his synesthetic color. To examine this further, we tested W.O. and nonsynesthetes on a visual search display in which the distractors had no synesthetic color. On each trial, observers searched for either a ᔕ (which is orange for W.O.) or a ᔕ (which has no synesthetic color) among a background of ᔕs (which also have no synesthetic color). Both W.O. and nonsynesthetes showed no difference in searching for the two types of targets among the nonsense distractors.

So according to our thinking, searching for a target that has a very different synesthetic color from that of the distractors is not entirely analogous to the true, preattentive pop out that occurs when a target's real color differs from the real color of the distractors. Thus, attention may very well be involved in color-graphemic synesthesia, thereby allowing a synesthete to more rapidly reject a distractor and accept a target in a visual search task, but not in a manner requiring the inducer to achieve the level of conscious recognition before eliciting a synesthetic color, as suggested by Mattingley et al. (2002). After all, W.O. was more than 500 ms faster than nonsynesthetes when searching for a target that differed from its distractors in synesthetic color. It is hard to reconcile this finding with the claim that synesthesia is elicited by stimuli that are already available for conscious report. Once a target is available for conscious report, the search task is finished. Why would a synesthete wait an additional 200–300 ms (see Grossenbacher & Lovelace, 2001) for the synesthetic color to appear? And how could that confer an advantage over searching among items with no synesthetic color to guide them?

Results from other groups also seem to suggest that synesthetic color can be available before conscious awareness of the identity of the inducer stimulus. For example, Wagar, Dixon, Smilek, and Cudahy (2002) found that synesthetic color eliminated object-substitution masking (Enns & DeLollo, 1997), and Ramachandran and Hubbard (2001b) outlined some results suggesting that synesthetic color can attenuate crowding effects (He, Cavanagh & Intriligator, 1996). As mentioned earlier, Ramachandran and Hubbard (2001a) found that synesthetes were more accurate at locating geometric arrangements of letters embedded among distractor letters when the letters had different synesthetic color. Although Ramachandran and Hubbard (2001b) attribute this improved accuracy to a true pop-out effect, their experimental design did not allow the determination of a pop-out effect in the classical visual search sense (Treisman & Gelade, 1980; see also Rich & Mattingley, 2001).

Finally, Smilek et al. (2001) had observers search for a target digit among a variable number of distractor digits. But rather than using targets and distractors that had similar or different synesthetic colors (like Palmeri, Blake, Marois, Flanery & Whetsell, 2002, and Ramachandran & Hubbard, 2001a), they instead varied the color of the background to be congruent or incongruent with the synesthetic color of the target. Synesthetes were significantly faster at locating the target when the display background color was incongruent with the synesthetic color of the target. In order for the incongruence of real color and synesthetic color to influence target search, synesthetic color must be bound to alphanumeric form before the explicit conscious identification of the target.

So, to sum up, we are led to take an intermediate position on the question of the degree to which an inducer must be processed before eliciting a synesthetic color. Requiring complete identification and conscious awareness of an inducer before the elicitation of the synesthetic color seems inconsistent with several sets of results, and the one finding pointing to this conclusion can be questioned on methodological grounds. At the same time, the evidence for preattentive pop out of synesthetic color is primarily anecdotal, and the failure to find flat visual search functions undermines the analogy between genuine color pop out and speeded visual search aided by synesthetic colors (but see Smilek et al., 2001).

What Is the Neural Basis of Synesthesia?

Given the results summarized in the previous sections, it is impossible to believe that synesthesia is simply metaphorical speech or the product of bizarre minds. Synesthetic colors have a genuine perceptual reality that allows synesthetes to exploit their color experiences when performing visual tasks or when memorizing and recalling otherwise arbitrary material. The reality of synesthetic color, then, brings to center stage the question: How does form recognition ultimately elicit a color experience in the brains of synesthetes?

Virtually all neural models of synesthesia propose that it arises from an atypical pattern of connectivity between form processing and color processing centers of the brain. Figure 4.3 displays a simple schematic diagram of the putative pathways involved in form recognition and color recognition, as adapted from depictions presented in recent reviews by Grossenbacher and Lovelace (2001) and Rich and Mattingley (2002). Visual processing is organized in parallel, roughly hierarchical systems with early areas processing primitive visual features that feed forward to areas processing more complex scenic elements that ultimately provide input to areas involved in form recognition or color recognition. According to traditional views, these concurrent systems ultimately converge upon multimodal areas supporting high-level cognitive processes. As shown in the diagram, feedforward connections are almost always accompanied by dense feedback connections. Horizontal connections between form and color-processing areas may also be present.

In this scheme, at least three possible routes emerge for eliciting a synesthetic color experience from an alphanumeric form (but see Cytowic, 1993, for an alternative conceptualization). One possibility is that synesthesia arises at a very late stage of processing where outputs from form recognition and color recognition are associated. Interaction at this late stage would imply that synesthesia is largely conceptual in nature, with associations between colors and forms simply being stronger versions of the kinds of semantic associations nonsynesthetes experience (e.g., "apple" and "red"). It is difficult,

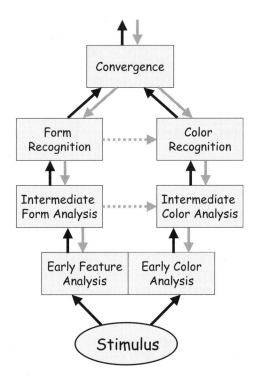

Figure 4.3. Schematic of possible pathways by which form evokes the synesthetic experience of color. Adapted from Grossenbacher and Lovelace (2001) and from Rich and Mattingley (2002).

however, to reconcile this idea with the strong evidence, reviewed earlier, for the perceptual reality of synesthesia. It is nevertheless conceivable that the convergence of color and form information occurs at earlier, more perceptual stages of processing. However, although some visual cortex areas such as V4 are known to be sensitive to both color and form (Gallant, Shoup & Mazer, 2000), there is as yet no evidence that a given brain region responds both to alphanumeric characters and to colors.

Another possibility is that synesthesia arises from disinhibited feedback from the convergence areas shown at the top of the flow diagram (Grossenbacher & Lovelace, 2001). The form pathway is used to recognize alphanumeric characters, ultimately leading to activity in high-level areas of convergence from multiple modalities. In nonsynesthetes, top-down feedback is sufficiently inhibited to prevent anomalous synesthetic experiences in nonstimulated modalities (except perhaps when under the influence of hallucinogenic drugs). In contrast, these feedback connections are disinhibited in synesthetes (for unspecified reasons), leading to representations of a concurrent synesthetic color experience when viewing an alphanumeric inducer stimulus. How far back into the color processing pathway a concurrent stimulus is represented may determine whether a synesthete is a projector, who sees the inducer itself as colored, or an associator, who experiences the color in the mind's eye. For this model to work, disinhibition must be highly selective and idiosyncratic among color-graphemic synesthetes, for we know that color experiences are highly reliable and differ widely among these individuals. In terms of neural organization, the disinhibited-feedback theory implies that the brains of synesthetes and nonsynesthetes are wired the same, but for some reason the modulation of specific feedback connections is attenuated in synesthetes.

A third possibility is that synesthetes have patterns of horizontal cross-wiring that are at least quantitatively, if not also qualitatively, different from that of nonsynesthetes (see Harrison & Baron-Cohen, 1997). As illustrated in figure 4.3, such cross-wiring could take place at different stages of form processing and color processing; once the form pathway makes contact with the color pathway via these horizontal connections, feedback to earlier stages in the color pathway could result as well (e.g., see Grossenbacher & Lovelace, 2001; Rich & Mattingley, 2001). It is reasonable to presume that the likelihood of strong cross-wiring is greater between physically adjacent neural areas (e.g., see Ramachandran & Hubbard, 2001b).

What could be the etiology of such cross-wiring? Maurer (1993; see also this volume) has proposed that all infants are born with extensive cross-wiring between modalities, which would mean, of course, that all infants routinely experience synesthesia. But, according to Maurer, this rich nexus between sensory areas is usually lost during the course of normal development. According to this hypothesis, synesthesia is retained into adulthood because cross-wiring endures owing to a failure of the pruning process (perhaps because of an unusually high density of connections to begin with). The notion of cross-wiring is broadly consistent with neurodevelopmental data documenting early diffuse projections followed by massive pruning (e.g., see Huttenlocher & Dabholkar, 1999). Finally, there is some behavioral evidence implying that young infants may not segregate modalities properly (Maurer, 1993), as the cross-wiring hypothesis would predict.

Restricting our attention to color-graphemic synesthesia, what can be inferred about the putative underlying cross-wiring? First, it seems clear that the inducing event must be the recognition of an alphanumeric character. Indeed, to our knowledge, there have been no demonstrations of synesthetic experience from simple visual features, such as oriented lines, gratings, or simple geometric shapes. Moreover, the color experiences elicited by visually similar alphanumeric characters are often quite different—for example, L.R. sees B as orange but P as green. Conversely, color experiences for dissimilar characters are often identical: L.R. sees D and Y as the same shade of green. Finally, color experiences also depend on context, with identical ambiguous characters taking on different colors (see figure 4.1a). These various characteristics of color-graphemic synesthesia place serious constraints on the patterns of underlying cross-wiring, and they certainly defy explanation in terms of cross-wiring at stages of early feature analysis.

The appeal of the cross-wiring model to account for synesthesia resides in its simplicity: activation of a grapheme-encoding area leads, via aberrant connectivity, to color perception. However, for cross-wiring to be considered a serious explanatory concept, it should account for several key characteristics of synesthesia; including its specificity (familiar names but not other names induce colors), its variety (it can occur not only between aspects of the same modality, such as visual form and color, but also between anatomically and functionally distant modalities, such as taste and touch) and its unidirectionality (e.g., form induces color, but not vice versa). Finally, it is also worth considering alternatives to cross-wiring models. In particular, there is no a priori reason to rule out the possibility that synesthetes possess a functionally novel brain area, absent in the rest of us, that both processes the inducing stimulus (e.g., a letter) and evokes the color experience.

In thinking about how to untangle these alternative accounts, we are skeptical about whether behavioral results alone will allow us to draw firm conclusions about how the brains of synesthetes and nonsynesthetes are wired. We are more optimistic about the possibility of using recently developed brain imaging techniques to learn how cortical areas within the brains of synesthetes are interconnected. In particular, analytical procedures are now available for estimating the levels of functional connectivity between areas (Biswal, Yetkin, Haughton & Hyde, 1995; Büchel, Cowl & Friston, 1998; Friston & Büchel, 2001; Hampson, Peterson, Skudlarski, Gatenby & Gore, 2001). Assuming brain regions underlying processing of the inducer stimulus and the evoked color experience can be isolated, it should be possible to assess the strength of the correlation of activity between these areas. If there are unusually strong connections between these areas, then their activity should be more strongly correlated than in control observers. Another, complementary technique for assessing patterns of connectivity is diffusion tensor imaging, which can estimate the presence and density of anatomical connections between brain regions (Le Bihan et al., 2001).

What Is the Neural Locus of the Synesthetic Experience?

The discussion above focused on the difficult issue of connectivity among brain areas putatively involved in synesthesia. A potentially more tractable question with neuroimaging concerns the neural locus of the induced synesthetic quality: What brain areas are uniquely activated when an individual has a synesthetic experience? More specifically, which areas are associated with the induction of the synesthetic experience (e.g., form computation), and which are associated with its expression (e.g., color perception)? From the outset, it should be kept in mind what exactly we may hope to learn about synesthesia from functional brain imaging. To be sure, neuroimaging is unlikely to reveal anything about the etiology of synesthesia or anything about synesthesia's underlying genetic, molecular, or cellular mechanisms. However, this technique has the potential to pinpoint brain areas activated during the synesthetic experience. In turn, these activation maps can reveal the extent to which the neural networks underlying synesthesia overlap with those underlying normal color processing, color perception, color imagery, or high-level cognitive processing. In addition, with functional brain imaging we should ultimately be able to determine whether common principles or mechanisms operate across different forms of synesthesia. In the following paragraphs, we summarize and discuss the handful of functional brain-imaging studies that have attempted to determine the neural locus of synesthesia.

Cytowic (1989) performed the first neuroimaging study of synesthesia, in this case an individual who experienced specific shapes associated with specific tastes. Using the nontomographic Xenon-133 inhalation technique, Cytowic observed widespread decreased blood flow in the cerebral cortex during synesthetic experiences, but more accurate localization of specific brain activity was not possible using this imaging technique.

Using positron-emission tomography (PET), Paulesu and colleagues (1995) were able to provide a more specific neural locus for the synesthetic experience of six women with color-phonemic synesthesia (i.e., color experience triggered by hearing phonemic utterances). Synesthetic observers and nonsynesthetic controls listened to a series of individual spoken words or a series of individual pure tones. For synesthetes only, the contrast of words versus tones yielded significant activation in the right middle frontal gyrus and insula and in the left posterior inferior temporal cortex. The location of these activations, as well as the lack of activation in early visual cortex, led the authors to conclude that color-phonemic synesthesia results from brain areas involved in language and feature integration, but not from activity in areas of cortex involved in early visual processing.

Using functional magnetic resonance imaging (fMRI), Weiss, Shah, Toni, Zilles, and Fink (2001) studied a single observer who experienced color-phonemic synesthesia, but only for names of personally familiar people. In a blocked-trials design, the observer was shown familiar names or unfamiliar names presented in either colored letters or in achromatic letters. The observer's task was to indicate by pressing a button whether each name induced synesthesia or not. Of particular interest was the comparison of brain activity for familiar names versus unfamiliar names. Synesthesia-inducing familiar names activated retrosplenial cortex and extrastriate cortex bilaterally.

The authors concluded that the observer's synesthesia was attributable to an interaction between the retrosplenial cortex, which has been implicated in emotional processing and judgments of personal familiarity (Maddock, 1999; Shah et al., 2001) and extrastriate regions of cortex involved in color processing (Beauchamp, Haxby, Jennings & DeYoe, 1999).

Aleman, Rutten, Sitskoorn, Dautzenberg, and Ramsey (2001) used fMRI to test an individual who experienced color-phonemic synesthesia, focusing in particular on possible activation within primary visual cortex during performance of two contrasting tasks. In the first task, the observer passively listened to words. In the second task, the observer listened to single letters and was asked to covertly generate as many words as possible that began with that letter (a word generation task). The control condition for both tasks involved listening to the regular presentation of pure tones. Analysis of blood-oxygen-level–dependent signals in area V1, identified based on anatomical landmarks, revealed activation in both experimental tasks relative to the control task. In addition, whole brain analyses detected several other activation sites, including the posterior inferior temporal cortex and prefrontal cortex. The authors concluded that the activation of primary visual cortex in their synesthete was consistent with the perceptual reality of synesthesia because it activates the same neural substrates critical for sensory perception. While we do not doubt their conclusion, we believe it is premature to conclude that synesthesia is associated with V1 activation. In our experience, it is difficult to delineate V1's borders based on anatomical landmarks (which is what Aleman et al. did), whereas functional isolation of V1 is straightforward using the well-validated technique of retinotopic mapping (Engel, Glover & Wandell, 1997). In addition, activated regions in Aleman et al.'s study were peppered throughout the brain, raising uncertainty about the specificity of the visual cortex activation.

Finally, Nunn et al. (2001) reported the most thorough imaging experiment on synesthesia to date, scanning 13 color-phonemic synesthetes and 28 control observers. Their first experiment consisted of a block design of passive listening to words and passive listening to pure tones. Not surprisingly, the words versus tones contrast revealed language-related areas activated for both synesthetes and controls. More important, for synesthetes this contrast also highlighted a left inferior temporal activation not observed in nonsynesthetes. The locus of this activation was in the neighborhood of visual cortex areas V4/V8, which are purported color-processing regions of the human brain (Hadjikhani, Liu, Dale, Cavanagh & Tootell, 1998). In addition, no primary visual cortex activation was observed for either synesthetes or controls. These findings suggest that color-phonemic synesthesia recruits a key locus of normal color processing. However, the second experiment of Nunn et al. showed that while this same left inferior temporal area was recruited by physically real color stimuli (compared to achromatic stimuli) in control observers, they were not in synesthetes. The authors argued that the left V4/V8 is involved in color-phonemic synesthesia, and that the participation of this area in synesthetic color perception may reduce or prevent its availability for normal color processing. These results seem to imply that brain areas involved in synesthetic and physical color perception may be segregated. Perhaps this could explain why synesthetes report so little confusion between real and synesthetic colors occupying the same part of the visual field.

The most striking characteristic of the functional imaging data summarized above is the almost complete absence of overlap of activations across the four PET and fMRI studies. Given the diversity of synesthetic experiences, it is not unreasonable to expect that various types of synesthesia would have their own distinct neural substrates. Indeed, the imaging experiments discussed above focused on shape–taste synesthesia (Cytowic, 1989), color-phonemic synesthesia (Aleman et al., 2001; Nunn et al., 2001; Paulesu et al., 1995), and color–familiar-name synesthesia (Weiss et al., 2001). Still, it is baffling why there is no overlap in brain activations even among the subset of studies that have investigated the same form of (color-phonemic) synesthesia (Aleman et al., 2001; Nunn et al., 2001; Paulesu et al., 1995).

We suspect that these divergent findings are attributable, in part, to differences in the experimental designs used in these studies. First, most of the imaging experiments have not used objective methods to determine whether observers were indeed experiencing synesthesia during scanning sessions. Second, some of the studies (Aleman et al., 2001; Cytowic, 1993; Weiss et al., 2001) did not scan nonsynesthetic individuals, so little can be concluded about the specificity of the reported brain activations for synesthesia. Third, most of the studies did not explicitly distinguish between the inducing and expressing substrates of synesthesia. Fourth, the control conditions and synesthesia-inducing conditions differed in ways other than just the mode of induction of synesthesia. For instance, three of the imaging studies compared spoken words to tones (Aleman et al., 2001; Nunn et al., 2001; Paulesu et al., 1995), even though there are potentially important differences between words and tones (e.g., semantic content) besides their differential ability to induce color synesthesia. Ideally, the control task should be identical to the experimental task in all respects except for its ability to induce synesthesia. Admittedly, it is challenging to devise control conditions that closely match the stimulus qualities of the synesthetic inducers without inducing synesthesia. For this reason, it may be preferable to avoid subtraction techniques altogether (Friston, Holmes, Poline, Price & Frith, 1996) and, instead, to capitalize on parametric approaches (Braver et al., 1997) or on fMRI adaptation techniques (Grill-Spector, Kushnir, Edelman, Itzchak & Malach, 1998). The latter approach offers particularly great promise in isolating areas specifically involved in synesthesia without having to rely on the comparisons of synesthesia-inducing and non–synesthesia-inducing tasks.

Finally, another significant challenge for brain imaging studies of synesthesia is to distinguish activations attributable to learned associations between words and colors from those attributable to genuine sensory events. It is entirely possible that one could observe synesthesia-like patterns of activation in nonsynesthetes who were instructed to imagine colors when they were presented words, or in nonsynesthetes who were trained to associate particular colors and words. One study (Nunn et al., 2001) attempted to address this possibility by scanning control observers who had been moderately trained to associate colors with words. While in the scanner, words were heard over headphones and nonsynesthetic observers alternated in blocked fashion between imagining the color of the words or thinking of the name of the color associated with the word. Contrasting the imaging versus thinking blocks, no significant activation was observed in left V4/V8, the area activated in synesthetes in the main experiment. However, one important limitation of this control study is that the contrast was not between words and tones, as in the main experiment contrasting synesthetes and nonsynesthetes, but between imagining a color versus thinking of the name of a color. Arguably, it may be difficult to think of the name of a color without imagining that color as well, especially given that the original training consisted in auditory word presentation and visual presentation of the color. Thus, it is not too surprising that V4/V8 failed to show significant activity modulation in these trained control observers, given that the critical contrast was far more stringent than that applied to synesthetes.

To sum up, the small number of extant imaging studies on synesthesia and the inconsistency of their findings preclude any overarching conclusions about the neural basis of this condition. Moreover, these studies have aimed at localizing specific areas activated during the synesthetic experience, yet extant theories of synesthesia focus more on how brain areas are (anomalously) interconnected. Clearly, greater progress will be achieved when theories and experiments converge on the same well-formulated questions. As mentioned earlier, potentially powerful fMRI and MRI techniques for assessing interconnectivity may help promote this convergence. Even then, however, a complete account of the neural basis of synesthesia faces the daunting challenge of the diversity of synesthetic experiences. This alone makes it unlikely that synesthesia will be distilled to a common neurobiological substrate. Nevertheless, it is possible that all forms of synesthesia arise from the same general neurobiological process, such as anomalous cross-wiring between brain regions. To be sure, the successful approach to understanding synesthesia must deploy carefully crafted perceptual tasks carried out hand in hand with brain imaging studies assessing functional activations and anatomical connections techniques. Only then do we stand a chance of distinguishing fact from fiction about the exotic experiences characteristic of synesthesia.

Closing Remarks

We close by considering a question that was raised by a student in one of our classes after hearing a lecture on synesthesia: Given all the challenging problems in the area of perception, why spend so much time and energy studying a condition that most of us can barely imagine, let alone ever experience? No doubt most of the authors of chapters in this volume would offer an answer that goes something like this: By studying exceptional individuals, we learn something about ourselves. After all, there is a long tradition in psychology of studying people with deficits in cognitive ability: visual neglect, amnesia, aphasia—the list goes on and on. The rationale is simple: We can learn about normal function by examining deviations from normal and, where possible, by relating those deviations to underlying neural abnormalities. To give just one example, the existence of brain areas specialized for color vision was first realized upon discovering rare cases of individuals suffering achromatopsia, acquired colorblindness consequent to neural damage specifically localized to occipito-temporal regions of the brain (Zeki, 1990). Clinical case studies provide revealing glimpses of normal neural mechanisms gone awry.

Likewise, studies of individuals with exceptional ability offer the tantalizing opportunity to learn about the potentials of the human brain and, moreover, how those potentials were realized developmentally. Thus, for example, students of music perception rely heavily on case studies of musical geniuses to glean insight into the bases of creativity and skill acquisition (e.g., Jourdain, 1997). The same can be argued for the study of synesthesia: For reasons yet to be learned, some people have brains organized in ways that promote highly organized, idiosyncratic associations between sensory qualities. No longer can we dismiss this remarkable propensity as the creation of a crazed mind; synesthesia is grounded in perceptual reality. Having affirmed this characteristic of synesthesia, researchers are now poised to tackle the difficult questions surrounding this fascinating condition. Moreover, we have at our disposal an array of revealing behavioral tests that can be refined for use in neuro-imaging experiments that go beyond simply asking what areas of the brain "light up" when someone is having a synesthetic experience. And, who knows, in the course of this work, we may stumble upon a means for evoking synesthetic-like experiences in the rest of us.

In the final analysis, though, we study these unusual, gifted individuals because they are utterly fascinating. The authors of this chapter will never forget the first opportunity we had to interview W.O.—here was an individual whose descriptions of his perceptual world challenged our conceptualizations of what it means to perceive. We still cannot imagine how the letter C can be seen as blue even though it is printed in black ink, but we are convinced that C is blue for W.O. (and is yellow for L.R.). And we are thankful that W.O., L.R., and others like them are sufficiently patient with our burning curiosity to allow us the opportunity to probe deeper into their colorful visual worlds.

Acknowledgments   Some of the work described in this chapter was supported by grants from the National Eye Institute (EY07760, EY013358), the National Institute of Mental Health (MH61370), and the National Science Foundation (BCS-9910756).

References

Aleman, A., Rutten, G.-J.M., Sitskoorn, M.M., Dautzenberg, G., & Ramsey, N.F. (2001). Activation of striate cortex in absence of visual stimulation: An fMRI study of synesthesia. *Neuroreport, 12,* 2827–2830.

Beauchamp, M.S., Haxby, J.V., Jennings, J.E., & DeYoe, E.A. (1999). An fMRI version of the Farnsworth-Munsell 100-Hue test reveals multiple color-selective areas in human ventral occipitotemporal cortex. *Cerebral Cortex, 9,* 257–263.

Biswal, B., Yetkin, F.Z., Haughton, V.M., & Hyde, J.S. (1995). Functional connectivity in the motor cortex of resting human brain using echo-planar MRI. *Magnetic Resonance Medicine, 34,* 537–541.

Braver, T.S., Cohen, J.D., Nystrom, L.E., Jonides, J., Smith, E.E., & Noll, D.C. (1997). A parametric study of prefrontal cortex involvement in human working memory. *Neuroimage, 1,* 49–62.

Büchel, C., Coull, J.T., & Friston, K.J. (1998). The functional anatomy of attention to visual motion: a functional MRI study. *Science, 283,* 1538–1544.

Cytowic, R.E. (1989). *Synesthesia: A union of the senses.* New York: Springer-Verlag.

Cytowic, R.E. (1993). *The man who tasted shapes: A bizarre medical mystery offers revolutionary insights into emotions, reasoning, and consciousness.* New York: G.P. Putnam's Sons.

Dixon, M.J., Myles, K.M., Smilek, D., & Merikle, P.M. (2002, April). *Not all synaesthetes are created equal: Distinguishing between projector and associator synaesthetes.* Paper presented at the 2nd Annual Meeting of the American Synesthesia Association, San Diego, California.

Dixon, M.J., Smilek, D., Cudahy, C., & Merikle, P. M. (2000). Five plus two equals yellow: Mental arithmetic in people with synaesthesia is not coloured by visual experience. *Nature, 406,* 365.

Engel, S.A., Glover, G.H., & Wandell, B.A. (1997). Retinotopic organization in human visual cortex and the spatial precision of functional MRI. *Cerebral Cortex, 7,* 181–192.

Enns, J.T., & DeLollo, V. (1997) Object substitution: A form of masking in unattended visual locations. *Psychological Science, 4,* 135–139.

Felleman, D.J., & Van Essen, D.C. Distributed hierarchical processing in the primate cerebral cortex. *Cerebral Cortex, 1,* 1–47.

Friston, K.J., & Büchel, C. (2001). Attentional modulation of effective connectivity from V2 to V5/MT in humans. *Proceedings of the National Academy of Sciences, USA, 97*, 7591–7596.

Friston, K.J., Holmes, A., Poline, J.B., Price, C.J., & Frith, C.D. (1996). Detecting activations in PET and fMRI: Levels of inference and power. *Neuroimage, 4*, 223–235.

Gallant, J.L., Shoup, R.E., & Mazer, J.A. (2000). A human extrastriate area functionally homologous to macaque V4. *Neuron, 27(2)*, 227–235.

Grill-Spector, K., Kushnir, T., Edelman, S., Itzchak, Y., & Malach, R. (1998). Cue-invariant activation in object-related areas of the human occipital lobe. *Neuron, 21*, 191–202.

Grossenbacher, P.G., & Lovelace, C.T. (2001). Mechanisms of synaesthesia: Cognitive and physiological constraints. *Trends in Cognitive Sciences, 5*, 36–41.

Hadjikhani, N., Liu, A.K., Dale, A.M., Cavanagh, P., & Tootell, R.B.H. (1998). Retinotopy and color sensitivity in human visual cortical area V8. *Nature Neuroscience, 1*, 235–241.

Hampson, M., Peterson, B.S., Skudlarski, P., Gatenby, J.C., & Gore, J.C. (2002). Detection of functional connectivity using temporal correlations in MR images. *Human Brain Mapping, 15*, 247–262.

Harrison, J.E., & Baron-Cohen, S. (1997). Synaethesia: A review of psychological theories. In S. Baron-Cohen & J.E. Harrison (Eds.), *Synaesthesia: Classic and contemporary readings* (109–122). Cambridge, MA: Blackwell.

He, S., Cavanagh, P., & Intriligator, J. (1997). Attentional resolution and the locus of visual awareness. *Nature, 383*, 334–337.

Huttenlocher. P.R., & Dabholkar, A.S. (1997). Regional differences in synaptogenesis in human cerebral cortex. *Journal of Comparative Neurology, 387*, 167–178.

Jourdain, R. (1997). *Music, the brain and ecstasy.* New York: Quill/HarperCollins.

Kim, C-Y., Blake, R., Palmeri, T., Marois, R., & Whetsell, W. (2003). Synesthetic colors act like real colors and interact with real colors. Meetings of the Visual Sciences Society, Sarasota FL.

Kolers, P.A., & von Grünau, M. (1976). Shape and color in apparent motion. *Vision Research, 16*, 329–336.

Le Bihan, D., Mangin, J.F., Poupon, C., Clark, C.A., Pappata, S., Molko, N., & Chabriat, H. (2001). Diffusion tensor imaging: Concepts and applications. *Journal of Magnetic Resonance Imaging, 13*, 534–546.

MacLeod, C.M. (1991). Half a century of research on the Stroop effect: An integrative review. *Psychological Bulletin, 109*, 163–203.

MacLeod, C.M., & Dunbar, K. (1988). Training and Stroop-like interference: Evidence for a continuum of automaticity. *Journal of Experimental Psychology: Learning, Memory and Cognition, 10*, 304–315.

Maddock, R.H. (1999). The retrospenial cortex and emotion: New insights from functional neuroimaging of the human brain. *Trends in Neuroscience, 22*, 310–316.

Mattingley, J.B., Rich, A.N., Yelland, G., & Bradshaw, J.L. (2001). Unconscious priming eliminates automatic binding of colour and alphanumeric form in synaesthesia. *Nature, 410*, 580–582.

Maurer, D. (1993). Neonatal synesthesia: Implications for the processing of speech and faces. In B. de Boysson-Bardies, P. Jusczyk, P. MacNeilage, J. Morton, & S. deSchonen (Eds.), *Developmental neurocognition: Speech and face processing in the first year of life* (pp. 109–124). Dordrecht: Kluwer.

McCollough, C. (1965). Color adaptation of edge-detectors in the human visual system. *Science, 149*, 1115–1116.

Mills, C.B., Boteler, E.H., & Oliver, G.K. (1999). Digit synaesthesia: A case study using a Strooplike test. *Cognitive Neuropsychology, 16*, 181–191.

Navon, D. (1977). Forest before trees: The precedence of global features in visual perception. *Cognitive Psychology, 9*, 353–383.

Nunn, J.A., Gregory, L.J., Brammer, M., Williams, S.C.R., Parslow, D.M., Morgan, M.J., Morris, R.G., Bullmore, E.T., Baron-Cohen, S., & Gray, J.A. (2001). Functional magnetic resonance imaging of synesthesia: Activation of V4/V8 by spoken words. *Nature Neuroscience, 5*, 371–375.

Odgaard, E.C., Flowers, J.H., & Mradman, H.L. (1999). An investigation of the cognitive and perceptual dynamics of a colour-digit synaesthete. *Perception, 28*, 651–664.

Palmeri, T.J., Blake, R., Marois, R., Flanery, M.A., & Whetsell, W. (2002). The perceptual reality of synesthetic colors. *Proceedings of the National Academy of Science, USA, 99*, 4127–4131.

Paulesu, E., Harrison, J. Baron-Cohen, S., Watson, J.D.G., Goldstein, L., Heather, J., Frackowial, R.S.J., & Frith, C.D. (1995). The physiology of coloured hearing: A PET activation study of colour-word synaesthesia. *Brain, 118*, 661–676.

Ramachandran, V.S., & Hubbard, E.M. (2001a). Psychophysical investigations into the neural basis of synaesthesia. *Proceedings of the Royal Society of London, B, 268*, 979–983.

Ramachandran, V.S., & Hubbard, E.M. (2001b). Synaesthesia: A window into perception, thought and language. *Journal of Consciousness Studies, 8*, 3–34.

Rich, A.N., & Mattingley, J.B. (2002). Anomalous perception in synaesthesia: A cognitive neuroscience perspective. *Nature Reviews Neuroscience, 3*, 43–52.

Shah, N.J., Marshall, J.C., Zafiris, O., Schwab, A, Zilles, K., Markowitsch, H.J., & Fink, G.R. (2001). The neural correlates of person familiarity: A functional magnetic resonance imaging study with clinical applications. *Brain, 124*, 804–815.

Smilek, D., Dixon, M.J., Cudahy, C., & Merikle, P.M. (2001). Synaesthetic photisms influence visual perception. *Journal of Cognitive Neuroscience, 13*, 930–936.

Smilek, D., Dixon, M.J., Cudahy, C., & Merikle, P.M. (2002). Synesthetic color experiences influence memory. *Psychological Science, 13*, 548–552.

Stroop, J.R. (1935). Studies of interference in serial verbal reactions. *Journal of Experimental Psychology, 18*, 643–662.

Treisman, A.M., & Gelade, G. (1980). A feature-integration theory of attention. *Cognitive Psychology, 12*, 97–136.

Wagar, B.M., Dixon, M.J., Smilek, D., & Cudahy, C. (2002). Coloured photisms prevent substitution masking in digit colour synaesthesia. *Brain and Cognition, 48*, 606–611.

Weiss, P.H., Shah, N.J., Toni, I., Zilles, K., & Fink, G.R. (2001). Associating colours with people: A case of chromatic-lexical synaesthesia. *Cortex, 37*, 750–753.

Zeki, S. (1990). A century of cerebral achromatopsia. *Brain, 113*, 1721–1777.

5

Binding of Graphemes and Synesthetic Colors in Color-Graphemic Synesthesia

Daniel Smilek, Mike J. Dixon, and Philip M. Merikle

M ost people experience their visual environment as consisting of meaningful whole objects. How does the visual system combine, or in other words bind, various visual and semantic properties together to create the experience of perceiving meaningful whole objects? We address this question by describing the unusual conscious experiences that accompany color-graphemic synesthesia. Individuals with color-graphemic synesthesia report experiencing vivid colors whenever they view achromatic graphemes. For some of these individuals, the synesthetic colors are experienced as color overlays that appear to be atop, or in other words, bound to, the visually presented graphemes. We were interested in studying color-graphemic synesthesia in the hope that the unusual binding that occurs in synesthesia might inform us about the processes involved in the general experience of perceiving objects as meaningful wholes.

In this chapter, we describe a series of studies designed to investigate the role that attention and awareness play in binding graphemes and synesthetic colors. Taken together, the results of these studies suggest that at least for some synesthetes, synesthetic colors are bound to graphemes before the synesthetes attend to and become aware of the graphemes, and the meaning of graphemes can play a role in binding synesthetic colors to the graphemes. On the basis of these results, we conclude that for some synesthetes, graphemes and synesthetic colors are bound into meaningful whole objects before the graphemes are attended and the synesthetes become aware of the graphemes.

Color-Graphemic Synesthesia

For individuals who have color-graphemic synesthesia, letters and digits elicit highly specific conscious experiences of color (also known as photisms). For any given synesthete, the color-graphemic pairings are consistent across time (see Dixon, Smilek, Cudahy & Merikle, 2000; Mattingley, Rich, Yelland & Bradshaw, 2001; Odgaard, Flowers & Bradman, 1999). For example, C., a color-graphemic synesthete whom we have studied extensively (e.g., Dixon et al., 2000; Smilek, Dixon, Cudahy & Merikle, 2001), has experienced 2 as red and 3 as purple for as long as she can remember. Although color-graphemic pairings are consistent across time for each synesthete, color-graphemic pairings differ widely across synesthetes. For example, J., another synesthete whom we have studied, has very different color-graphemic pairings than C. For J., 2 is orange rather than red and 3 is green rather than purple.

Color-graphemic synesthesia is also automatic in the sense that synesthetes report that they cannot intentionally suppress their synesthetic color experiences. The automaticity of synesthetic colors has been demonstrated numerous times using variants of the Stroop task (e.g., Dixon et al., 2000; Mattingley et al., 2001; Mills, Boteler & Oliver, 1999; Odgaard et al., 1999; Wollen & Ruggiero, 1983). For instance, in one or our studies (Dixon et al., 2000), C. was presented with displays that contained a single colored digit. There were two key conditions. In one condition, the color of the digit was the same as C.'s synesthetic color for the digit (congruent condition). In another condition, the color of the digit presented on each trial was different from C.'s synesthetic color for the digit (incongruent condition). C.'s task was to ignore the synesthetic color elicited by the digit and to name the video color of the digit as fast as possible. The rationale underlying the experiment was that if synesthetic colors are elicited automatically, then the synesthetic colors should interfere with color naming on incongruent trials, leading to slower reaction times on incongruent trials compared to congruent trials. The results showed that C.'s color-naming reaction times were, in fact, much slower on incongruent trials (797 ms, 2.8% errors) than on congruent trials (552 ms, 1.4% errors). In contrast, a group of eight nonsynesthetes showed no differences in their reaction times to stimuli that, for C., were congruent or incongruent. These results demonstrate that C.'s synesthetic colors could not be inhibited and that they indeed occur automatically.

Even though synesthetic experiences appear to be consistent and automatic for all synesthetes, it is important to note that there are substantial individual differences among color-graphemic synesthetes with respect to the way they experience their synesthetic colors. Our investigations have revealed that there are at least two different kinds of color-graphemic synesthetes (Dixon, Smilek, Wagar & Merikle, in press). For some synesthetes, whom we refer to as associators, synesthetic colors are experienced in the mind's eye. For other synesthetes, whom we refer to as projectors, synesthetic colors are experienced as color overlays bound to the visually presented graphemes. Because projector synesthetes experience synesthetic colors as being bound to graphemes, our investigations of the binding of synesthetic colors and graphemes have focused primarily on projector synesthetes.

The Role of Attention and Awareness in Binding

When shown a visual grapheme, projector synesthetes often report that they become aware of the grapheme and the synesthetic color associated with the grapheme simultaneously. These reports of their subjective experiences suggest that projector synesthetes experience colored graphemes as bound entities. If so, this implies the possibility that graphemes and synesthetic colors are bound *before* synesthetes attend to and become aware of the graphemes. Experimental investigations of this possibility have led to two different views. One view, which is consistent with the subjective reports of synesthetes, holds that graphemes and synesthetic colors are bound together before attention and awareness (e.g., Blake, Palmeri, Marois & Kim, this volume; Palmeri, Blake, Marois, Flanery & Whetsell, 2002; Smilek et al., 2001; Smilek & Dixon, 2002; Smilek, Dixon & Merikle, in press; Wagar, Dixon, Smilek & Cudahy, 2002). The contrasting view holds that graphemes and synesthetic colors are bound together only after synesthetes attend to and become aware of the graphemes (e.g., Mattingley et al., 2001; Robertson, 2001, 2003). In the following sections, we discuss the experimental evidence supporting each of these views.

Support for Binding before Attention and Awareness

Digits Embedded in Colors   Our initial studies (see Smilek et al., 2001) investigating the role of awareness in the binding of synesthetic colors to graphemes were based on the following idea: If a synesthetic color experience is activated before awareness of the grapheme that elicited the color experience, then a grapheme might be more difficult to see when it is presented against a background that is the same color as the synesthetic color elicited by the grapheme than when it is presented against a background that is different in color than the synesthetic color elicited by the grapheme. For example, if a synesthete is presented with a black 2 and the associated red synesthetic color is activated before awareness of the 2, then the 2 might, under certain conditions, be more difficult to perceive against a red background than, for example, a blue background. In contrast, if synesthetic color is activated after awareness of a grapheme, then the relationship between the background color and the synesthetic color elicited by a grapheme should have no effect on a synesthete's ability to perceive the grapheme. We have used this general idea in several experiments to evaluate whether synesthetic colors are activated and bound to graphemes before awareness.

In one experiment (see Smilek et al., 2001), the synesthete C.'s task was to identify black digits that were briefly presented and followed by a pattern mask. On each trial, a single digit was presented and the color of the background was varied so that it was either the same or different as the color C. experiences when viewing the digit. Following the logic described above, we expected that if C.'s synesthetic color is activated before she becomes aware of a digit, then she should be less accurate identifying masked digits on "same background" than on "different background" trials.

As predicted, the results of the experiment showed that C. was less accurate identifying a black digit when it was presented against a background that was the same color as her synesthetic color for the digit (e.g., a synesthetically perceived "red" 2 against a red background) than when it was presented against a background that was a different color from her synesthetic color for the digit (e.g., a synesthetically perceived "red" 2 against a blue background). In contrast to C.'s results, a group of seven nonsynesthetes showed no difference between the two conditions. These results suggest that C.'s synesthetic colors influenced whether or not she became aware of the graphemes. As such, the results are consistent with the idea that C.'s synesthetic colors are activated before her awareness of graphemes.

In another experiment based on the same rationale (see Smilek et al., 2001), C. was presented with displays consisting of a black target digit embedded among a varying number of black distractor digits. The displays remained on the screen until C. responded, and her task was to localize the target digit as quickly as possible. We used the digits 2 and 4 as possible targets and the digit 8 for the distractors. For C., the digits 2, 4, and 8 elicit red, blue, and black synesthetic colors, respectively, so in each display, only the target digit elicited a chromatic synesthetic experience. As in the previous experiment, the color of the background was varied such that it was either the same as or different from C.'s synesthetic color associated with the target digit on that trial. Therefore, on half the trials, the background of the displays was red, which is C.'s color for 2, and on the other half of the trials the background of the displays was blue, which is C.'s color for 4. Consonant with the logic described above, we predicted that if C.'s synesthetic color is activated before her awareness of the target digit, then she should be slower localizing the target digit on "same background" trials than on "different background" trials. As expected, the results showed that

C was slower localizing the target digits on same background trials than on different background trials. In contrast to C.'s results, a group of seven nonsynesthetes did not show any difference in performance between the two types of trials. Taken together, these findings are consistent with the findings of the previous experiment and further corroborate the conclusion that C.'s synesthetic colors are activated before her awareness of graphemes.

In addition to the overall performance difference between same background and different background trials, there was another pattern of findings in C.'s data consistent with the idea that her synesthetic colors are activated before she attends to and becomes aware of graphemes. The slope of the search function for detecting the target digits on different background trials was shallower than the slope of the search function for detecting the target digits on same background trials. In other words, her search for the target digits was more efficient on different background than on same background trials. These findings indicate that C.'s attention was more efficiently guided to the target digit on different background trials than on same background trials. A reasonable supposition is that C.'s attention was attracted to the target digits more effectively on different background trials than on same background trials because her synesthetic colors made the target digits stand out more from the background colors on different background trials. As such, the results suggest that the synesthetic colors associated with the target graphemes were activated before the target graphemes were attended and guided C.'s attention to the target digits.

To further test the possibility that synesthetic colors are activated before graphemes are attended, we tested another synesthete, J. (Smilek et al., in press) using a visual search task similar to the one we used with C. In this study, J. searched for one of two possible target characters (the digits 2 or 5) presented among a varying number of distractor characters (0,), #). We chose the distractors 0,), and # because J. does not experience synesthetic colors for these characters. The color of the background of the displays was varied so that on half of the trials the background was orange (J.'s synesthetic color for 2) and on the other half of the trials the background was pink (J.'s synesthetic color for 5). Using these conditions, the color of the background in each display was either the same as or different from J.'s synesthetic color for the target digit in the display. If the synesthetic color elicited by a target digit guides or attracts attention, then for J., as was found for C., the slope of the search function for detecting target digits on different background trials should be shallower than the slope of the search function for detecting target digits on same background trials. The results were consistent with the prediction, the slope of the search function for detecting target digits on different background trials was shallower than the slope of the search function for detecting target digits on same background trials. In contrast, for seven nonsynesthetes, there was no difference between the slopes of the search functions for detecting the target digits on the two types of trials. These results indicate that the synesthetic colors associated with the target graphemes were activated before the graphemes were attended and that the synesthetic colors guided or attracted attention to the graphemes.[1]

Four-dot Masking   Wagar et al. (2002) used the four-dot masking procedure developed by Enns and Di Lollo (1997) to provide further evidence that C.'s synesthetic colors draw attention to black graphemes. Wagar et al. first tested eight nonsynesthetes. In the key conditions, the nonsynesthetes were briefly presented (i.e., 16.67 ms) a black target digit (2, 4, 5, or 7) embedded in a display containing 15 black distractor digits (the digit 8). The target digit was surrounded by four black dots, and the nonsynesthetes were told to try to name the digit within the four dots. Critically, on half of the trials, the four dots surrounding the target digit disappeared from the screen at the same time that the target and distractor digits disappeared from the screen, whereas on the other half of the trials, the target and distractor digits disappeared from the screen, but the four dots remained on the screen for an additional 320 ms. The nonsynesthetes made significantly more errors naming the target digits within the four dots when the dots remained on the screen for 320 ms following the offset of the digits than when the offset of the dots coincided with the offset of the digits (see table 5.1). The generally accepted explanation of this four-dot masking effect is that when attention is distributed across multiple items in a display (i.e., a target embedded in distractors), the initial percept of the target digit surrounded by the four dots is replaced by the percept of the four trailing dots alone (Enns & Di Lollo, 1997).

Wagar et al. (2002) also showed that the four-dot masking effect could be prevented from occurring for the nonsynesthetes by presenting the target digits in color.[2] When the eight nonsynesthetes were presented with colored target digits (e.g., a red 2 embedded in black 8s and surrounded by the four-dot mask), they made significantly fewer errors than when they were presented

Table 5.1. Number of errors (maximum = 48) identifying target digits surrounded by four-dot masks.

	No trailing mask	Trailing mask
Nonsynesthetes (*N* = 8)		
Black targets	5 (4.31)	18 (4.07)
Colored targets	5 (4.27)	4 (4.12)
Synesthete C.		
Black targets	2	5

The offsets of the targets, distractors, and masks occurred either simultaneously (no trailing mask) or the offset of the mask occurred 320 ms after the offsets of the targets and distractors (trailing mask). Mean errors and (standard deviations) are presented for the nonsynesthetes.

with black target digits (see table 5.1). This finding suggests that the non-synesthetes made fewer errors because their attention was attracted to the colored target digits, thereby preventing four-dot masking from occurring.

In the final phase of this study, Wagar et al. (2002) tested C. using black targets (i.e., 2, 4, 5, and 7) and black distractors (i.e., 8s). For C., her synesthetic colors for 2, 4, 5, and 7 are red, blue, green, and yellow, respectively, whereas her synesthetic color for the digit 8 is black. Thus, if a target digit such as a 2 is embedded among 15 distractor 8s, the synesthetic color for the target digit should stand out from the distractors in the display. The prediction was that C.'s endogenously generated synesthetic colors for target digits should act like the externally presented colors for the nonsynesthetes. In other words, even with black targets and distractors, C.'s synesthetic colors for the digits 2, 4, 5, and 7 should draw her attention to the targets and eliminate the masking caused by the four dots. Consistent with this prediction, the results showed that C.'s performance (5 errors) was 3 standard deviations below the mean performance of the nonsynesthetes (18 errors) in the condition with black target digits and the trailing mask (see table 5.1). In fact, C.'s error rate was comparable to that of the nonsynesthetes when they attempted to detect colored targets in the trailing-mask condition (4 errors). From these results, Wagar et al. concluded that C.'s endogenously generated synesthetic colors served to draw her attention to the target digits and prevent masking in the same way as the exogenously presented colors served to draw the nonsynesthetes' attention to the target digits. The clear implication of these findings is that C.'s synesthetic colors for digits are activated before she actually attends to the digits.

Perceptual Grouping   Evidence consistent with the idea that synesthetic colors are bound to graphemes before the graphemes are attended to and brought into awareness has also been found in studies of perceptual grouping. For example, Ramachandran and Hubbard (2001) have found evidence suggesting that the binding of synesthetic color to graphemes influences how items in a display are grouped together. Ramachandran and Hubbard tested two synesthetes, J.C. and E.R., who report that they see synesthetic color "spatially in the same location as the form" (p. 979). In their key experiment, Ramachandran and Hubbard presented matrices composed of approximately 45 small black graphemes (e.g., Hs, Ps, and Fs) to J.C. and E.R., as well as to 40 nonsynesthetes. Before being shown a matrix for 1 s, both the synesthetes and the nonsynesthetes were informed that although the Ps and Fs would appear in random locations, the Hs would be aligned within the matrix to form a distinctive shape (i.e., square, rectangle, diamond, or triangle). All participants were instructed to indentify the shape formed by the Hs. Ramachandran and Hubbard (2001) found that the synesthetes were more accurate than the nonsynesthetes at identifying the shapes formed by the designated grapheme and suggested that the synesthetes' superior performance was due to the fact that they grouped the graphemes on the basis of their synesthetic color experiences. This finding is completely consistent with the idea that synesthetic colors are activated before awareness of graphemes. It is difficult to conceive of how grouping based on synesthetic colors could have aided shape identification unless the synesthetic colors were bound to the graphemes before the synesthetes first became aware of the graphemes.

We conducted a perceptual grouping experiment with C. that was similar to the experiment reported by Ramachandran and Hubbard (2001). In our experiment, C. and nine nonsynesthetes were shown matrices composed of multiple instances of a target grapheme (e.g., 7) that were embedded among multiple fragments of graphemes and arranged to form one of four possible shapes (i.e., square, rectangle, diamond, or triangle). Examples of these matrices are shown in the top half of plate 5.1. Before being shown each matrix, C. and the nonsynesthetes were told the name of the target grapheme (e.g., 7) that would be aligned to form a shape within the matrix. C. and the nonsynesthetes were asked to identify the shape formed by the grapheme as quickly as possible, and each matrix was left on screen until the shape was named.

Our experiment differed from the experiment conducted by Ramachandran and Hubbard (2001) in an important way. In our experiment, we varied the background color of the matrices, so that on half the trials, the background color was different from the synesthetic color for the target grapheme, and on the remaining trials, the background color was the same as the synesthetic color for the target grapheme. An example of a different background matrix is shown in the top left of plate 5.1, and a depiction of C.'s perception of this matrix is shown in the bottom left of plate 5.1. We predicted that when C. viewed the different background matrices, her projected synesthetic colors would enable her to group the target graphemes by their synesthetic colors and thus aid her in identifying the shapes formed by the graphemes. In other words, given that C. experiences a yellow overlay when she views a black 7, she should group the (synesthetically) yellow 7s together and readily detect the "yellow" square standing out from the purple background. In contrast, when C. viewed a same background matrix, we expected her projected synesthetic color to blend into the background and thus make it more difficult for her to identify the shape formed by the target grapheme than when she viewed a different background matrix. Examples of a same background matrix and C.'s presumed perception of the matrix are shown on the right side of the plate 5.1. Here, C.'s synesthetically yellow 7s blend into the background, and therefore the expectation was that she should find it more difficult to identify the embedded shape in same background matrices than in different background matrices. In a manner consistent with our expectations, the results showed that C. was much faster at identifying the shapes made by the target graphemes in different background matrices than in same background matrices. In contrast, none of the nine nonsynesthetes tested using the identical matrices showed a difference between same background and different background matrices. These findings are entirely consistent with the findings reported by Ramachandran and Hubbard (2001), and they provide further support for the idea that synesthetic colors can be activated and bound to graphemes before awareness of the graphemes.

Support for Binding after Attention and Awareness

Despite considerable evidence suggesting that synesthetic colors are bound to graphemes before the graphemes are attended, there are also at least two experimental findings that seem to support the contrary view that synesthetic colors are activated only after graphemes are attended. One such finding was reported by Robertson (2003; see also this volume), and the other finding was reported by Mattingley and colleagues (2001; see also this volume). For the reasons described below, we believe that neither finding offers strong support for the view that synesthetic colors are activated only after synesthetes attend to and become aware of the graphemes.

Robertson (2003) tested two synesthetes, C.P. and A.D., using displays consisting of four colored dots, arranged so as to form two pairs of dots. One pair of dots was located to the left of fixation and the second pair of dots to the right of fixation. The pairs of dots were used to set the size of the attentional window. In one condition, the pair of dots were located 8° from fixation so that there was a large attentional window, whereas in the other condition, the pairs of dots were located 0.3° from fixation to form a small attentional window. To induce a synesthetic color on each trial, a display with two identical achromatic digits (e.g., 7) was presented 200 ms before the onset of each four-dot display. The digits were always located 8° to the left and right of fixation so that they were within the large attentional window but outside the small attentional window. The synesthetic color induced by the digits on each trial was either congruent or incongruent with the color of the dots, which the synesthetes were to name as quickly as possible.

The predictions for the experiment were straightforward. If attention is required to bind synesthetic colors and graphemes, then the time required to name the colors of the dots should be greater on incongruent than congruent trials when the digits are presented within the (large) attentional window, and there should be no difference between incongruent and congruent trials when the digits are presented outside the (small) attentional window. In contrast, if synesthetic colors and graphemes are bound before a synesthete attends to the graphemes, the time required to name the colors of the dots should be greater on incongruent than on congruent trials, independent of whether the digits are presented within the (large) attentional window or outside the (small) attentional window.

The results of the experiment seem more consistent with the idea that synesthetic colors are bound to graphemes before the graphemes are attended than with the view that synesthetic colors are bound to graphemes only after the graphemes are attended. The critical finding supporting this conclusion is that it took both C.P. and A.D. longer to name the colors of the dots on incongruent than congruent trials both when the color-inducing digits were presented within the attentional window and when the color inducing digits were presented outside the attentional window. On the other hand, the difference in color-naming times between incongruent and congruent trials was also larger when the digits were presented within the attentional window than when they were presented outside the attentional window. Although this latter finding suggests that attention may modulate the strength of a synesthetic color experience (see Robertson, 2003), the clear implication of the results of this experiment taken as a whole is that attention is not a necessary condition for the binding of synesthetic colors and graphemes.

Mattingley and colleagues (2001; see also this volume) have also reported findings that seem to suggest that synesthetic colors are activated only after synesthetes attend to graphemes and become aware of them. In their experiment, a group of synesthetes was shown a sequence of displays on each trial consisting of a lowercase letter (i.e., the prime), a mask, and a color patch (i.e., the target). The synesthetes' task on each trial was to name the color of the target as fast as possible. The color of the target was varied so that it was either congruent or incongruent with the synesthetic color elicited by the letter used as the prime. Awareness of the prime was varied by varying the exposure duration of the letter prime. In one condition, the primes were presented for 500 ms so that the synesthetes were definitely aware of the primes. In two other conditions, the primes were presented for 56 ms or 28 ms so that the synesthetes were generally unaware of the primes.

The results showed that when the primes were presented for 500 ms, the synesthetes were considerably slower at naming the color of the targets on incongruent trials than on congruent trials. These results indicate that when the synesthetes were aware of the primes, the synesthetic colors associated with the primes were activated and influenced how fast the colors of the targets were named. However, when the primes were presented for either 56 or 28 ms, such that the synesthetes were generally unaware of the primes, the difference between the reaction times to name the target colors on congruent and incongruent trials was statistically nonsignificant. Based on these results, Mattingley and colleagues (2001) suggested that "the obligatory binding of colour and form in synesthesia can be broken when inducing stimuli are masked, rendering them unavailable for conscious report" (p. 582).

There are at least three reasons that caution needs to be exercised when interpreting the findings reported by Mattingley et al. (2001; this volume).

1. There may, in fact, have been priming by synesthetic color even when the synesthetes were unaware of the primes. The conclusion reached by Mattingley and colleagues is based on their failure to find statistically significant differences between the reaction times to name the target colors on congruent and incongruent trials when the primes were presented for either 56 or 28 ms. As noted by Blake et al. (this volume), this failure to find statistically significant differences may be more indicative of the lack of sufficient experimental power to detect a difference than to a true absence of an effect of the primes.

2. Color perceived without awareness may not be an effective prime. A critical assumption underlying the experiment is that color can be perceived without awareness and that when color is perceived without awareness, it can prime a subsequent response. Despite the central importance of this assumption, Mattingley and colleagues present no evidence to support it. To better interpret their findings, what is needed is a control experiment in which it is demonstrated that color per se (e.g., a color patch) can prime a subsequent response even when the color is presented under conditions (e.g., masking) that preclude awareness.

3. The findings, if true, may apply only to associator synesthetes. As noted previously, our studies have revealed that color-graphemic synesthetes can be classified as either associators or projectors (Dixon et al., in press). Associator synesthetes are the most common type of color-graphemic synesthete, and they typically report that they experience synesthetic colors in their "mind's eye." Projector synesthetes, on the other hand, account for just 5 or 6% of all color-graphemic synesthetes, and they report experiencing synesthetic colors as colored overlays bound to the graphemes. Much of the evidence reported to date suggesting that synesthetic colors are bound to graphemes before the graphemes are attended to has come from experiments with projector synesthetes. In contrast, Mattingley and colleagues (2001) tested only associator synesthetes. Thus, it is possible that the inconsistency between the conclusion reached by Mattingley and colleagues (2001, this volume) and the conclusion we and others (e.g., Blake et al., this volume; Palmeri et al., 2002) have reached may very well be attributable to individual differences between the synesthetes tested in the different experiments.

Summary

When all of the evidence is considered, we believe that the findings indicate that, at least for projector synesthetes, graphemes and synesthetic colors are bound together before the synesthetes attend to and become aware of the graphemes. As such, the experimental evidence is consistent with the subjective reports of projector synesthetes. They always report that they experience colored graphemes, and they never report that they experience black graphemes that subsequently become colored. This being said, it is important to note that there are considerable individual differences among color-graphemic synesthetes. Therefore, future research may show important differences in how graphemes and colors are bound in different types of color-graphemic synesthesia.

The Role of Meaning in Binding

Given that synesthetic colors are bound to graphemes before synesthetes, or at least projector synesthetes, attend to and become aware of the graphemes, we wondered whether the meaning of the graphemes influenced the binding of the synesthetic colors with the graphemes. The initial evidence suggesting that meaning may be involved in the binding of synesthetic color to graphemes came from the subjective reports of several synesthetes. We asked the synesthetes to report the color they experienced when viewing ambiguous graphemes such as the grapheme 5, which can be interpreted as either the digit 5 or the letter S. The synesthetes reported that their synesthetic colors depended on their interpretations of the graphemes. For example, when the synesthete J. was shown the ambiguous grapheme 5, she reported that she experienced a pink synesthetic color when she interpreted the ambiguous grapheme as the digit 5, but she experienced a green synesthetic color when she interpreted the grapheme as the letter S. J.'s report of her subjective experiences suggested the possibility that her synesthetic colors depend not only on the shapes of the graphemes but also on her interpretations of the graphemes or, in other words, the meanings of the graphemes.

To corroborate these subjective reports with experimental data, we (Dixon et al., in press) conducted a Stroop experiment with the synesthete J. In this experiment, we presented a number of ambiguous graphemes that could be interpreted as either a digit or a letter. To manipulate the interpretations of the graphemes, we varied the context in which they were presented. On some trials, the ambiguous grapheme was embedded in a string of digits (i.e., a digit context), whereas on other trials the ambiguous grapheme was embedded in a string of letters (i.e., a letter context). We reasoned that interpretation of the ambiguous graphemes should be biased by the context. In other words, when an ambiguous grapheme (e.g., 5) was presented in the context of digits, J. should be biased to interpret the grapheme as a digit (e.g., 5), whereas when the same ambiguous grapheme was presented in the context of letters, J. should be biased to interpret the grapheme as a letter (e.g., S). The critical issue addressed by the experiment was whether the context, and presumably J.'s interpretation of the ambiguous graphemes, influenced her synesthetic color experiences. If synesthetic color experiences depend on the meaning of graphemes, then we would expect J. to experience different synesthetic colors for a given ambiguous grapheme depending on the context (letter or digit) in which the grapheme was presented.

To measure whether the conceptual context influenced J.'s synesthetic color experiences, we presented ambiguous graphemes embedded in strings of either letters or digits. Immediately after the presentation of each string of letters or digits, J. was presented with the ambiguous grapheme by it-self to probe the color experience elicited by the grapheme. The ambiguous graphemes used as probes were presented in color, and J.'s task was to name the video color of each probe as fast as possible. Each probe (e.g., 5) was presented in one of two video colors: the color consistent with J.'s digit in-terpretation of the probe (e.g., pink) or the color consistent with J.'s letter interpretation of the probe (e.g., green). If J. interpreted each probe in a manner consistent with the bias induced by the context, then the video color of each probe would be either congruent or incongruent with the synesthetic color experience elicited by the probe.

We expected that J. would be much slower at naming the video color of a probe when it was incongruent with her synesthetic color elicited by the probe than when it was congruent with her synesthetic color elicited by the probe. However, because a congruently colored probe in one context was an incongruently colored probe in the other context, we expected that an iden-tical probe would lead to relatively slow responses in one context but to faster responses in the other context. Therefore, if synesthetic color depends on the meaning of graphemes, we would expect that the reaction time for naming the video color of a probe would strongly depend on the context in which the probe was presented. The results of the experiment are shown in figure 5.1. The figure indicates that, as expected, the reaction times for naming the color

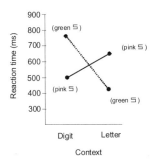

Figure 5.1. J.'s reaction times to name the video colors of ambiguous graphemes presented in digit or letter contexts. The figure shows one of the four ambiguous graphemes used in the study.

of a given probe strongly depended on the context in which the probe was presented. These results suggest that synesthetic colors elicited by ambiguous graphemes depend, at least in part, on the meaning of the graphemes. Furthermore, the findings imply that the binding of synesthetic colors and graphemes does not simply involve binding of shapes with synesthetic colors, but that it also involves the meanings of the graphemes.

Concluding Comments

We believe that the findings described in this chapter have important implications regarding the binding of synesthetic colors to graphemes in color-graphemic synesthesia. The evidence suggests that for some synesthetes, synesthetic colors are activated before graphemes are attended to, and synesthetic colors depend on the meaning of graphemes. Taken together, these findings lead to the conclusion that at least for some color-graphemic synesthetes, namely, projector synesthetes, graphemes are processed as meaningful whole objects and are bound with synesthetic colors before the graphemes are attended to and synesthetes become aware of the graphemes. This general conclusion is not only consistent with the empirical findings, but it is also consistent with the projector synesthetes' descriptions of their subjective experiences, which indicate that graphemes and synesthetic colors seem to come into awareness as meaningful whole objects.

How might graphemes and synesthetic colors be bound into meaningful whole objects in the visual system? We believe that graphemes and synesthetic colors are bound together through activation of various brain areas by "feed-forward" and "feed-backward" pathways in the visual system (see Grossenbacher & Lovelace, 2001; Smilek et al., 2001). Specifically, information about a visually presented grapheme is propagated through feed-forward pathways to areas of the brain that process the meaning of the graphemes (i.e., anterior fusiform; see Allison, McCarthy, Nobre, Puce & Belger, 1994). Following partial activation of meaning, the area of the brain that processes meaning sends signals, through feed-backward pathways, to the area of the brain that processes color (i.e., V4). We believe that the reciprocal activation of these various brain areas results in the activation of a circuit that leads to the experience of graphemes and synesthetic colors as bound, meaningful whole objects. As our review of the experimental evidence suggests, the activation of such circuits occurs even before synesthetes attend to and become aware of the graphemes.

Acknowledgments   This research was made possible by operating grants from the Natural Sciences and Engineering Research Council of Canada awarded to M.J.D. and P.M.M., as well as postdoctoral scholarships from the Natural Sciences and Engineering Research Council of Canada, Killam Trusts, and the Michael Smith Foundation for Health Research awarded to D.S.

Notes

1. Palmeri et al. (2002; see also Blake et al., this volume) have reported findings based on visual search experiments that are consistent with the idea that synesthetic colors are bound to graphemes before synesthetes become aware of the graphemes. They tested the synesthete W.O. with search displays containing target and distractor graphemes that elicited either the same synesthetic colors or different synesthetic colors. They found that W.O.'s search for the target graphemes was more efficient (i.e., search functions were shallower) when the target and distractors elicited different synesthetic colors than when the target and distractors elicited similar synesthetic colors.

2. This part of the study is not reported in Wagar et al. (2002).

References

Allison, T., McCarthy, G., Nobre, A., Puce, A., & Belger, A. (1994). Human extrastriate visual cortex and the perception of faces, words, numbers and colors. *Cerebral Cortex, 5,* 544–554.

Dixon, M.J., Smilek, D., Cudahy, C., & Merikle, P.M. (2000). Five plus two equals yellow. *Nature, 406,* 365.

Dixon, M.J., Smilek, D., Wagar, B., & Merikle, P.M. (in press). Grapheme-color synesthesia: When 7 is yellow and D is blue. In E. Calvert, C. Spence, & B. Stein (Eds.), *Handbook of multisensory processing.* Cambridge, MA: MIT Press.

Enns, J.T., & Di Lollo, V. (1997). Object substitution: A new form of masking in unattended visual locations. *Psychological Science, 8,* 135–139.

Grossenbacher, P.G., & Lovelace, C.T. (2001). Mechanisms of synesthesia: Cognitive and physiological constraints. *Trends in Cognitive Science, 5,* 36–41.

Mattingley, J.B., Rich, A.N., Yelland, G., & Bradshaw, J.L. (2001). Unconscious priming eliminates automatic binding of color and alphanumeric form in synesthesia. *Nature, 410,* 580–582.

Mills, C.B., Boteler, E.H., & Oliver, G.K. (1999). Digit synesthesia: A case study using a stroop-type test. *Cognitive Neuropsychology, 16,* 181–191.

Odgaard, E.C., Flowers, J.H., & Bradman, H.L. (1999). An investigation of the cognitive and perceptual dynamics of a color-digit synesthete. *Perception, 28,* 651–664.

Palmeri, T.J., Blake, R., Marois, R., Flanery, M.A., & Whetsell, Jr. W. (2002). The perceptual reality of synesthetic colors. *Proceedings of the National Academy of Science, USA, 99,* 4127–4131.

Ramachandran, V.S., & Hubbard, E.M. (2001). Psychological investigations into the neural basis of synesthesia. *Proceedings of the Royal Society of London, B, 268,* 979–983.

Robertson, L.C. (2001). Color my i's blue. *Nature, 410,* 533.

Robertson, L.C. (2003). Binding, spatial attention and perceptual awareness. *Nature Reviews, 4,* 93–104.

Smilek, D., & Dixon, M.J. (2002). Towards a synergistic understanding of synesthesia: Combining current experimental findings with synesthetes' subjective descriptions. *Psyche* [on-line], *8.* Available: http://psyche.cs.monash. edu.au/v8/psyche-8-01-smilek.html

Smilek, D., Dixon, M.J., Cudahy, C., & Merikle, P.M. (2001). Synesthetic photisms influence visual perception. *Journal of Cognitive Neuroscience, 13,* 930–936.

Smilek, D., Dixon, M.J., & Merikle, P.M. (2003). Synesthetic photisms guide attention. *Brain and Cognition, 53,* 364–367.

Wagar, B.M., Dixon, M.J., Smilek, D., & Cudahy, C. (2002). Colored photisms prevent object-substitution masking in digit-colour synesthesia. *Brain and Cognition, 48,* 606–611.

Wollen, K.A., & Ruggiero, F.T. (1983). Colored-letter synesthesia. *Journal of Mental Imagery, 7,* 83–86.

6

Synesthesia and the Binding Problem

Noam Sagiv and Lynn C. Robertson

For a synesthete, certain stimuli or the thought of certain concepts may be accompanied by perceptual qualities not normally experienced by most people (e.g., Cytowic, 1997). For some synesthetes, letter shapes may induce a color (e.g., A is red, B is blue); others may experience gustatory qualities when hearing words ("Jeremy" tastes like shellfish consommé), or see moving colored shapes when listening to music (e.g., Sibelius's "Valse Triste" may evoke the sight of slowly drifting pink dots). These correspondences are consistent across time and idiosyncratic, though some trends have been observed (e.g., Day, this volume; Shanon, 1982; Ward, Simner, & Auyeung, in press).

This may sound very odd to most people, and it is often hard to believe for those of us who have never had such experiences. Indeed, a central issue in synesthesia research has been the development of methods to test the perceptual reality of such reported phenomena. Such methods have been developed and have demonstrated that synesthesia is indeed a real perceptual phenomenon (Blake et al., this volume; Palmeri, Blake, Marois, Flanery & Whetsell, 2002; Ramachandran and Hubbard, 2001a, this volume; Smilek, Dixon, Cudahy & Merikle, 2001, this volume). Given the peculiarity of synesthetes' reports, it is not surprising that theories of synesthesia have begun to focus on the question of how synesthetes' brains may be different from the brains of nonsynesthetes, as evident in other chapters of this book. However, one simple question has been largely overlooked: What does synesthesia share in common with normal perception? In particular, what cognitive and neural mechanisms ordinarily used in perception are essential for synesthesia?

Odd as it may sound, synesthesia does share much in common with normal perception. First, although particular synesthetic colors, tastes, and so on, may sometimes be hard to describe, they are still experienced as having one or more of the familiar sensory qualities. Synesthesia is not a sixth sense (see Tyler, this volume) as some are temped to declare. Additionally, synesthetic qualities are consistent. Just as nonsynesthetes' experience of seeing one particular color induced by certain wavelengths is consistent across time, the same can be said about synesthetic aspects of stimuli. In fact, consistency of reported correspondences has been widely accepted as one diagnostic criterion for synesthesia. A color-graphemic synesthete who perceives the letter H as crimson always sees H this way. He or she will consistently choose the same crimson color patch among similar color patches across testing sessions that can be months or years apart. Moreover, crimson becomes a property of the letter H, just as redness is a property of strawberries. The color crimson is bound to the letter H, in the sense that it consistently co-occurs with it.

The idea that synesthetic correspondences are, in fact, prevalent in human cognition is not new (e.g., Marks, 1987; Merleau-Ponty, 1962; Ramachandran and Hubbard, 2001b). However, little is known about whether binding of synesthetic stimulus properties (in this example synesthetic color to shape) obeys the rules of normal binding of surface properties such as color and shape, and in particular whether attention plays a central role in synesthetic binding as it appears to do in normal perception.

We begin this chapter by briefly reviewing how binding is thought to occur for nonsynesthetes (sometimes referred to as normal perceivers). The visual system must solve several binding problems to make correct inferences about the world around us (e.g., Treisman, 1996). However, the problem of correctly combining color, shape, and other surface features into objects has been a hotly debated issue (for a review, see Wolfe & Cave, 1999). According to one popular theory, Feature Integration Theory (FIT), proposed by Treisman and Gelade (1980), this type of binding is achieved by engaging spatial attention. When binding fails (e.g., under conditions of divided attention), wrong combinations of features may be seen. For instance, if a blue A and green X are presented briefly and attention is focused elsewhere, a person might see a green A and blue X. These incorrect combinations of features are known as illusory conjunctions (e.g., Treisman & Schmidt, 1982) and reflect early independence of feature registration, which must then be bound into the colored shape we see.

Many deny that feature binding is a problem at all (e.g., Garson, 2001; Shadlen & Movshon, 1999), and there are ongoing debates about whether the brain works in a way that creates a binding problem in the first place. There is, however, ample behavioral evidence that binding is a problem, at least as operationally defined by paradigms requiring judgments about feature conjunctions. Other behavioral evidence has been derived from the study of neurological patients. Neuropsychological data have perhaps offered the most persuasive evidence that binding is more than a theoretical construct.

For some individuals with brain injury resulting in spatial deficits, binding can be a real problem that occurs in everyday life. As FIT would predict, illusory conjunctions happen more frequently when spatial attention is disrupted (for a review, see Robertson, 1999, 2004).

The case of R.M. is perhaps the most remarkable example. R.M. suffered from Balint's syndrome produced by bilateral parietal lesions. He nearly completely lost all spatial information outside that of his own body and consequently showed illusory conjunctions even in free viewing conditions (Bernstein & Robertson, 1998; Friedman-Hill, Robertson & Treisman, 1995; Robertson, Treisman, Friedman-Hill & Grabowecky, 1997; see Humphreys, Cinel, Wolfe, Olsen & Klempen, 2000, for confirming evidence). While neurophysiological data suggest that color and shape are initially processed in different areas of the cortex in ventral visual pathways (e.g., Felleman & Van Essen, 1991; Livingstone & Hubel, 1988), data from R.M. show that accurate integration of such features requires dorsal pathway input (e.g., spatial processing of the parietal lobe).

The neuropsychological approach of studying patients with certain lesions and deficits to learn how the brain might work has taught us a great deal. But studying positive phenomena, in which something is added rather than missing, also has much to offer. Synesthesia is such a case and is another example of abnormal binding that is a type of "hyperbinding." In this case, a property such as color that is not part of the stimulus itself is nevertheless bound to it in perception.

In one sense this may be thought of as the converse to the binding problem observed in R.M. For R.M., colors and shapes appear to be independently registered (as they are for normal perceivers), but the features are not bound correctly, presumably due to an inadequate spatial signal from the parietal lobes. However, for some synesthetes this signal may not be necessary for binding, perhaps due to a more direct link between brain areas that encode separate features than is present for the rest of us (e.g., Ramachandran and Hubbard, 2001b). This may lead to preattentive binding (binding that occurs without the need for attention). It would seem that the strongest test of this proposal would be with color-graphemic synesthetes, especially those who see synesthetic colors bound tightly to shapes.

Even within the color-graphemic category of synesthesia, the percept varies widely across individuals. Some synesthetes report that the color is projected externally, while others do not (e.g., Smilek and Dixon, 2002). As reported throughout this volume, synesthetic colors do influence performance, and they are not a delusion. Another important distinction is whether the color is seen as a surface feature of the grapheme (either projected on the actual presented grapheme or a second visualized copy some synesthetes report seeing) or is seen in a different location. Our focus has been on the type that most resembles normal feature binding, where letters or digits induce an externally projected color that appears as a surface feature of a grapheme (e.g., Smilek et al., 2001). For these synesthetes, the synesthetic color somehow coexists in the same space as the actual surface color but without mixing.

Our studies were designed to explore the role of attention, and in particular spatial attention, in this type of synesthesia. Is attention necessary for synesthetic binding, as it appears to be for normal feature binding? One popular account of synesthesia is that certain brain areas are abnormally and more directly connected than in nonsynesthetes (Baron-Cohen, Harrison, Goldstein & Wyke, 1993). Particularly, in the case of color-graphemic synesthesia, Ramachandran and Hubbard (2001b) propose that these would most likely connect two ventral cortical areas: the color area V4/V8 (e.g., Hadjikhani, Liu, Dale, Cavanagh & Tootell, 1998; Zeki & Marini, 1998) and the grapheme area (e.g., Nobre, Allison & McCarthy, 1994). To date, there is no direct evidence for the anatomical claims about hyperconnectivity giving rise to synesthesia. Nevertheless, if this theory is correct, it could be the case that cross-talk between ventral areas subserving synesthesia occur directly and without parietal input. Moreover, as synesthetic features are not actually present in the scene, perhaps there is no a priori reason to believe that attention should play a role. Alternatively, because in many cases, perceived synesthetic features do have a well-defined spatial location and extent, it may rely on parietal mechanisms that support spatial attention after all. Indeed, we found that synesthesia does require attention and appears to follow at least some of the rules of normal feature binding (Robertson, 2003; Robertson & Sagiv, 2002; Sagiv, 2001; Sagiv, Heer, & Robertson, in preparation). Here we review some of these findings, but first we introduce our participants.

A.D. and C.P. are both color-graphemic synesthetes. Both report that letters and digits evoke colors that are determined by the graphemic shape (e.g., 5 and S have similar colors; see plate 6.1). Both synesthetes are in their late 20s, and both report that they have always seen letters and digits this way, at least as far back as they can remember. They provided us with R,G,B values that best matched their synesthetic colors when presented with an achromatic number or digit, and on a consistency test given several months later they chose the same colors. Both reported that synesthetic colors were externally projected on the grapheme surface (i.e., experienced as a surface feature as illustrated in plate 6.2, and coexisting with the actual surface color.

Synesthesia Facilitates Visual Search: Pop Out or Guided Search?

One challenge in designing experiments to study synesthesia is selection of objective measures that can verify its presence. A common design used for this purpose is a variant of Stroop-like methods (e.g., Bergfeld-Mills, Howell Boteler & Oliver, 1999; Dixon, Smilek, Cudahy & Merikle, 2000; Odgaard, Flowers & Bradman, 1999), in which effects of a task-irrelevant variable on color naming are evaluated. A typical finding with synesthetes is that reaction time (RT) to judge a color patch is influenced by a task-irrelevant synesthetic color evoked by an achromatic stimulus in the display. RT is faster when the color patch is consistent with the synesthetic color than when it is inconsistent. Others sought to document the perceptual reality of synesthesia by embedding a complex target in a multi-item achromatic display (e.g., Ramachandran and Hubbard, 2001a). The evidence using this method demonstrated that synesthetic colors could facilitate search in otherwise monochromatic grapheme displays. However, the nature of this facilitation at first was poorly understood: Ramachandran and Hubbard described it as pop out, implying that binding of synesthetic color to grapheme shape occurs preattentively. This is indeed a plausible outcome of cross-activation between grapheme and color areas in brain via direct connections between these areas. In the displays used by Ramachandran and Hubbard, both distractors and targets induced synesthetic colors. Under such conditions, it is hard to know whether the facilitation was due to a true pop out of the target's synesthetic color or to faster rejection of distractor items based on their synesthetic color (i.e., guided search rather than pop out of synesthetic color induced by a yet-to-be detected target).

We began to explore these issues by attempting to replicate the visual search findings under more restrictive conditions. We only used distractors that did not induce synesthetic colors and compared RTs to detect targets that were either synesthetic inducers or not. Sample displays are shown in figure 6.1. In one display the target was a 180°-rotated L, and the distractors were 90° rotated Ts. These were not referred to as Ls and Ts until after the experimental data were collected. The same displays were used in another condition, except now they were rotated 180°, making the L upright and an obvious letter, while the Ts remained rotated. As a result of this manipulation, all the physical features of the displays were equated between the two display conditions, and in neither case were the distractors synesthetic inducers. The critical difference was that in one case the target was a synesthetic inducer and in the other case it was not. We refer to the two conditions as "inverted" and "upright" in reference to the target. All stimuli were achromatic (gray) items on a white background.

Other than the change in the target's potential as a synesthetic inducer, the subjects engaged in a standard visual search experiment. They were asked to indicate whether the target was present or not, and response speed was emphasized. The target was present on half the trials, and set size was either 4, 9, or 16. Stimulus density was equated across set size.

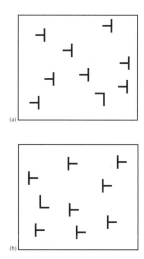

Figure 6.1. Sample search displays (with target present) used in experiment 1. (a) Initial inverted block, a nonletter target; (b) second upright block, a letter target.

As can be seen in plate 6.3, visual search was quite normal; RTs increased with set size, and slopes were steeper for target-absent than target-present conditions (in target-present conditions, search can be terminated as soon as the target is found). Critically, neither subject showed any evidence of (or even a trend toward) faster search rates for targets that induced a color (Ls) compared with targets that did not induce a color (inverted Ls); in other words, there was no interaction of set size and target orientation on those trials when the target was present. When distractors were not synesthetic inducers, synesthetic properties of the target did not make a difference, meaning that, at least for A.D. and C.P., synesthetic colors do not pop out. Rather, the synesthetic experience only began upon target detection when it became the focus of attention.

These findings are consistent with the subjective reports of both our participants who reported seeing the color associated with the letter L, but only upon detecting the target (and only when it was upright). Neither reported knowing the target was there as a consequence of seeing the corresponding synesthetic color before target detection.

Processing without awareness has been reported in a wide variety of tasks in different subject populations. However, our findings shed doubt on preattentive binding in synesthesia. Binding of the synesthetic color with the inducing shape required attention to the inducing stimulus. The data also suggest that the synesthetic properties of distractors can account for the improvement in visual search for other synesthetes tested in other laboratories.

Synesthetic color may help synesthetes group distractors into clusters of similar color, making them easier to reject, perhaps via a special form of guided search (Wolfe, 1994). Alternatively, the synesthetic color induced by distractors as the search proceeds may help synesthetes avoid returning to those distractors that have been rejected. The colors may group the distractors in ways they do not for normal perceivers, making the search more efficient. Palmeri et al. (2002; see also Blake et al., this volume) also provided confirming evidence that synesthetic color guides search but does not actually precede target detection. Like Ramachandran and Hubbard (2001a), they too found that synesthetes were faster than controls in finding a target grapheme among distractor graphemes. However, in a later experiment, they showed that this advantage disappeared when meaningless symbols (that do not induce color) were used as distractors. Their study also helps rule out other explanations of our findings based on factors such as the smaller set sizes or constant density we used, or that our findings are unique to the two synesthetes who participated in our study. In addition, A.D. and C.P. were tested by Hubbard and Ramachandran (2002) using their displays and procedures and showed an advantage over control subjects detecting the embedded target shape among letter distractors.

Other results reported by Ramachandran and Hubbard (2001a, 2001b) may also be explained along similar lines. In one experiment, grouping elements into rows or columns by synesthetes was determined by similarities of synesthetic colors induced by items in the display. However, given that stimuli were available for a prolonged time and speed was not a variable, these findings were probably not due to pop out. In another experiment, synesthetes were asked to identify a single achromatic target among four achromatic distractors (a crowding paradigm that normally produces performance decrements in naming the target for nonsynesthetes). The displays were placed in peripheral vision with a digit target in the center of these displays surrounded by digit distractors. In contrast to normal perceivers who are slower to name the target under such conditions, synesthetes were faster at naming the central target. However, here too, the distractors were synesthetic inducers, and it would be interesting to see whether this effect would be replicated with distracters that do not induce color surrounding a target that does.

Other recent studies have been concerned with the question of whether attention is necessary for synesthetic binding. The largest group of synesthetes ($N = 15$) was studied by Mattingley, Rich, Yelland, and Bradshaw (2001; see also Rich & Mattingley, this volume). They found that under conditions sufficient to produce letter priming from below threshold achromatic letter primes, synesthetic color priming was not observed. The synesthetic color only primed when the inducer was perceived.

In sum, synesthesia acts rapidly enough to influence perception and performance. However, it appears that the majority of color-graphemic

synesthetes do not bind synesthetic color to graphemic shape preattentively and that awareness of the inducing grapheme is generally necessary
for synesthetic colors to be experienced (an exception reported by Smilek
et al. will be discussed later). But can attention modulate synesthesia at
suprathreshold levels? If attention is required for synesthetic binding, then
manipulations of spatial attention may modulate the strength of the experience as well.

Attention Modulates Synesthesia

In the previous section we reviewed results consistent with the conclusion
that synesthetic colors do not pop out of a cluttered array, but rather are experienced when inducers become the focus of attention and the inducing shape
reaches visual awareness. To directly assess the role of attention, particularly
spatial attention, we conducted a second experiment. In this experiment we
varied the size of the attentional window so that it either included or did not
include task-irrelevant but clearly visible digit inducers placed on both sides
of fixation. Sample displays are shown in plate 6.4. On each trial two identical
achromatic digits (either 2 or 7) appeared 200 ms before presentation of a
target. The target was four identically colored dots. Subjects were asked to
report the color of the dots as rapidly as possible by pressing a key, and the
dots were either a consistent or inconsistent color to that induced by the 2s
or by the 7s. Target dots appeared either close to fixation, which was at the
center of the screen, or more peripherally, closer to the color-inducing digits.
The position of the target dots was blocked to encourage subjects to focus
attention either narrowly or widely before a trial began. It is also important
to note that the position of the inducer digits was the same in both blocks and
never changed throughout each block of trials. By changing only target dot
position, the inducer digits would be within a wide attentional window when
dots were expected in more peripheral locations and outside the attentional
window when dots were expected close to fixation. Note that to optimize the
occurrence of synesthesia, the digits always appeared before the target dots.[1]

We compared RTs to judge the color of the target dots that were either
congruent or incongruent with the synesthetic color of the inducers. Congruency effects between synesthetic color and actual target color have been
frequently used as an objective measure of synesthesia. RT to colored shapes
congruent with the synesthetic color are typically faster than to incongruently colored shapes, and we have obtained a similar result with A.D. and C.P.
in other experiments. Here we also manipulated attention to determine its
effects on the inducers. If attention can modulate synesthesia, we predicted
that a smaller congruency effect would be observed when attention was
focused narrowly and the inducer digits were outside the focus of attention.

Indeed, this is what we found; the congruency effect was markedly reduced when inducers where outside the attentional window. This was demonstrated by a significant interaction between color congruency and attention for both A.D. and C.P. (plate 6.5). In A.D.'s case the difference in RT between the incongruent and congruent case dropped from 74 ms to 35 ms when the inducers were outside the window of attention (attention narrowly focused), and for C.P. the effect was even larger—from 256 ms to 69 ms.

In sum, inducers had a smaller effect when they were outside the focus of spatial attention, even though they were in the same retinal location as when attention was spread widely. Consistent with these findings, both subjects reported experiencing more vivid colors when the target dots were farther in the periphery.

Of course, with such simple displays, inattention would not be expected to be complete, and some residual effect would be expected even when inducers were not within a narrowly focused attentional window. This means that whether or not some processing of the synesthetic properties of graphemes took place without attention could not be addressed with this study alone. However, these results clearly demonstrate that attention substantially modulates the strength of synesthesia.

Several other studies (some by contributors to this volume) also support a central role for attention in synesthesia. These include modulation by attentional load (Rich and Mattingley, this volume) and synesthete's reports when viewing hierarchical stimulus (e.g., a large 5 made by the placement of smaller 2s). The reported color depends on whether synesthete's attend to the global or local stimulus levels (Mattingley et al., in press; Palmeri et al., 2002; Ramachandran and Hubbard, 2001b). Also, synesthetes' reports are generally consistent with the finding that paying attention makes a difference.

The literature as a whole also suggests that synesthesia is automatic, which is one of the attributes that on the surface suggests that it should not require attention. In fact, automaticity is typically one of the requirements for diagnosing synesthesia (Cytowic, 1997). However, the evidence as a whole suggests that once the inducer is attended, synesthesia appears automatically (Mattingley et al., 2001). It happens without effort, but awareness of the inducer shape or identity appears to be necessary, at least for the majority of synesthetes and clearly for those we tested.

Synesthesia and Visual Awareness

In our studies reported in the last two sections the stimuli were presented above threshold, so no direct test of an attentional role in binding was performed. However, other studies have examined synesthesia at or near perceptual threshold and have reported conflicting results in terms of whether synesthetic binding occurs preattentively. In the largest study of synesthetes yet reported, Mattingley et al. (2001) presented evidence suggesting that synesthesia without awareness is unlikely, at least for a mixed group of 15 color-graphemic and color-phonemic synesthetes. However, some findings reported by Smilek and colleagues appear to provide at least one counter example. In a study reported in the *Journal of Cognitive Neuroscience*, Smilek et al. (2001) described a color-graphemic synesthete, C., who, like A.D. and C.P., projects synesthetic colors externally (a "projector" as categorized by Smilek & Dixon, 2002), onto the surface of the inducing shape. C. was less likely to detect an achromatic (black) digit presented on a colored background that was congruent with the synesthetic color of that digit than a background color that was incongruent. This pattern was replicated using different methods with C., including visual search, and suggests that the synesthetic color was bound to the digit preattentively (see Smilek et al., this volume).

Since C., A.D., and C.P. all bind colors within the boundaries of the shape, we attempted to replicate Smilek et al.'s (2001) findings with our subject A.D. (C.P. was unavailable for this experiment). Unlike C., A.D. was able to detect the letters equally well whether the background color was congruent or incongruent. In addition to the original design, we also ran a simpler, modified version of this experiment with only two possible graphemes and two possible background colors (rather than nine as used by Smilek et al.). We reasoned that RT measures would be less susceptible to strategic biases that might be introduced when errors were the dependent measure (e.g., using the background color as a default guess or, conversely, avoiding it when uncertain). Thus, we asked A.D. to determine as rapidly as possible which of two black letters was presented on each trial. In 50% of the trials letters were presented on a background congruent with the synesthetic color of the presented letter and in 50% letters were presented on a background that was incongruent (the color normally induced by the other possible letter in the stimulus set).

For the original design, we found no differences in error rates between background colors. In the reaction time version, RT to correctly identified letters was significantly shorter in the congruent condition (641 ms) than in the incongruent condition (711 ms). It appears that for A.D. synesthesia does not occur preattentively. Performance was affected by the background, perhaps at some later stage of processing or decision-making.

Coexistence of Stimulus and Synesthetic Color

The above differences between C. and A.D. may simply be yet another piece of evidence that synesthesia has wide individual differences. However, a spontaneous comment by A.D. piqued our interest. She told us that the digit she saw was both black and the induced color at the same time. When probed about the locations of the two colors, A.D. reported that she didn't know how to explain it, but that both appeared on the shape in the same location at the same time. Her comments are consistent with several synesthetes we and others have interviewed in that they claim to see both the real color and the induced color at the same time (although not always as tightly coupled as for A.D.).

When two colors exist in the same place, they mix, but this does not appear to be the case with synesthetic colors and colors carried by wavelengths in the stimulus. When one color (we are including black) is generated by wavelengths from the stimulus and another by its shape, the two colors appear to coexist. How might this be explained? Suppose a red A is presented in the middle of a computer screen to a synesthete who sees green whenever an A is present. In such a case the brain should activate three feature maps (location, shape, color) registering one location signal (central), one shape signal (A), and two color signals (red and green). The question is how the visual system handles the extra color.

There are several possible solutions: to inhibit the stimulus color completely; to see two colors, one bound to the shape's location and one off to the side; to replicate the shape in another location and bind the color to it; or, as A.D. reports, to somehow see both colors in the same location in the same shape (see Robertson, 2003, for a detailed way in which the brain might manage this). Other synesthetes seem to solve the problem differently, reporting that the color is anywhere from slightly off the shape to hovering elsewhere or as an aura. Still others claim they see the color as real but in their mind (not projected into the world), which may represent a qualitatively different type of synesthesia (Smilek & Dixon, 2002) or a point on a continuum with one end represented by tightly bound sensations and the other by normal metaphors, a position that Ramachandran and Hubbard (2001b) favor.

To our knowledge no one has yet attempted to quantify the report that two colors can coexist at the same location at the same time, but several questions immediately arise that may be relevant for understanding individual differences in color-graphemic synesthetes such as C. and A.D. To what extent, if any, does either a synesthetic or stimulus color dominate, and do they compete for awareness? Do they alternate in perception so quickly for some synesthetes that they appear to be present in the same place at the same time but are actually not? At least some synesthetes report that synesthetic percepts are more easily accessed in the dark (Tyler, this volume), bringing forth the possibility that the stimulus color dominates under stronger lighting conditions and the synesthetic color under weaker lighting conditions. To what extent can controlled attention modulate the dominance of one color over the other?

This discussion brings us back to the question of how C. might solve the binding problem presented by two color signals, one shape signal and one location signal. Assuming that she, like other synesthetes, sees the stimulus color and her synesthetic color together, the question then becomes why dark gray (the digit color used by Smilek et al. [2001] in the camouflage experiments) was not sufficient to detect the target on a colored background. Why would background color congruency with the synesthetic color have any effect? Perhaps C.'s visual system inhibits stimulus color, leaving only the synesthetic color and the background color. Under such circumstances a dark gray digit (or any other colored digit) would be replaced with its synesthetic color. If this is the explanation for why dark gray was not sufficient for C. to detect the digit in a colored background, this still means the induced color replaced the dark gray before C. became aware of the presented digit (preattentive inhibition and preattentive binding). It seems that under normal viewing conditions C does detect letters and their actual color, but whether the dynamics of her perception under more restricted conditions generalizes to other synesthetes remains an open question. This then would be consistent with hyperconnectivity between feature maps and the hypothesis that we originally tested but found no support for; namely, that binding under such conditions would be preattentive in synesthetes with tightly bound color-graphemic synesthesia.

Neural Contributions to Color Synesthesia

It is possible that C. represents an extreme case of quick, automatic, and vivid synesthesia, while the majority of other synesthetes, including other projector synesthetes, depend on attention at least to some extent. If such individual differences exist, we should be able to trace their neurophysiological origins. Candidates for neural bases of such differences include:

1. Quantitative differences of abnormal cortico-cortical hyperconnectivity as might be directly tested with diffusion-weighted imaging measures.
2. Qualitative differences in connectivity (e.g., the level of visual processing hierarchy at which abnormal connections are present). Such differences may be evident in the time course of electrophysiological correlates of synesthesia (Sagiv et al., 2003).
3. Quantitative differences in functional organization of the visual cortex: What proportion of color-sensitive tissue is dedicated to processing of synesthetic color? This may correlate with the likelihood that synesthesia will influence detection of certain stimuli. Further differences may

manifest in varying degrees of inhibition between putative stimulus and synesthetic color-responsive areas.

4. Qualitative differences in functional organization of the visual cortex: Do some synesthetes have shared circuits for stimulus and synesthetic color while others split the color area into two functionally segregated modules? One would expect that in the latter case, more accurate perception of actual stimulus properties may be permitted in parallel with the synesthetic experience. Imaging techniques such as functional magnetic resonance adaptation (Grill-Spector & Malach, 2001) would be valuable for assessing such differences. As noted above, both A.D. and C.P. reported that the synesthetic color does not replace the actual color, but rather they coexist.

Neuroimaging data have not been reported for most the synesthetes who have been tested in behavioral studies. From the handful of studies that have reported imaging data, a particularly interesting result is that areas of the brain that are active during colored-hearing synesthesia include those that normally correlate with perceived color (even though no color is presented; Nunn et al., 2002). Interestingly, for the subjects in the Nunn et al. study, there was a division of labor between hemispheres in regions that respond to externally presented color. One was more responsive to the color of the stimulus and the other to the synesthetic color. We hope that future studies will tell whether this pattern generalizes and will provide more quantitative information on the dynamics of activity correlated with normal and synesthetic color perception or, alternatively, whether the degree of overlap in activity correlates with the ability to report both colors.

Another intriguing finding in the Nunn et al. (2002) data was that the angular gyrus and inferior parietal lobes were just as active as V4/V8 when synesthesia was induced. In fact, parietal activity has been present in all studies of synesthesia reported to date, but these findings have been downplayed or ignored for some reason. For instance, using PET, Paulesu et al. (1995) found strong activation bilaterally in the occipital/parietal junction which the authors considered puzzling.

Parietal activation in the functional imaging study of Nunn et al. (2002) was within areas of damage in R.M. and other Balint's syndrome patients. Recall that RM had severe binding deficits between color and shape as a result of spatial deficits (Robertson et al., 1997). In light of these findings and the parietal activation observed with synesthetes, we suggest that the spatial attentional signal generated by the parietal lobes also plays a major role in color-graphemic synesthesia. The hyperconnectivity suggested by others seems to require consideration of both dorsal and ventral visual pathways, although it would be interesting to know whether the synesthetes who do show evidence of preattentive binding (Smilek et al., 2001, this volume) activate only ventral areas during synesthesia.

Discussion

Although we expected to find evidence for preattentive binding with synesthetes, especially those demonstrating a strong spatial coupling between inducer shape and evoked color, this hypothesis was not supported. We had reasoned that if hyperconnectivity between ventral cortical visual areas that process shape and color was the underlying neural cause of the most common forms of synesthesia (color-graphemic and color-phonemic), evidence for preattentive binding would be present, and this would reduce the reliance on attentional mechanisms. Instead, our results demonstrated that attention of the inducer was needed before synesthesia arose and that spatial attention modulated the strength of synesthesia. These findings are in need of explanation considering other evidence that synesthetic binding can occur before awareness (Smilek at al., 2001) and results demonstrating that synesthesia can increase visual search efficiency (Palmeri et al., 2002; Ramachandran and Hubbard, 2001a).

The evidence demonstrating that search is more efficient is relatively easy to explain. In fact, our data are in accord with the results of Palmeri et al.'s (2002) last experiment, which has not received the attention it deserves. When Palmeri et al. used distractors that did not evoke a unique color, they observed that search for a synesthesia-evoking target was no longer more efficient than search for a target that has no synesthetic properties.

The fact that synesthetes are able to find a conjunction target faster than normal perceivers is consistent with guided search models of visual search (Wolfe, 1994), but with a twist. For a synesthete who begins searching a display of shapes in an area that does not contain the target, all the distractors within the window of attention will turn the synesthetic color. As spatial attention moves across the display, other items will turn colored, and items already scanned will remain colored, producing general areas of color that act also as a cue that those areas have already been searched. This process would increase search efficiency and reduce rescanning of distractor regions or overlapping regions of attention, and this explanation is consistent with the visual search literature and synesthesia. Increased search efficiency does not occur when the target and distractors produce the same color or when the distractors are not themselves inducers.

The evidence for preattentive binding presented by Smilek et al. (2001) is more difficult to explain, and the synesthete they reported (C.) may in fact reflect a form of synesthesia that produces preattentive binding of synesthetic color with a shape. If true, this finding would also reflect the variability of synesthesia, even for those in the same category (e.g., projector color-graphemic). It would also suggest that the brain might solve the binding problem in different ways when confronted with two colors but only one shape, and it would predict different interactions between cortical areas for different synesthetes that may vary in time or in neural connectivity between areas that are normally separate. Synesthesia may arise as a function of many constellations, with some synesthetic phenomena appearing more rapidly, more vividly, and more projective than others depending on the underlying neural machinery. The level at which binding occurs will also vary as a result.

In sum, although simple explanations of binding are not adequate to explain color-graphemic synesthesia, the role of attention in its occurrence has been supported across laboratories and with the majority of synesthetes who have been tested. Spatial attention changes the emergence and the strength of color-shape binding for synesthetes. Visual search studies demonstrate that attention must be directed to a target (or distractor inducer) location in a cluttered array before synesthesia appears, and methods that change the size of an attentional window influence the intensity or probability of synesthetic perception. Consistently, parietal and posterior temporal cortical activity correlates with color synesthesia, as observed when nonsynesthetes search for a conjunction of color and another feature. These similarities may indicate common mechanisms for feature binding even when one of the features does not exist in the external stimulus.

Acknowledgments We thank Jeffrey Heer, Arvin Hsu, Alexandra List, Joseph Brooks, Krista Schendel, Edward Hubbard, and Anina Rich for helpful discussions. Preliminary results were presented at the first annual meeting of the American Synesthesia Association at Princeton, New Jersey, May 2001 and at the 9th Annual Meeting of the Cognitive Neuroscience Society, April 2002. This work has been supported by a Veterans Administration Senior Research Career Scientist Award and National Institute of Neurological Disorders and Stroke grant MH62331 to L.C.R. and the Elizabeth Roboz Einstein Fellowship in Neuroscience and Human Development to N.S.

Note

1. The choice of a 200-ms interval between inducers and targets was not arbitrary. Event-related potentials (ERPs) to orthographic versus nonorthographic material first diverge about 150 ms after stimulus presentation (Bentin, Mouchetant-Rostaing, Giard, Echallier & Pernier, 1999). We reasoned that minimally we should allow sufficient time for digits to be categorized to induce color. Indeed, preliminary ERP data from A.D. and C.P. show electrophysiological markers of synesthesia beginning between 150–200 ms (Sagiv, Knight & Robertson, 2003). Thus, we chose a stimulus onset asynchrony (SOA) of 200 ms. Furthermore, a control study using a similar design in control subjects showed that this SOA is sufficient to avoid confounding of the results by the different target–distractor distance (a concern for flanker paradigms in which the target and the distractors are presented synchronously).

References

Baron-Cohen, S., Harrison, J., Goldstein, L.H., & Wyke, M. (1993). Coloured speech perception: Is synaesthesia what happens when modularity breaks down? *Perception, 22*, 419–426.

Bentin, S., Mouchetant-Rostaing, Y., Giard, M.H., Echallier, J.F., & Pernier, J. (1999). ERP manifestations of processing printed words at different psycholinguistic levels: Time course and scalp distribution. *Journal of Cognitive Neuroscience, 11*, 235–260.

Bentin, S., Sagiv, N., Mecklinger, A., Friederici, A., & von Cramon, D.Y. (2002). Priming visual face-processing mechanisms: Electrophysiological and fMRI evidence. *Psychological Science, 13(2)*, 190–193.

Bergfeld-Mills, C., Howell Boteler, E., & Oliver, G.K. (1999). Digit synaesthesia: A case study using a stroop-type test. *Cognitive Neuropsychology, 16(2)*, 181–191.

Bernstein, L.J., & Robertson, L.C. (1998). Independence between illusory conjunctions of color and motion with shape following bilateral parietal lesions. *Psychological Science, 9*, 167–175.

Cytowic, R. (1997). Synaesthesia: Phenomenology and neuropsychology. In S. Baron-Cohen & J.E. Harrison (Eds.), *Synaesthesia: Classic and contemporary readings* (pp. 17–39). Oxford: Blackwell.

Dixon, M. J., Smilek, D., Cudahy, C., & Merikle, P. M. (2000). Five plus two equals yellow. *Nature, 406*, 365.

Felleman, D.J., & Van Essen, D.C. (1991). Distributed hierarchical processing in the primate cerebral cortex. *Cerebral Cortex, 1*, 1–47.

Friedman-Hill, S.R., Robertson, L.C., & Treisman, A. (1995). Parietal contributions to visual feature binding: Evidence from a patient with bilateral lesions. *Science, 269*, 853–855.

Garson, J. W. (2001). (Dis)solving the binding problem. *Philosophical Psychology, 14*, 381–392 .

Grill-Spector, K., & Malach, R. (2001). fMR adaptation: A tool for studying the functional properties of cortical neurons. *Acta Psychologia, 107*, 293–321.

Hadjikhani, N., Liu, A. K., Dale, A. M., Cavanagh, P., & Tootell, R.B.H. (1998). Retinotopy and color sensitivity in human visual cortical area V8. *Nature Neuroscience, 1(3)*, 235–241.

Hubbard, E.M., & Ramachandran, V.S. (2002). Different types of synesthesia may depend on different brain loci. *Society for Neuroscience Abstracts, 28*, 220.2.

Humphreys, G.W., Cinel, C., Wolfe, J., Olson, A., & Klempen, N. (2000). Fractionating the binding process: Neuropsychological evidence distinguishing binding of form from binding of surface features. *Vision Research, 40*, 1569–1596.

Livingstone, M., & Hubel, D. (1988). Segregation of form, color, movement & depth: Anatomy, physiology and perception. *Science, 240*, 740–749.

Marks, L. (1987). Auditory-visual interactions in speeded discrimination. *Journal of Experimental Psychology: Human Perception and Performance, 13*, 384–394.

Mattingley, J.B., Rich, A.N., Yelland, G., & Bradshaw, J.L. (2001). Unconscious priming eliminates automatic binding of colour and alphanumeric form in synaesthesia. *Nature, 410,* 580–582.

Merleau-Ponty, M. (1962). *Phenomenology of perception.* New York: Routledge & Kegan Paul.

Nobre, A.C., Allison, T., & McCarthy, G. (1994). Word recognition in the human inferior temporal lobe. *Nature, 372(6503),* 260–263.

Nunn, J.A., Gregory, L.J., Brammer, M., Williams, S.C.R., Parslow, D.M., Morgan, M.J., Morris, R.G., Bullmore, E.T., Baron-Cohen, S., & Gray, J.A. (2002). Functional magnetic resonance imaging of synesthesia: activation of V4/V8 by spoken words. *Nature Neuroscience, 5,* 371–375.

Odgaard, E.C., Flowers, J.H., & Bradman, H.L. (1999). An investigation of the cognitive and perceptual dynamics of a colour-digit synaesthete. *Perception 28,* 651–664.

Palmeri, T.J., Blake, R., Marois, R., Flanery, M.A., & Whetsell, W. Jr. (2002). The perceptual reality of synesthetic colors. *Proceedings of the National Academy of Sciences, USA, 99(6),* 4127–4131.

Paulesu, E., Harrison, J., Baron-Cohen, S., Watson, J.D. G., Goldstein, L., Heather, J., Frackowiak, R.S.J., & Frith, C.D. (1995). The physiology of coloured hearing: A PET activation study of colour-word synaesthesia. *Brain, 118,* 661–676.

Ramachandran, V.S., & Hubbard, E.M. (2001a). Psychophysical investigations into the neural basis of synaesthesia. *Proceedings of the Royal Society of London B, 268,* 979–983.

Ramachandran, V.S., & Hubbard, E.M. (2001b). Synaesthesia—A window into perception, thought and language. *Journal of Consciousness Studies, 8,* 3–34.

Robertson, L.C. (1999). What can spatial deficits teach us about feature binding and spatial maps? *Visual Cognition, 6,* 409–430.

Robertson, L.C. (2003). Binding, spatial attention and perceptual awareness. *Nature Reviews Neuroscience, 4(2),* 93–102.

Robertson, L.C. (2004). *Space, objects, minds and brains.* Philadelphia: Psychology Press.

Robertson, L.C., & Sagiv, N. (2002, April). Seeing and binding: Lessons from a synesthete. Paper presented at the Ninth Annual Meeting of the Cognitive Neuroscience Society, San Francisco, CA.

Robertson, L.C., Treisman, A., Friedman-Hill, S.R., & Grabowecky, M. (1997). The interaction of spatial and object pathways: Evidence from Balint's Syndrome. *Journal of Cognitive Neuroscience, 9,* 254–276.

Sagiv, N. (2001, May). Synesthesia and visual attention. Paper presented at the First Annual National Meeting of the American Synesthesia Association, Princeton University, Princeton, NJ.

Sagiv, N., Knight, R.T., & Robertson, L.C. (2003, March, April). Electrophysiological markers of synesthesia. Paper presented at the 10th Annual Meeting of the Cognitive Neuroscience Society, New York.

Shadlen, M., & Movshon, J. (1999). Synchrony unbound: a critical evaluation of the temporal binding hypothesis. *Neuron 24,* 67–77.

Shanon, B. (1982). Colour associates to semantic linear orders. *Psychological Research, 44*, 75–83.

Smilek, D., & Dixon, M.J. (2002). Towards a synergistic understanding of synaesthesia: Combining current experimental findings with synaesthetes' subjective descriptions. *Psyche* [on-line], 8. Available: http://psyche.cs.monash.edu.au

Smilek, D., Dixon, M. J., Cudahy, C., & Merikle, P. M. (2001). Synaesthetic photisms influence visual perception. *Journal of Cognitive Neuroscience, 13*, 930–936.

Treisman, A. (1996). The binding problem. *Current Opinion in Neurobiology, 6*, 171–178.

Treisman, A., & Gelade, G. (1980). A feature integration theory of attention. *Cognitive Psychology, 12*, 97–136.

Treisman, A., & Schmidt, H. (1982). Illusory conjunctions in the perception of objects. *Cognitive Psychology, 14*, 107–141.

Ward, J., Simner, J., & Auyeung, V. (in press). A comparison of lexical-gustatory and grapheme-colour synaesthesia. *Cognitive Neuropsychology.*

Wolfe, J.M. (1994). Guided search 2.0: A revised model of visual search. *Psychonomic Bulletin and Review, 1*, 202–238.

Wolfe, J.M., & Cave, K.R. (1999). The psychophysical evidence for a binding problem in human vision. *Neuron, 24*, 11–17.

Zeki, S., & Marini, L. (1998). Three cortical stages of colour processing in the human brain. *Brain, 121(9)*, 1669–1685.

7

Can Attention Modulate Color-Graphemic Synesthesia?

Anina N. Rich and Jason B. Mattingley

I n this chapter we review our recent experiments targeting the issue of whether visual selective attention can modulate synesthetic experience. Our research has focused on color-graphemic synesthesia, in which letters, numbers, and words elicit vivid experiences of color. Although the specific associations between inducing stimuli and the colors they elicit are typically idiosyncratic, they remain highly consistent over time for individual synesthetes (Baron-Cohen, Harrison, Goldstein & Wyke, 1993; Baron-Cohen, Wyke & Binnie, 1987).

Subjective reports have provided rich insights into the experience of synesthesia (e.g., Dresslar, 1903; Dudycha & Dudycha, 1935; Ginsberg, 1923; Karwoski & Odbert, 1938; Motluk, 1994, 2000, 2001; Myers, 1911, 1914; Ox, 1999; Pierce, 1907; Seron, Pesenti & Noel, 1992). They cannot, however, elucidate the cognitive mechanisms that underlie the phenomenon. What these subjective data provide are valuable clues for the development of hypotheses, which can then be investigated empirically. Our approach has been to measure synesthesia objectively, rather than using self-report or introspective data as the experimental method. Although we recognize the value of analyzing data from individual participants given the heterogeneity of synesthesia, we have focused predominantly on group studies to build up a picture of potential mechanisms based on the commonalities between individuals who report similar experiences.

There is considerable debate surrounding the issue of the extent to which an inducing stimulus needs to be processed before it elicits a synesthetic color (Rich & Mattingley, 2002). Some researchers have suggested that synesthetic colors are elicited early in visual processing (Ramachandran & Hubbard, 2001a), before the explicit recognition of the inducing form (Palmeri, Blake, Marois, Flanery & Whetsell, 2002; Smilek, Dixon, Cudahy & Merikle, 2001).

In this chapter, we review evidence from our laboratory that suggests instead that synesthetic colors arise only after substantial processing of the inducing stimuli, and that this processing involves attention.

Measures of Competition: The Synesthetic Stroop Task

Most synesthetes report that their synesthetic colors occur automatically, without conscious effort. This hypothesis has been tested by setting synesthetic colors in competition with the demands of a task. If synesthetic colors really are involuntary, then synesthetes should not be able to suppress them, even when they interfere with performance of a task. Under these circumstances, we would expect synesthetes' performance to be poorer than when there is no such competition present.

Following earlier single-case studies (Mills, Boteler & Oliver, 1999; Odgaard, Flowers & Bradman, 1999; Wollen & Ruggiero, 1983), we tested a group of 15 color-graphemic synesthetes and matched nonsynesthetic controls on a task designed to assess the effects of such competition. In this synesthetic Stroop task, colored letters were presented individually on a computer screen and participants were asked to name the display color as quickly as possible (Mattingley, Rich, Yelland & Bradshaw, 2001b). The color of each letter was either the same as the synesthetic color induced by the letter (congruent) or different from this synesthetic color (incongruent). To illustrate, one synesthete, E.S., experiences red when she sees an achromatic (gray) letter A. Presenting a green A creates competition between the display color (green) and the synesthetic color of the letter (red) and is therefore an incongruent stimulus for E.S. (plate 7.1a). In contrast, a red A causes no competition and is therefore a congruent stimulus.

In the initial phase, synesthetes selected computer-generated colors that matched their synesthetic colors for a set of alphanumeric characters (letters A–Z, digits 0–9). They were then asked to rate how well the computer-generated color matched the synesthetic colour for each item. For each synesthete, the six best matched characters were selected to create a unique set of congruent and incongruent items for that individual. Control participants viewed exactly the same items as the synesthete to whom they were matched, thus controlling for any extraneous effects of particular letter–color pairings. Congruent and incongruent items were randomly intermingled within a block of trials. For a nonsynesthete, the identity of a particular letter should have no influence on the time it takes to name the color in which it is displayed. In contrast, if synesthetes are unable to suppress their synesthetic colours, the conflict between the synesthetic color elicited by the letter and the color it is displayed in should slow color-naming times relative to congruent trials.

Plate 7.1b shows the group results for synesthetes and controls (Mattingley et al., 2001b). Synesthetes were significantly slower to name display colors when the letter and color were incongruent than when they were congruent, whereas controls showed no such effects. This synesthetic congruency effect demonstrates that synesthetic colors interfere with color naming, suggesting that some aspect of their processing is not under voluntary control. In addition, this test provides a quantifiable and objective index of the effect of synesthetic colors on behavior, which can be used to answer other questions about the processing required to produce synesthetic experiences.

Masking Inducing Stimuli from Awareness

One way to examine the processing required for synesthetic colors to be elicited is to limit the processing of inducing stimuli (i.e., the letters that trigger synesthetic colors) and to observe the impact of this manipulation on a previously observed effect. We presented masked alphanumeric primes prior to colored targets and used the synesthetic congruency effect described above as our dependent measure. It is known that considerable processing of stimuli can occur before conscious perception (Snow & Mattingley, 2003). Words and objects that are presented briefly and masked such that participants cannot report them may nevertheless receive considerable unconscious processing, as evidenced by subsequent responses to target items (Dehaene et al., 1998, 2001). Some researchers suggest that, at least for some synesthetes, it is the visual appearance of alphanumeric characters that induces synesthesia rather than the conceptual nature of the stimuli (Ramachandran & Hubbard, 2001b). Other researchers suggest that access to meaning is required, but that this need not occur consciously; it has been proposed that under appropriate conditions synesthetic colors can be elicited without explicit identification of the inducer (Smilek et al., 2001). If synesthesia is induced by early analysis of stimuli before conscious vision, then masked alphanumeric characters should still trigger synesthetic colors despite being unavailable for conscious report. If, in contrast, stimuli need to be consciously perceived before they induce synesthesia, then masking them from awareness should prevent generation of synesthetic colors and hence eliminate any synesthetic congruency effects.

We explored these hypotheses using a masked priming paradigm (Mattingley et al., 2001b). In this task, participants were required to name the color of a target patch as quickly as possible. The prime, under unmasked conditions, either induced a synesthetic color that matched the target color (congruent) or did not match the target color (incongruent). The sequence of displays in a typical trial is illustrated in plate 7.2a. A forward pattern mask was presented for 500 ms. This was followed by an achromatic alphanumeric prime presented for one of three durations (blocked separately). The color target acted as a backward mask for the prime. The target remained visible until a response was given, or for a maximum of 4000 ms.

In a baseline task, we presented the prime for 500 ms so that it would be clearly visible to all participants, to verify that the synesthetic congruency effect occurred in this novel paradigm. Consistent with our synesthetic Stroop results, synesthetes were significantly slower to name target colors when these were preceded by an incongruent versus a congruent prime (plate 7.2c), whereas controls showed no such difference (plate 7.2d). In the masked priming conditions, primes were presented for either 56 or 28 ms, both of which were effective in eliminating awareness of the prime. Neither synesthetes (plate 7.2c) nor controls (plate 7.2d) showed any effect of synesthetic congruency on color-naming times at these prime durations. We verified in a separate block of trials that processing of the primes was limited under these masked conditions: Participants' ability to identify the primes was severely curtailed at 56 and 28 ms (plate 7.2b). In a separate task, we also verified that the identity of the masked primes was extracted unconsciously. We presented lowercase-letter primes for the same durations before presenting uppercase letter targets in either congruent (e.g., a → A) or incongruent (e.g., b → A) trials. Both groups were slower to name target letters in incongruent trials compared to congruent trials, demonstrating that the primes were processed to the level of letter recognition despite being masked from awareness.

From these experiments, we concluded that considerable perceptual processing was required for an inducing stimulus to elicit a synesthetic color. We proposed that in order for synesthetic colors to occur, there must be overt recognition of the identity of the inducer (Mattingley et al., 2001b).

Can Attention Modulate Synesthesia?

It is generally accepted that attention is capacity limited (Driver, 2001; Pashler, 1998; Treisman, 1988; Wolfe, 1998). Although elementary visual properties of the environment may be extracted rapidly and in parallel without apparent capacity limits, focused attention is assumed to be necessary for these basic features to be bound together to form cohesive representations for overt recognition (Treisman, 1998, 1999; Treisman & Gelade, 1980). Our masked priming results suggest that the binding of form and synesthetic color in color-graphemic synesthesia requires overt recognition of the inducing stimulus. It follows, then, that this binding should rely on attention.

We investigated the modulation of synesthetic binding by mechanisms of selective attention by manipulating the availability of attentional resources for processing inducing stimuli.

Because attention has limited capacity, it is possible to reduce the resources available for processing a given stimulus by requiring a concurrent task to be performed (Pashler & Johnston, 1998). If attention plays a crucial role in the generation of synesthetic colors, then diverting attention from inducing stimuli should attenuate synesthetic color experiences. Instead of reducing processing of the prime through visual masking, as in our previous experiment, we aimed to modulate prime processing by introducing an attentional load task during presentation of relevant inducing stimuli (Mattingley, Rich & Payne, 2004). If focused attention is required for a prime to induce synesthesia, the synesthetic congruency effects observed on color-naming times should be reduced or eliminated when attention is engaged by a secondary load task.

We tested color-graphemic synesthetes and matched nonsynesthetic controls on a variant of the priming task described above. Rather than using masking to limit processing of the inducing stimulus, we restricted the amount of attention available for prime processing by having participants perform a difficult gap-discrimination task that coincided with the appearance of the letter prime. The sequence of displays in a typical trial is illustrated in plate 7.3a. A fixation point was followed by a prime display, which was presented for 400 ms. Surrounding the letter prime was a large diamond with a single gap in each of the four sides. The attentional load task required discrimination of the relative size of the gaps in diagonally opposite sides of the diamond. The discriminability of the gaps was titrated to create two different load conditions. In the low-load condition, participants were around 98% correct in their gap discrimination judgments. In the high-load condition, the gaps were more similar in size so that performance for the group was around 78% correct (with chance being 50%). Immediately after the prime display, a colored target appeared. Participants were required to name the target color as quickly as possible before indicating which side of the diamond had the larger gap. As in the synesthetic priming paradigm outlined previously, the synesthetic color elicited by the letter prime could be congruent or incongruent with the target color to be named. Crucially, the prime was irrelevant to both the gap-discrimination and color-naming tasks and could therefore be ignored.

In a baseline (no-load) condition, participants were asked to ignore the gaps and to concentrate on the color-naming task exclusively. Synesthetes were slower to name target colors on incongruent versus congruent trials, whereas controls showed no difference, thus verifying the presence of a synesthetic congruency effect with these modified priming displays. Plate

7.3b shows results from the low- and high-load conditions for a single synesthete, M.M., whose performance is illustrative of that of the group. Under both load conditions, M.M. was significantly slower to name the target color when it was preceded by an incongruent versus congruent prime. Critically, the magnitude of the synesthetic congruency effect was substantially smaller in the high-load condition relative to the low-load condition. Thus, diverting attention from relevant inducing stimuli reduces the extent to which synesthetic colors are able to interfere with naming display colors. The small effect of congruency that was evident in the high-load condition suggests that synesthetic colors may still be elicited under conditions of reduced attention. It should be recalled, however, that participants performed at around 78% correct in discriminating gaps in the high-load task and so probably were still able to allocate some attention to the prime. The near ceiling-level performance in identifying primes, measured in a separate task involving identical displays, is consistent with this explanation.

The results of our attentional load experiment support the hypothesis that focused attention is important in color-graphemic synesthesia and can act as a powerful modulator of synesthetic experience. Also consistent with this proposal are the results of a second attentional experiment in which we investigated the impact of presenting multiple synesthetic inducers within a single stimulus, each of which elicits a different synesthetic color (Rich & Mattingley, 2003).

In these experiments, we modified standard Navon-type local–global stimuli to manipulate synesthetic congruency. In a typical local–global stimulus, small (local) letters form a large (global) letter of the same identity (consistent stimuli), or of a different letter (inconsistent stimuli). When viewing local–global stimuli, most people perceive both the local and global forms, but they can increase the salience of one level by voluntarily focusing their attention on it. When the task is to identify target forms, participants are typically faster to respond to targets that appear at the global level than those that appear at the local level, and global distractors slow identification of local targets more than local distractors slow identification of global targets (Navon, 1977). These effects can be reduced or eliminated by having participants focus attention preferentially at the local level, demonstrating the role of selective mechanisms in prioritising different aspects of a common stimulus (Robertson, Egly, Lamb & Kerth, 1993; Ward, 1982).

When synesthetes view achromatic local–global stimuli constructed from different local and global characters, they report perceiving the color associated with the form to which they are currently attending, rather than two distinct colors (one for each form) or a blend of colors (Mattingley, Rich, Yelland & Bradshaw, 2001a; Palmeri et al., 2002; Ramachandran & Hubbard, 2001a). Moreover, synesthetes report that as they switch their attention between local and global levels, the synesthetic color that is perceived changes accordingly (Ramachandran & Hubbard, 2001a). It seems likely that incongruent local and global forms compete for selection, in a manner analogous to other kinds of perceptual rivalry (Blake & Logothetis, 2002), and that the synesthetic color associated with the stronger competitor comes to dominate. We investigated this idea empirically, again using the synesthetic congruency effect as our dependent measure.

We presented color-graphemic synesthetes and matched nonsynesthetic controls with colored local–global stimuli (Rich & Mattingley, 2003). In our first experiment, we aimed to quantify the influence of synesthetic colors on naming display colors of local–global stimuli. As with conventional Navon-type displays, the identity of local and global letters could be the same or different. When they were the same, the synesthetic color they elicited could be either congruent (plate 7.4a) or incongruent (plate 7.4b) with the display color to be named. When local and global letters were different, the relationship between the display color and the synesthetic colors induced by the letters was manipulated: the global letter could elicit a synesthetic color that matched the display color, in which case the local letters were incongruently colored (plate 7.4c), or the local letters could elicit a synesthetic color that matched the display color, and the global letter was colored incongruently (plate 7.4d). Note that for both versions of these latter stimuli, the color of the display was congruent with the synesthetic color elicited by the letter at one level but incongruent with the synesthetic color elicited by the letter at the other.

The four stimulus types were randomly intermingled, making it impossible to predict the level at which synesthetic incongruency would arise for each trial. Participants were instructed to name the display color of each stimulus as quickly as possible and to ignore the letters themselves, which were always irrelevant to the task. Mean correct color-naming times for synesthete K.B., whose results are representative of those of the synesthetic group as a whole, are shown in Figure 7.1a. K.B. was slower when letters at either level (or both) were colored differently from her induced synesthetic color, compared with conditions in which the synesthetic and display colors matched. She was slowest of all for trials in which letters at the local and global levels had the same identity, but for which the display color was incongruent with her synesthetic color for this letter. Her fastest color-naming times occurred when the same letter appeared at both local and global levels and the display color matched her synesthetic color for that letter. When local letters were arranged to create a different global letter and the display color was congruent with only one of the forms (local or global), her color-naming times were intermediate between the two other conditions. The results of this experiment demonstrate that having two inducers within a single stimulus causes a significant synesthetic congruency effect, even when one of the synesthetic

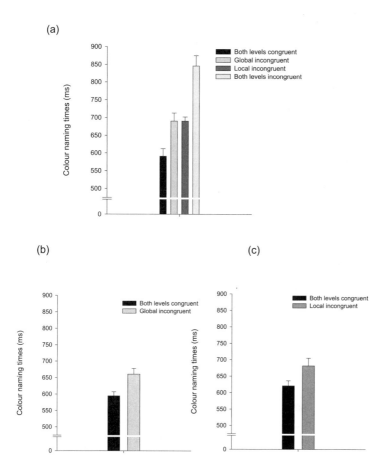

Figure 7.1. (a) Mean correct color-naming times for synesthete K.B. for the first local-global experiment in which all four conditions were randomly intermingled. (b) Mean correct color-naming times for K.B. for the 'attend global' condition of the second experiment in which incongruency only occurred at the local level. (c) Mean correct color-naming times for K.B. for the 'attend local' condition of the second experiment in which incongruency only occurred at the global level.

colors matches the display color. Under these circumstances, however, the effect is less pronounced than when only incongruent synesthetic colors are induced.

Following from this initial experiment, we then had synesthetes maintain attentional focus on one level (global or local) throughout a block of trials, in order to determine whether the synesthetic congruency effect can arise from letters that are actively ignored. Displays were constructed so that the letter at the attended level always elicited a synesthetic color that was *congruent* with the display color to be named, while the letter at the ignored level elicited a color that was either congruent or incongruent. Thus, in the *attend global* condition, all stimuli comprised congruently colored global letters that were formed by congruently or incongruently colored local letters (plate 7.4a,c); whereas in the *attend local* condition, stimuli were congruently colored local letters that comprised congruently or incongruently colored global letters (plate 7.4a,d). If attention modulates synesthetic experience, as we have suggested, then having participants selectively attend to congruently colored letters at one level of the display should reduce interference from incongruently colored letters at the ignored level.

Figures 7.1b and 7.1c show the mean correct color-naming times for synesthete K.B., separately for the *attend global* and *attend local* conditions. The magnitude of the synesthetic congruency effect was significantly reduced in the two focused attention conditions relative to the initial experiment in which there was no requirement to focus attention at one level. This provides evidence that diverting attention from incongruently colored stimuli reduces their influence on color-naming times. It is worth noting, however, that although our manipulations clearly reduced the synesthetic congruency effect, it was not eliminated entirely (see figure 7.1b,c). This implies that under conditions of reduced attention, letters can still trigger synesthetic colors, consistent with the findings from our priming experiments involving an attentional load task.

Results from attentional manipulations of the conventional Stroop effect, in which participants are asked to name the ink colors of color words (e.g., RED written in green; Stroop, 1935), have shown that directing attention to color-neutral words (e.g., CHAIR) reduces but does not eliminate interference from an incongruent color word presented in the same display (Brown, Gore & Carr, 2002). Other studies have shown that coloring just a single letter in a color word eliminates the Stroop effect (Besner, Stolz & Boutilier, 1997) and that cueing a single letter in the word compared to cueing all the letters reduces the impact of incongruent color-word stimuli (Besner & Stolz, 1999b). The general explanation for these modulations of the Stroop effect is that diverting attention from the word reduces the efficiency of semantic access and therefore reduces the conflict between the color word and the color to be named (Besner, 2001; Besner & Soltz, 1999a). Similarly, our manipulations of attention in the synesthetic Stroop task may have reduced the efficiency with which the inducing letters were able to activate the appropriate conceptual or semantic representations, including any synesthetic colors, and thus reduced the magnitude of the synesthetic congruency effect.

One interpretation for the remaining effect of synesthetic congruency in these experiments is that synesthetic colors can be induced by ignored stimuli. Alternatively, the effect may be due to residual attentive processing of the inducing stimuli, despite the attentional manipulations. This latter explanation is supported by the near-ceiling performance for prime identification in the attentional load task. In a recent set of experiments, we investigated these interpretations using a novel modification of the classic attentional blink paradigm (Raymond, Shapiro & Arnell, 1992), which allows one to measure the extent to which inducing stimuli are attended or consciously perceived.

In a typical attentional blink (AB) paradigm, stimuli appear successively at fixation in a rapid serial visual presentation (RSVP) stream. Participants are asked to identify one target (e.g., a white letter among black letters) and then to discriminate the presence of a probe (e.g., a black X) from distractor items (figure 7.2). When the probe appears within approximately 500 ms of the first target, participants are poorer at discriminating the probe than at longer intervals or when they are doing the probe task alone. This decrement in performance on the probe task when also identifying the initial target, relative to performance on the probe task alone, is known as the AB (Raymond et al., 1992). The original explanation proposed for the AB was that processing of the first target tied up available attentional resources for a certain period of time, and that other items, such as the probe, were not processed during this period (Raymond et al., 1992). Subsequent experiments revealed that substantial processing of the probe could occur despite participants being unable to explicitly report its presence in the stream (see Shapiro, Arnell & Raymond, 1997, for review). For example, Shapiro, Driver, Ward, and

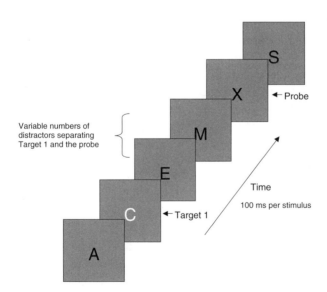

Figure 7.2. Sequence of events in a typical attentional blink paradigm in which the task was to identify the white letter (Target 1) and then discriminate the presence of a black X (the probe). The number of distractors between Target 1 and the probe was varied systematically.

Sorenson (1997) demonstrated that probe items could prime responses to a subsequent (third) target, despite being unavailable for conscious report. They showed better performance on a third target when it was related to the probe compared to when these items were unrelated. These results were found both for identity priming with letters and for semantic priming with words, providing evidence that probe stimuli that occur within the period of the AB may be processed to a semantic level.

We modified the typical AB paradigm with the aim of examining whether a letter that occurs within the period of the AB can induce a synesthetic color despite being unavailable for conscious report (Rich & Mattingley, 2004). We presented an RSVP stream of achromatic (dark gray) letterlike distractor stimuli, deliberately constructed so that they would not induce synesthetic colors. The first target (target 1), which was present on all trials, was a white disk with stripes that were oriented vertically, horizontally or obliquely ($\pm 45°$). Participants were asked to discriminate the orientation of the stripes by selecting one of four options from a separate display that appeared at the end of the RSVP stream (see plate 7.5a). On 50% of trials, an achromatic letter (the probe) appeared at a variable stimulus onset asynchrony (SOA) after target 1. Each stimulus in the stream was presented for 100 ms with an interstimulus interval of 17 ms. There were five SOAs (117, 233, 350, 467, and 817 ms), corresponding to varying numbers of distractors separating the two targets (0, 1, 2, 3, and 6). The number of distractors presented before target 1, and the number presented subsequent to the probe, varied randomly between 3 and 6 items, so that the length of each trial was unpredictable. At the end of the stream, a colored target appeared (plate 7.5a). The synesthetic color associated with the probe letter could be either congruent or incongruent with the subsequent colored target, and both these items were tailored individually for each synesthete and his or her matched control. We have tested a number of synesthetes using this modified AB paradigm, but here we present data from just a single synesthete, N.W.

In the first task (standard AB), we verified that an AB was present for the probe with our modified displays. Participants were asked to identify target 1 and to report whether a letter probe had appeared in the stream. A colored target appeared at the end of the stream, but in this task participants were not required to name the color, thus allowing them to concentrate on target 1 and the probe. In the second task (attend probe), we aimed to show that when attention could be devoted exclusively to the probe letter, a synesthetic congruency effect of the kind observed in our previous experiments could also be elicited in this new paradigm. Participants were required to name the target color as quickly as possible and then to indicate whether a letter was present in the stream. Color-naming times for congruent versus incongruent trials were then compared to assess the extent of any synesthetic congruency effect.

Normally, the AB is assessed by determining the proportion of correct probe responses when identification of target 1 is also required, relative to the proportion of correct responses when attention is devoted exclusively to the probe. Similarly, in our AB paradigm we compared the proportion of correct letter discriminations in the standard AB task with that of the attend probe task. Accuracy of probe discrimination for N.W. is presented in plate 7.5b. At SOAs of 233 and 350 ms, N.W.'s ability to discriminate the probe was significantly reduced when she had to respond to both target 1 and the probe, compared with when she had to respond to the colored target and the probe, thus demonstrating an AB. Plate 7.5c shows N.W.'s mean color-naming times for trials in which she correctly discriminated the presence of a probe letter. It is clear that for trials in which the probe letter elicited a synesthetic color that was incongruent with the target color, N.W.'s naming times were significantly slower than for trials in which the synesthetic and target colors were congruent. A synesthetic congruency effect can thus be induced by a single letter among letterlike distractors, despite a variable interval of 300–750 ms between the probe letter and colored target. This finding suggests that once elicited, representations of synesthetic colors can remain active for a considerable time and can resist disruption by subsequent distractor items.

Having established that a synesthetic congruency effect can be obtained using our RSVP task and that an AB arises for letters presented 233 and 350 ms after target 1, we then tested the influence of letter stimuli presented during the AB on color-naming times. In the critical third task, participants were required to name the target color as rapidly as possible and then to identify target 1. If the mere presence of a letter in the stream is sufficient to elicit a synesthetic color, then there should also be a significant synesthetic congruency effect at all SOAs in this task, just as was observed for the identical displays in the attend probe task. If, in contrast, inducing letters must be selectively attended (and thus available for conscious report) in order to trigger synesthetic colors, then the magnitude of any synesthetic congruency effect should be reduced or eliminated at SOAs corresponding to the period of the AB in this task.

Plate 7.5d shows the mean correct color-naming times for N.W., plotted separately for congruent and incongruent trials in which target 1 was correctly identified. Strikingly, there was no evidence for a synesthetic congruency effect at any SOA, suggesting that the demands of identifying target 1 eliminated synesthetic competition arising from letters that appeared well beyond the duration of the predetermined AB. This intriguing finding suggests that synesthetic color experiences may not arise automatically under all conditions, even when the stimuli that induce them can be accurately discriminated from a stream of visually similar distractors. The results cannot be due to participants simply ignoring items that appeared after target 1 because the number of items that appeared between target 1 and the colored target was varied unpredictably. The preliminary results from these novel manipulations of the AB phenomenon imply an even more powerful role for attention than suggested by our priming and local–global experiments. They also provide further fuel for the debate concerning the kind of representations of inducer stimuli that are both necessary and sufficient to produce synesthetic color experiences.

Conclusion

In this chapter we have reviewed a series of experiments focused on objective measurement of color-graphemic synesthesia and asked what role attention and awareness might play in the generation of these colors. We have relied on the replicable synesthetic congruency effect, in which synesthetes are slower to name display colors if these are preceded or accompanied by characters that induce different synesthetic colors. We have shown that this effect does not occur when the inducing stimulus is masked from awareness, and that it can be powerfully modulated by mechanisms of voluntary selective attention.

The studies conducted in our laboratory imply that the color experiences associated with letters, words, and digits rely on conscious representations of inducing stimuli. We found that representations of inducing characters at an early perceptual level of analysis are neither necessary nor sufficient to elicit synesthetic colors. Using three different paradigms, we have demonstrated a powerful role for visual selective attention in synesthetic color experiences, which is consistent both with our suggestion that attention is critical in synesthetic binding of form and color (Rich & Mattingley, 2002) and with the proposed role of attention in feature binding (Treisman, 1998; Treisman & Gelade, 1980).

Acknowledgments   Parts of this work were presented at the Annual Meeting of the Cognitive Neuroscience Society, San Francisco, California, April 2002. J.B.M. is supported by grants from the Australian Research Council, the National Health and Medical Research Council, and Unilever (U.K.); A.N.R. is supported by an Australian Postgraduate Award.

References

Baron-Cohen, S., Harrison, J., Goldstein, L.H., & Wyke, M. (1993). Coloured speech perception: Is synesthesia what happens when modularity breaks down? *Perception, 22,* 419–426.

Baron-Cohen, S., Wyke, M.A., & Binnie, C. (1987). Hearing words and seeing colours: An experimental investigation of a case of synesthesia. *Perception, 16*, 761–767.

Besner, D. (2001). The myth of ballistic processing: Evidence from Stroop's paradigm. *Psychonomic Bulletin and Review, 8*, 324–330.

Besner, D., & Stolz, J.A. (1999a). Unconsciously controlled processing: The Stroop effect reconsidered. *Psychonomic Bulletin and Review, 6*, 449–455.

Besner, D., & Stolz, J.A. (1999b). What kind of attention modulates the Stroop effect? *Psychonomic Bulletin and Review, 6*, 99–104.

Besner, D., Stolz, J.A., & Boutilier, C. (1997). The Stroop effect and the myth of automaticity. *Psychonomic Bulletin and Review, 4*, 221–225.

Blake, R., & Logothetis, N.K. (2002). Visual competition. *Nature Reviews Neuroscience, 3*, 13–21.

Brown, T.L., Gore, C.L., & Carr, T.H. (2002). Visual attention and word recognition in Stroop color naming: Is word recognition "automatic"? *Journal of Experimental Psychology: General, 131*, 220–240.

Dehaene, S., Naccache, L., Le, C.H.G., Koechlin, E., Mueller, M., Dehaene-Lambertz, G., van de Moortele, P. F., & Le Bihan, D. (1998). Imaging unconscious semantic priming. *Nature, 395*, 597–600.

Dahaene, S., Naccache, L., Cohen, L., Bihan, D.L., Mangin, L.F., Poline, J.B., & Riviere, D. (2001). Cerebral mechanisms of word masking and unconscious repetition priming. *Nature Neuroscience, 4*, 752–815.

Dresslar, F.B. (1903). Are chromaesthesias variable? A study of an individual case. *American Journal of Psychology, 14*, 308–382.

Driver, J. (2001). A selective review of selective attention research from the past century. *British Journal of Psychology, 92*, 53–72.

Dudycha, G.J., & Dudycha, M.M. (1935). A case of synesthesia: Visual-pain and visual-audition. *Journal of Abnormal and Social Psychology, 30*, 57–69.

Ginsberg, L. (1923). A case of synesthesia. *American Journal of Psychology, 34*, 582–589.

Karwoski, T.F., & Odbert, H.S. (1938). Color-music. *Psychological Monographs, 50*, 1–60.

Mattingley, J.B., Rich, A.N., & Payne, J. (2003). The effects of attentional load on colour-graphemic synesthesia. Manuscript submitted for publication.

Mattingley, J.B., Rich, A.N., Yelland, G., & Bradshaw, J.L. (2001a). Investigations of automatic binding of colour and form in synesthesia. Paper presented at the TENNET, Montreal, Canada.

Mattingley, J.B., Rich, A.N., Yelland, G., & Bradshaw, J.L. (2001b). Unconscious priming eliminates automatic binding of colour and alphanumeric form in synesthesia. *Nature, 410*, 580–582.

Mills, C.B., Boteler, E.H., & Oliver, G.K. (1999). Digit synesthesia: A case study using a Stroop-type test. *Cognitive Neuropsychology, 16*, 181–191.

Motluk, A. (1994, August). The sweet smell of purple. *New Scientist, 32*–37.

Motluk, A. (2000, April). The number purple: Crossed wires in the brain give colour to numbers. *New Scientist, 19*.

Motluk, A. (2001, March). Sounds like a rose to me. *New Scientist, 50*.

Myers, C.S. (1911). A case of synesthesia. *British Journal of Psychology, 4,* 228–238.

Myers, C.S. (1914). Two cases of synesthesia. *British Journal of Psychology, 7,* 112–117.

Navon, D. (1977). Forest before trees: The precedence of global features in visual perception. *Cognitive Psychology, 9,* 353–383.

Odgaard, E.C., Flowers, J.H., & Bradman, H.L. (1999). An investigation of the cognitive and perceptual dynamics of a colour-digit synesthete. *Perception, 28,* 651–664.

Ox, J. (1999). Color me synesthesia. *Leonardo, 32,* 7–8.

Palmeri, T.J., Blake, R., Marois, R., Flanery, M.A., & Whetsell, W. (2002). The perceptual reality of synesthetic colors. *Proceedings of the National Academy of Sciences USA, 99,* 4127–4131.

Pashler, H. (Ed.). (1998). *The psychology of attention.* Cambridge, MA: MIT Press.

Pashler, H., & Johnston, J.C. (1998). Attentional limitations in dual-task performance. In H. Pashler (Ed.), *Attention* (pp. 155–189). East Sussex: Psychology Press.

Pierce, A.H. (1907). Gustatory audition: A hitherto undescribed variety of synesthesia. *American Journal of Psychology, 18,* 341–352.

Ramachandran, V.S., & Hubbard, E.M. (2001a). Psychophysical investigations into the neural basis of synesthesia. *Proceedings of the Royal Society of London, B, 268,* 979–983.

Ramachandran, V.S., & Hubbard, E.M. (2001b). Synesthesia—a window into perception, thought and language. *Journal of Consciousness Studies, 8,* 3–34.

Raymond, J.E., Shapiro, K.L., & Arnell, K.M. (1992). Temporary suppression of visual processing in an RSVP task: an attentional blink? *Journal of Experimental Psychology: Human Perception and Performance, 18,* 849–860.

Rich, A.N., & Mattingley, J.B. (2002). Anomalous perception in synesthesia: A cognitive neuroscience perspective. *Nature Reviews Neuroscience, 3,* 43–52.

Rich, A.N., & Mattingley, J.B. (2003). The effects of stimulus competition and voluntary attention on colour-graphemic synesthesia. *NeuroReport, 14,* 1793–1798.

Rich, A.N., & Mattingley, J.B. (2004). An attentional blink for synesthetic colours? Manuscript in preparation.

Robertson, L.C., Egly R., Lamb, M.R., & Kerth, L. (1993). Spatial attention and cuing to global and local levels of hierarchical structure. *Journal of Experimental Psychology: Human Perception and Performance, 19,* 471–487.

Seron, X., Pesenti, M., & Noel, M.P. (1992). Images of numbers, or "When 98 is upper left and 6 sky blue." *Cognition, 44,* 159–196.

Shapiro, K.L., Arnell, K.M., & Raymond, J.E. (1997). The attentional blink. *Trends in Cognitive Sciences, 1,* 291–295.

Shapiro, K., Driver, J., Ward, R., & Sorensen, R.E. (1997). Priming from the attentional blink: A failure to extract visual tokens but not visual types. *Psychological Science, 8,* 95–100.

Smilek, D., Dixon, M.J., Cudahy, C., & Merikle, P.M. (2001). Synesthetic photisms influence visual perception. *Journal of Cognitive Neuroscience, 13,* 930–936.

Snow, J.C., & Mattingley, J.B. (2003). Perception, unconscious. In L. Nadel (Ed.), *Encyclopedia of cognitive science* (pp. 517–526). London: Macmillan.

Stroop, J.R. (1935). Studies of interference in serial verbal reactions. *Journal of Experimental Psychology, 18,* 643–662.

Treisman, A. (1988). Features and objects: The fourteenth Bartlett memorial lecture. *The Quarterly Journal of Experimental Psychology, 40A,* 201–237.

Treisman, A. (1998). Feature binding, attention and object perception. *Philosophical Transactions of the Royal Society of London, B, 353,* 1295–1306.

Treisman, A. (1999). Solutions to the binding problem: Progress through controversy and convergence. *Neuron, 24,* 105–110.

Treisman, A., & Gelade, G. (1980). A feature-integration theory of attention. *Cognitive Psychology, 12,* 97–136.

Ward, L.M. (1982). Determinants of attention to local and global features of visual forms. *Journal of Experimental Psychology: Human Perception and Performance, 8,* 562–581.

Wolfe, J.M. (1998). What can 1 million trials tell us about visual search? *Psychological Science, 9,* 33–39.

Wollen, K.A., & Ruggiero, F.T. (1983). Colored-letter synesthesia. *Journal of Mental Imagery, 7,* 83–86.

Part III

Consciousness and Cognition

8

Synesthesia: A Window on the Hard Problem of Consciousness

Jeffrey Gray

Philosophical and Scientific Background

After millennia of philosophical speculation, the problem of consciousness has finally entered the experimental laboratory. Though this development is of recent date (just a few decades or so), it is now rapidly gathering speed. The fundamental assumption underlying it—that empirical research has a good chance of resolving the issues that have not yielded to philosophical argument—is open to question. But, if one does accept this assumption (as I do), then scientific progress may have a profound impact on our understanding of human nature, of the place of human experience in the universe, and conceptions of core religious and spiritual issues such as the existence or nature of the soul, the possibility of a nonmaterial afterlife, or the nature of meditative experience. Fortunately, the methods of natural science do not depend on the beliefs held by individual scientists concerning these (or other) issues. One may therefore put such beliefs aside and use standard scientific approaches to see what they can deliver on even this difficult terrain.

Functionalism and the Hard Problem of Consciousness

To date, scientific investigation in the field of consciousness studies has been restricted almost entirely to what Chalmers (1996) calls the "easy" problems (while nonetheless admitting that, in standard scientific terms, their resolution presents formidable difficulties, both technical and theoretical). Solutions to the easy problems are essentially descriptive and correlational.

They consist in answers to questions such as, How much of behavior is accomplished by processes of which one is conscious, and how much by unconscious processes? Are there systematic differences between these two classes of process, or between the two classes of behavior with which they are associated? What, if any, are the differences in neural location or in types of neural function that are associated with consciously and unconsciously achieved behavior, respectively?

Some of these easy questions now have reasonably clear answers, at least in preliminary form. So, for example, it is clear that most behavior (certainly a great deal more than is apparent to simple introspection) is accomplished by processes of which the subject remains completely or in large part unaware (Velmans, 1991). It is also reasonably well established that the contents of consciousness are largely and perhaps entirely perceptual; that is, they occur as visual, auditory, olfactory, or gustatory percepts or combinations of these (Gray, 1995). Other easy questions, however, are only just beginning to yield to empirical inquiry. There remain, for example, widely different but defensible hypotheses concerning what Crick (1994) has called the "neural correlates of consciousness"—that is, the sites and types of neural processing in the brain that most closely correlate with particular conscious experiences. These range from the claim that it is only ever the activity of the whole brain that serves as a neural correlate of consciousness (Dennett, 1991) to the proposal that, for visual consciousness, it is necessary and sufficient to have activity in relatively small regions of the visual system in which particular features (such as color, motion, contours, faces) are computed (Barbur, Watson, Frackowick & Zeki, 1993; fftyche et al., 1998; Zeki and Bartels, 1998). So, on this ("Zeki's") hypothesis, activity in the area known as V4 (Zeki et al., 1991) or V8 (Hadjikhani, Liu, Dale, Cavanagh & Tootell, 1998) is necessary and sufficient for the experience of color, activity in V5 is necessary and sufficient for the experience of visual motion, and so on (see Gray, 2004).

In contrast, empirical research on the hard problem of consciousness (Chalmers, 1996) has barely begun. This is the problem (put in scientific as distinct from philosophical terms) of causal mechanism: How do the seemingly utterly disparate realms of, on the one hand, brain processes and behavior and, on the other hand, consciousness mesh with one another? (I use the nontechnical term "mesh with" advisedly, since all of the more respectable terms, such as "interact with," "cause," "supervene upon," come loaded with a variety of philosophical baggage that is best avoided.) No matter how close and detailed the sets of correlations among brain processes, behavioral functions, and conscious experiences that eventually emerge from studies of the easy problems, these will not by themselves explain the mechanisms underlying the correlations. This state of affairs is, of course, not special to the hard problem of consciousness: It is a general maxim of both philosophy and science that correlation does not establish cause or causal mechanism. There is one way, however, in which this part of the hard problem of consciousness is special. It is held by some philosophers that it is impossible in principle to give a causal account of the relations between conscious experience on the one hand and, on the other hand, the brain and behavioral processes with which conscious experience is correlated. In other words, for these philosophers, the hard problem is not merely hard, it is intractable. My contrary view is simply stated. Conscious experience is a feature of the natural world. It is generally the case that other features of the natural world are susceptible of investigation by, and explanation within, natural science. The reasons claimed to demonstrate that consciousness is an exception to this rule are strongly disputed even within philosophy. It is reasonable, therefore, for science to try to tackle the hard problem in its own way.

Everything we know empirically about consciousness suggests that this is created by the human brain (though not necessarily uniquely by the human brain). As already noted, conscious experience is largely or entirely perceptual. Work on the neural correlates of visual consciousness is largely consistent with Zeki's hypothesis (Zeki, 1993) that activity in relatively restricted regions of the cortex creates conscious awareness of particular visual features, such as an experience of color or of motion (Gray, 2004). We need, therefore, a word to describe such elements of perception. The philosophical term "qualia" (singular, "quale"), stripped of its philosophical overtones, fits the bill well. Thus the hard problem may be phrased for scientific purposes as: How does the brain create qualia? Unfortunately, the dominant view within contemporary science (cognitive science, psychology, artificial intelligence, and, to a slightly lesser extent, neuroscience) is functionalism, and functionalism is so structured that it prevents this question from ever being properly put, let alone answered. (Dennett's well-known 1991 book, *Consciousness Explained*, is a good example of functionalist thought.)

Consider as a specific version of the hard problem this question: How should one explain the difference between two subjective experiences of color, say of red and green? I take functionalism to approach a question of this kind in the following way. It starts by eliminating from the question the qualia of red and green as such. For these, it substitutes as the explicandum the repertoire of behavioral responses by which a person demonstrates the capacity to discriminate between red and green. This repertoire would include, for example, pointing to a red color when requested to do so, using the word "red" appropriately in relation to the color red, stopping at red traffic lights, stating that a tomato is red, and so on. Next, functionalism seeks an understanding of the mechanisms by which these discriminating behavioral "functions" are discharged. This understanding may be sought at a black-box level, as in the familiar box-and-arrow diagrams of cognitive psychology, neural networks, computer simulations, and so on, or in the circuitry of the actual brain systems that connect the inputs to the outputs of each discriminating behavioral function. A full function for a given difference between qualia then consists in a detailed account of the corresponding differences in inputs, outputs, and the mechanisms that mediate between input and output. If such a full functional account is given, then, according to functionalism, there is no further answer to the original question: What is the difference between the subjective experiences (the qualia) of red and green? To continue asking this question in the face of a complete functionalist account would be a meaningless activity, for, according to functionalism, qualia just are the functions (input-mechanism-output) by which they are supported.

From this formulation of functionalism one can draw the following primary inference: For any discriminable difference between qualia, there must be an equivalent discriminable difference in function. There is also a second, complementary inference: For any discriminable functional difference, there must be a discriminable difference between qualia. Clearly, there are ways in which the complementary inference may be false, for there are many forms of behavior that are not accompanied by qualia at all. So, for example, the pupil of the eye constricts if illumination increases and dilates if illumination decreases; but one is not aware of either of these changes. However, in the case of a behavioral domain normally accompanied by qualia, it seems reasonable that, whenever functionalism draws the primary inference, it should also draw the complementary one. Let us return to the example of red and green. The primary inference is that, if someone claims to have different red and green experiences, then there must be different functions (input-mechanism-output) to support this claim. The complementary inference would be that, if someone manifests different functions (input-mechanism-output) for each of which there is an associated quale, then these qualia must also differ. The two inferences together constitute a claim for identity between qualia and functions within the domain of color vision. Functionalism generalizes this identity claim across all domains and all qualia.

If functionalism is correct, then, there is no point in asking the question, how does the brain create qualia?, because we already know in principle all there is to know—that is, how the brain carries out behavioral functions (all remaining easy problems aside), and qualia just are functions. However, functionalism has never been exposed to empirical test. Rather, it is simply taken for granted as a foundational axiom. Yet the primary and complementary inferences drawn above are not in principle immune to empirical test. Furthermore, because functionalism purports to provide a perfectly general account of how conscious experiences mesh with brain and behavior, it would take only one clear empirical demonstration of a counter-instance to these inferences to invalidate the functionalist doctrine. We have reported studies of colored-hearing synesthesia that go far to demonstrate just such a counter-instance (Gray et al., 2002; Nunn et al., 2002).

Colored-Hearing Synesthesia

Synesthesia is a condition in which, in otherwise normal individuals, stimulation in one sensory modality reliably elicits the report of a sensation in another modality; a synesthete is a person who reports experiences of this kind. The etymology of the word is from the Greek "syn" meaning "together" and "aesthesis" meaning "sensation." Cytowic (2002) translates this into the graphic phrase, "a union of the senses." The senses so unified are bewildering in their variety: sounds can evoke colors; tastes can evoke shapes; colors can evoke smells; pain or sexual orgasm can evoke colors, and so on. The most common varieties of synesthesia are ones in which words or numbers, whether spoken or seen, evoke colors. Synesthaesia in all of its forms is relatively rare. Estimates of its prevalence differ widely, from a low of 1 in 25,000 to a high of 1 in 300; a best guess at present is about 1 in 2000. There is a preponderance of female synesthetes; estimates converge on about a 6:1 female:male ratio. Synesthesia runs in families in a pattern suggestive of transmission by way of a gene on the female or X chromosome. X-linked genes are usually recessive; however, any X-linked gene for synesthesia would need to be dominant to account for the greater abundance of female synesthetes (Cytowic, 2002). This hypothesis, however, has not yet been tested on a sufficiently large sample to establish its adequacy. Despite this evidence for familial transmission, even within a group of family members sharing the same type of synesthesia (e.g., seeing colors in response to words), synesthetic experiences are completely idiosyncratic: no two synesthetes report the same set of experiences. All synesthetes report that they have had their synesthetic experiences for as far back as they can remember. Most of them, however, never talk about these experiences, having learned at an early age that nonsynesthetes generally regard them as odd or even crazy. However, apart from occasional, relatively minor cognitive deficiencies (e.g., in arithmetic or spelling), synesthetes are otherwise normal. Sometimes they are even able to use their synesthetic experience to achieve supernormal performance, particularly in the domain of memory (Luria, 1968). Almost always they value their synesthetic experiences, finding in them pleasure, and even joy.

I defined synesthesia above conservatively: as a condition in which stimulation in one sensory modality reliably elicits the report of a sensation in another. However, if the arguments advanced here are to hold, it must be the case that the report is veridical, in two senses. First, the report must be more than mere confabulation—there must be some experience that is separate from the report and is reliably reported. Second, that experience must be perceptual, if we are to base arguments about qualia upon it. Over the last decade evidence has accumulated to support both these assumptions. The key experiments have studied two of the most common groups of synesthetes, those in whom spoken words evoke experiences of color (colored-hearing synethesia) or in whom numbers and letters presented visually in black and white are seen in color (color-graphemic synesthesia).

First, Baron-Cohen, Harrison, Goldstein, and Wyke (1993) introduced a "test of genuineness," with which they demonstrated the reliability of reports of colored-hearing synesthesia. Their subjects gave essentially identical reports of their color experiences in response to a list of words when retested at a year's interval, with no warning that they would be retested at that time. In contrast, the similarity of reported word–color associations in a group of nonsynesthete controls retested, with warning, after a period of just a month was strikingly inferior. All synesthetes participating in our experiments, described below, are required to pass a modified form of this test of genuineness.

Second, a number of recent experiments using psychophysical techniques have clearly demonstrated the perceptual nature of the synesthetic experience. I give here just one example (Ramachandran and Hubbard, 2001a). It is characteristic of visual perception that items in a display that differ in a feature from other background items in the same display "pop out"—that is to say, they are seen automatically and involuntarily as being different from the background items, and immediately grouped together as separate from the background items. Suppose, for example, you are looking at a display in which most of the items are in red but a few are in green. You will at once detect the green items as standing out from the red. There will be no need for you to search the display to find these items. Taking advantage of this visual pop out, Ramachandran and Hubbard presented subjects with a black-against-white display of 2s and 5s, computer-generated so that the 5s were mirror images of the 2s. The 5s were disposed among the background 2s so as to form a triangle. Nonsynesthetes found it hard to detect the triangle and took more time to do so. Color-graphemic synesthetes, in contrast, for whom the 2s and 5s elicited different color sensations (e.g., red and green, respectively), at once saw the triangle standing out in one color against a background of a different color. It is virtually impossible to account for this and similar observations except by giving credit to the synesthetes' own reports that they see the numbers in color, even though they are in fact presented in black against white. These perceptual characteristics set true synesthesia apart from mere verbal associations or metaphor.

Third, this evidence from psychophysical experiments is supported by data from neuroimaging experiments, in which the brain is visualized in action during the act of perception. In a first experiment of this kind, using positron emission tomography (PET), Paulesu et al. (1995) presented a list of spoken words to a group of colored-hearing synesthetes and to nonsynesthete controls. The synesthetes, but not the controls, responded with activity in the visual system. In this experiment, the activity was observed at relatively high levels of the visual system, in visual association cortex, a finding that has been interpreted by Grossenbacher and Lovelace (2001) as indicating that synesthetic experiences of color "result from partial activation of higher-order visual cortical networks, rather than arising at the earliest levels of cortical visual processing" (page 38).

However, our group (Nunn et al., 2002) has recently reinvestigated this issue, using essentially the same materials and procedure as Paulesu et al. (1995), but taking advantage of the greater temporal and spatial resolution afforded by functional magnetic resonance imaging (fMRI). In both colored-hearing synesthetes and nonsynesthete controls, matched for sex (all female), handedness, and verbal intelligence, we measured regional blood oxygen level dependent (BOLD) activity in response to a list of spoken words (relative to auditory stimulation by tones as a baseline condition). We related the resulting pattern of BOLD activity to that obtained in a standard test of brain activation by color. In this test, regional BOLD activity is measured in response to presentations of "Mondrians" (patterns made up of irregular rectangles, each of a different color, like those painted by the artist Piet Mondrian), as compared to a baseline condition of the same patterns in black and white. We performed two experiments, one in which the pattern of BOLD activation by colored Mondrians was derived from earlier data obtained at the Institute of Psychiatry on nonsynesthetes (Howard et al., 1998), and a second in which we remeasured this pattern both in a further group of nonsynesthete controls and in the synesthete subjects. The results of the two experiments were essentially identical. They demonstrated that the synesthetes, but not the controls, activated the extrastriate visual system in response to spoken words, confirming in this broad respect the findings reported by Paulesu and colleagues. However, the activation was located lower down in the visual system, exactly in the region known from previous reports (e.g., Howard et al., 1998), and replicated in our own Mondrian experiment, to be the earliest point at which the brain computes colors as such (as distinct from information merely about wavelength of light falling upon different points in the retina); viz, the area in the fusiform gyrus known as V4 or V8. Thus, these findings, like those reported by Ramachandran and Hubbard (2001a), support the hypothesis that synesthetic color experiences arise at an early stage of visual processing and are truly perceptual in nature.

Function verus Tissue

I have so far presented functionalism without contrasting it to any alternative approach to the understanding of qualia. In the present context, the most relevant contrast is with what can be called, for want of a better word, a "tissue" approach. The "want of a better word" reflects the fact that this alternative to functionalism has been articulated far less clearly than functionalism itself. Indeed, it is not clear that it has ever been articulated at all.

Functionalism more or less inevitably leads to the conclusion that, if a system displays behavior of a kind that, in us, is associated with conscious experience, then the components out of which the system is made are irrelevant. So, for example, if a computer or a robot is able to discharge a sufficiently broad range of high-level functions in a manner comparable to a human being, then (so it is claimed) the computer or robot will also have conscious experiences like those that a human being has while discharging the same functions. A contrary view, however, holds that there is something special about the actual components out of which brains are made and that this something provides a necessary condition for consciousness. The best known version of this view stresses the physics of the components, as in the quantum gravitational theory of consciousness proposed by Penrose and Hameroff (see Woolf & Hameroff, 2001). As yet, and surprisingly, there has been no clear statement of a theory in which consciousness depends upon specifically biological, as distinct from general physical, properties of the brain. Views of the tissue kind are sometimes explicitly proposed as being superior to functionalism, as in the case of Penrose and Hameroff, but more often it is left unclear whether they are incompatible with functionalism.

Despite this lack of conceptual articulation, here I use as a contrast to functionalism the tissue approach. This choice is dictated by the parallel afforded by the contrast to the two most plausible accounts of the etiology of synesthesia. These hold that synesthesia is based upon either (1) early and strong associative learning, or (2) an unusual form of hard wiring in the synesthete brain. The parallel I draw recognizes equivalences between, on the one hand, hypothesis 1 and functionalism and, on the other hand, hypothesis 2 and the tissue approach. More specifically, hypothesis 2 holds that, as the result of an extra, hard-wired projection in the synesthete brain, activity in the inducing sensory pathway (e.g., colored hearing, auditory speech analyzers) leads automatically to further activity in the induced pathway (subserving color vision), and that activity in the induced pathway is sufficient, without regard to the nature of any associated ongoing functions, to trigger the associated conscious experience (of color). I refer to this putative process as synesthetic "sparking over." Applied to colored hearing, the sparking over hypothesis includes Zeki's hypothesis that activity in V4/V8 is necessary and sufficient for the conscious experience of color. No more general hypothesis is offered as to the nature of the events in the induced pathway (e.g., in V4/V8) that are sufficient for synesthetic conscious experience to spark over. To do so would be to propose a novel solution to the hard problem—one that I do not have.

As we have seen, synesthetes generally report that they have had synesthesia as far back as they can remember. They do not normally report any specific learning experience that might have led to their associating, for example, a particular word with a particular color. However, such learning may have taken place at a sufficiently early age to fall into the period of infantile amnesia. Thus, one possible explanation for synesthesia is that the individuals concerned form exceptionally strong and enduring associations between words and colors at an early age. The alternative, hard-wiring account (as introduced above) is that the synesthete brain has abnormal projections that link one part of the brain (the sensory system in which the inducing stimulus is processed) to another (the sensory system in which the synesthetic percept is induced). So, in the case of colored hearing, there would be a projection, not existing in the nonsynesthete brain (or even in the brains of individuals with other types of synesthesia) from the parts of the brain that process heard and/or seen words to the color-selective region (V4/V8) of the visual system. This abnormal projection might arise because the synesthete has a genetic mutation that promotes its growth or one that prevents it from being pruned during early development, since at this time the brain normally has an abundance of so-called exuberant connections that are no longer found in the adult brain (Dehay, Bullier & Kennedy, 1984). As we have seen, the likelihood of a genetic basis for synesthesia is strengthened by the strong tendency for the condition to run in families. There is at present no easy way to test directly the hard-wiring hypothesis because this would require anatomical investigation of the brain (although the MRI method of diffusion tensor imaging may offer a way forward; Jones et al., 2002). What my group has tried to do, therefore, is to test the associative learning hypothesis.

We performed two experiments. In the first (Nunn et al., 2002) we gave nonsynesthetes extensive over-training on a series of word–color associations closely matched to those reported by our colored-hearing synesthetes. In the second (Gray et al., 2002), we similarly over-trained both colored-hearing synesthetes and nonsynesthetes on a series of associations between short melodies and colors (the colored-hearing synesthetes had no spontaneous color experiences in response to nonspeech sounds, including music). After training on these associations we presented the words (to the nonsynesthetes) or the melodies (to both synesthetes and nonsynesthetes) during fMRI scanning. Subjects were tested in this way with instructions either to predict the associated color or to imagine it. Our training criteria were strict: subjects had to attain five all-correct runs through the list of associations before they entered the scanner. Furthermore, after initial fMRI scanning, they were given additional training in the scanner to the same rigorous learning criterion and then scanned again. Nonetheless, there was no activation in V4/V8 in any of these testing conditions ("predict" and "imagine" instructions given before and after retraining in the scanner) either in the nonsynesthetes presented with words or in the synesthetes or nonsynesthetes presented with melodies. These experiments show that neither strong associative learning nor imagining colors is sufficient to activate the color-selective region of the brain that is automatically activated by words in colored-hearing synesthesia. They also show that colored-hearing synesthetes are not especially gifted in associative learning. They did not learn the melody–color associations any more quickly than controls; and they did not show any activation in V4/V8 in response to the melodies after learning. Thus, whether in synesthetes or nonsynesthetes, associative learning is unable to mimic what happens spontaneously when synesthetes are tested in the modality in which they spontaneously have their synesthetic experiences.

Does Hard Wiring Underlie Colored Hearing Synesthesia?

It is difficult to reject a hypothesis on the basis of negative findings alone. We cannot rule out the possibility that, despite the considerable effort we put into overtraining our subjects, we were unable to achieve the strength of the early learning that might conceivably underlie word–color associations in colored-hearing synesthesia. Perhaps there is something special about the period of early learning that cannot be duplicated in adult subjects. Nonetheless, the complete absence in these experiments of any activation in the color-selective regions of the visual system, except in the case of spontaneous synesthetic word–color associations, casts considerable doubt on the hypothesis that the latter are the fruit of normal associative learning.

Given this conclusion, we are left by default with the hard-wiring hypothesis. In colored-hearing synesthesia, the behavioral evidence suggests that the critical stimuli that elicit perceived colors are linguistic, taking in some subjects a phonetic form and in others a graphemic form. Thus the pathway responsible for inducing synesthetic colors most likely originates in regions in which the auditory and visual representations of phonemes and graphemes are located (Ramachandran and Hubbard, 2001b). Our fMRI data do not directly throw further light upon the inducing pathway, nor would they be expected to do so, since this pathway is presumably activated to a similar degree in synesthetes and nonsynesthetes presented with words, and, indeed, this assumption fits our fMRI observations (Nunn et al., 2002). Our data do, however, sharpen hypotheses concerning the likely route from the inducing to the induced pathway.

The colored-hearing synesthetes in our experiments responded to spoken words by activating the color-selective region of the visual system without activation at any earlier point in the visual pathways, such as V1 or V2, although these regions are activated when subjects are presented with colored visual stimuli. This pattern of results—similar activation in more central parts of the visual pathway, but V1/V2 more clearly activated by the more normal route of stimulation—has been reported also in studies of color afterimages (Hadjikhani et al., 1998), motion aftereffects (Tootell et al., 1995), and illusory motion (Zeki, Watson, & Frackowiak, 1993). In contrast, imagining colors is insufficient to activate either of these regions, V1/V2 or V4/V8 (Gray et al., 2002; Howard et al., 1998; Nunn et al., 2002). These contrasting patterns of activation are consistent with the common introspection that afterimages and aftereffects are true visual percepts, whereas merely imagined visual features are not.

Overall, then, these results suggest, in agreement with Zeki's hypothesis, that activation of modules in the visual system specialized for the analysis of particular visual features, such as color (V4/V8) or motion (V5), is both necessary and sufficient (not requiring supplementation by activity in regions earlier in the visual pathway) for the conscious experience of that visual feature. This generalization is also supported by data on hallucinatory experiences in the Charles Bonnet syndrome. This is a condition, occurring after sudden deterioration in normal vision (due to a detached retina or glaucoma, for example), in which the patient experiences vivid involuntary visual hallucinations. The content of the hallucinations differs from patient to patient. In an experiment by ffytche et al. (1998), each patient described the hallucinatory experience and indicated its start and finish while lying in the MRI scanner. There was an excellent correlation between the content of the hallucinations and the region of the visual system activated. So, hallucinations of color were accompanied by activity in area V4/V8 in the fusiform gyrus; hallucinations of faces, by activity in a closely adjacent part of the fusiform gyrus known to be specialized for face perception; and hallucinations of objects, by activity in a further region of the fusiform gyrus known to have this specialization. In no case was there activity in V1. From this point of view, then, word–color synesthesia can be viewed as an example of illusory experience in which the triggering stimulus (words) occurs with very high frequency, as compared to triggers for other illusions, such as color afterimages or motion aftereffects (which follow upon prolonged inspection of the inducing color or motion, respectively, and so occur with much lower frequency). In all these cases, once the relevant visual module (V4/V8 for color, V5 for motion, etc.) is activated (provided the activation reaches a sufficient degree of intensity; ffytche, in press; Moutoussis and Zeki, 2002), the illusory experience occurs automatically.

A further important aspect of our findings is that we saw activation in colored-hearing synesthetes presented with spoken words in left V4/V8 only. Given the left lateralization of cortical language systems, this left-lateralized activation may relate to the fact that it is speech sounds rather than sounds in general that elicit the synesthete's color experiences. Both the lack of activation in V1/V2 and the left lateralization of the activation in V4/V8 were observed in two independent experiments (Nunn et al., 2002), so these appear to be robust findings. Also consistent with these results, in their PET study of colored-hearing synesthetes, Paulesu et al. (1995) found subthreshold activation of left, but not right, V4/V8. Thus the abnormal projection that hypothetically underlies colored hearing appears to travel from left-lateralized cortical language systems directly (without involvement of regions lower in the visual system; see above) to left V4/V8. This conclusion is in good agreement with inferences drawn from other data by Ramachandran and Hubbard (2001a, 2001b). It is not yet clear, however, whether this left lateralization tells us anything special about synesthesia or merely about the language systems that act as the inducing pathway for the particular kinds of synesthesia studied by both our group and theirs. We hope to study this issue further.

A final result from our fMRI study of colored-hearing synesthetes (Nunn et al., 2002) deserves mention. The data from the experiment using fMRI to investigate the brain region activated by color showed good agreement between synesthetes and nonsynesthete controls, but only in the right hemisphere. In this hemisphere, both groups showed activation of V4/V8. However, left V4/V8 was activated by colored (vs. black-and-white) Mondrians only in nonsynesthetes. Thus, in the synesthetes, left (but not right) V4/V8 was activated by spoken words and right (but not left) V4/V8 by colored Mondrians. These data raise the interesting possibility that, in colored-hearing synesthesia, the putative abnormal projection from left cortical language systems to left V4/V8 prevents the normal dedication of the latter region (together with its right-sided homologue) to color vision. This hypothesis is testable using standard psychophysical methods.

Taken together, these results and the inferences derived from them present the following picture. Colored-hearing synesthetes are endowed with an abnormal extra projection from left-lateralized cortical language systems to the color-selective region (V4/V8) of the visual system, also on the left. Whenever the synesthete hears or sees a word, this extra projection leads automatically to activation of the color-selective region. Activation of this region is sufficient to cause a conscious color experience, with the exact nature (idiosyncratic in a given synesthete) of that experience depending on the particular set of V4/V8 neurons activated. There is no evidence that the experienced color plays any functional role in the synesthete's auditory or visual processing of words. (In the next section, evidence is presented that, indeed, the experienced color may actively interfere with such processing.) Thus, there is no relationship between the occurrence of the synesthete's color experiences and the linguistic function that accompanies them. This conclusion appears to be incompatible with the functionalist analysis of conscious experience.

The Alien Color Effect

The data reviewed so far strongly support the conclusion that colored hearing is based on an abnormal, probably genetically determined, projection hard-wired into the brain. Conversely, these data lend no support to the hypothesis that this condition results from any special form of associative learning. This section presents additional experimental data that further weaken the associative learning hypothesis. These data come from a study of a subgroup of colored-hearing synesthetes who experience the "alien color effect" (ACE; Gray, 1999). In this phenomenon, the names of colors induce a color experience that is different from the color named. So, for example, the word "red" might give rise to the experience of green, the word "yellow" might give rise to an experience of red, and so on. For a given colored-hearing synesthete, the ACE may affect all, some, or no color names.

As is the case for synesthesia in general, the ACE appears to have been present since early childhood. Now, consider the opportunities for associative learning that this situation entails. A young child with the ACE would frequently encounter circumstances under which someone makes a statement of the form: "see the red bus coming round the corner." From statements such as these, the child has normal opportunities to learn the visual color to which the word "red" applies. Synesthetes do, indeed, learn color names normally (Rich and Mattingley, 2002). So, in the example given above, as well as seeing a red bus come round the corner just after being told about the bus, the child with ACE would also experience a different color, such as green, upon hearing the word red. Thus she must frequently encounter opportunities for associative learning provided by chains such as: word red, experience of green, and sight of red bus. If the first part of this chain, word red followed by green experience, were due to associative learning in the first place, one would expect it to be unlearned by these further associative learning opportunities. This, certainly, is what happens in countless experiments on so-called counter-conditioning or reversal learning with both animal and human subjects. Thus, the existence of the ACE is incompatible with the associative learning account of word-color synesthesia.

Given the scope of the conclusions for functionalism that we seek to draw from the hard-wiring account of synesthesia, it was important to validate the ACE experimentally. As in other recent reports of Stroop-like interference (see below) arising from synesthetic experiences (Mattingley et al., 2001), my group therefore sought evidence that the ACE might delay the speed of color naming. We assessed a group of colored-hearing synesthetes for the degree to which they displayed the ACE and divided them into groups accordingly (Gray et al., 2002). We calculated % ACE for each subject as the percentage of visually presented color names that elicited alien color experiences. We then measured their speed of color naming in a conventional Stroop test. This compares the speed of naming the color in which a row of Xs is presented (as the control condition) to the speed of naming the ink color in the Stroop condition. In the latter condition, the subject is shown name of a color (e.g., the word "red") that is incongruent with the color of the ink (e.g., green) in which it is written. The difference in speed of naming between the control and Stroop conditions provides a measure of the degree to which the color name interferes with the processing of the name of the ink color. We also included a further condition in which the speed of color naming is slowed even further by negative priming. This is like the Stroop condition, but with the added complication that the correct color name response on trial N is the same as the one which had to be inhibited on trial $N - 1$. We anticipated that, if the ACE as reported by the subjects is a real phenomenon, then in naming the ink color they would suffer interference from the alien color and, further, that this interference would be exacerbated by the Stroop and/or negative priming effects. Thus, we predicted that, the greater % ACE, the slower would be the naming of the ink color, especially in the Stroop and negative priming conditions.

Colored-hearing synesthetes were assigned to one of three groups ($N = 10$ per group), with 0–35%, 35–70%, and 70–100% ACE, respectively. In addition, we tested a nonsynesthete control group. Across all groups we found significant Stroop and negative priming effects, and these were unaffected by either synesthesia (as also found for the Stroop effect by Mattingley et al., 2001) or the ACE. Superimposed upon these effects, however, there was a general slowing of color naming across all conditions in subjects with the ACE. This effect was graded: the greater the % ACE reported, the slower the color naming. These results confirm the reality of the self-reported ACE. The slowed color naming was observed as strongly in the control condition, in which the subject had only to name the ink color in which four Xs were presented, as in the Stroop and negative priming conditions. Quantitatively, the degree of the ACE-induced slowing (if one compares full ACE color-naming speed to that of the nonsynesthetes) was about the same as the size of the Stroop effect. Thus, interference from the ACE is separate from interference due to either the Stroop effect or negative priming. This implies that ACE interference arises in a separate brain system—a prediction we are currently testing with fMRI. Note that the interference caused in color naming by the ACE must precede the subject's overt utterance of the correct color name. This interference is presumably due, therefore, to activation of the synesthetic, incongruent color by subvocal retrieval of the ink color name.

The reality of the ACE, demonstrated in this experiment, casts further doubt on the possibility that colored-hearing synesthesia could be the result of any associative learning process. Every time a color name occurs in association with the perception of the color named, and therefore also in conjunction with the alien color experience triggered by the name, as presumably occurred in the experiment just described (Gray et al., 2002), there is an opportunity for normal associative learning to reverse the aberrant association that putatively underlies the ACE. Yet the ACE persists unchanged from childhood to adulthood. It is extremely unlikely, therefore, that the ACE is established as the result of an initial stage of normal associative learning. By extension, it is also unlikely that colored hearing synesthesia in general rests upon such an associative basis.

Conclusions

Overall, the results of these experiments (see also Ramachandran and Hubbard, 2001b) give rise to the following conclusions.

1. Colored-hearing synesthesia does not result from aberrant associative learning.
2. Colored-hearing synesthesia is most likely due to an extra, abnormal, left-lateralized projection from cortical language systems to the color-selective region (V4/V8) of the visual system.
3. On this analysis, excitation in synesthetes by heard or seen words of cortical language systems transmits excitation obligatorily to the color-selective region of the visual system.
4. Activation of the color-selective region of the visual system is sufficient to lead, automatically and involuntarily, to the conscious experience of color, with the specifics of the color experience depending on the particular pattern of neuronal firing caused in V4/V8 by excitation received from cortical language areas. Conclusions 3 and 4 together constitute the hypothetical process of sparking over, as postulated earlier in this chapter.
5. The occurrence of the synesthetic color experience in colored-hearing synesthesia plays no functional role in relation either to speech or language perception or to color vision. An intriguing gloss on this conclusion is provided by Ramachandran and Hubbard's (2001b) description of a color-graphemic synesthete with anomalous color vision who "claimed to see numbers in colors that he could never see in the real world ('Martian colors')" (26). Such colors imply that, if a pattern of V4/V8 neuronal firing induced in synesthesia differs from any elicited, indeed ever elicited color, via the normal visual pathway, it can nonetheless give rise to a color experience specific to the pattern per se and not to any visually linked functional relationships.

These conclusions are incompatible with a functionalist account of colored-hearing synesthesia. In particular, this condition provides a counterexample to what I called above the complementary inference from functionalism; namely, that, for any discriminable functional difference, there must be a corresponding discriminable difference between qualia. In colored-hearing synesthesia two quite different functions, comprehension of spoken language and color vision, share the same color qualia. Within the behavior of any given colored-hearing synesthete there is a clear functional separation between the seeing of a color presented via the normal visual channel, on the one hand, and the perception of that same color triggered by a word, on the other hand. Yet, apparently, neither the qualia nor their neural bases (with a qualification concerning hemispheric lateralization, to which I turn below) produced by these two functional routes differ. Notice that these inferences are drawn on a within-subject basis. The same synesthete subject experiences and reports on the qualia activated via the two different functional routes. This important feature of our experimental design eliminates the problem of the so-called privacy of conscious experience. This problem would arise only if we were attempting to compare qualia between different subjects.

It is, of course, difficult to affirm a lack of difference in qualia with certainty. It could be argued, for example, that the synesthetic color experience differs from normal color experiences in at least two ways and therefore fails to provide a counter-instance to the complementary inference.

First, synesthetic color is always and necessarily combined with an auditory experience—that is, of the inducing word. Note, however, that these two experiences remain separate, as distinct from what happens in cases of perceptual binding, in which, for example, the shape, motion, and color of a moving object (a red kite, say, flying in the sky) are fully integrated into one visual percept, even though each of these attributes is computed in a different brain region. The combination of word and color in colored-hearing synesthesia is more like the simultaneous experience of the sound of a violin and the sight of its being played. The two modalities of experience are tightly synchronized but perceptually separate. Thus, there is no more reason to regard synesthetic color as not constituting a perceptual experience in its own right, separate from the associated auditory experience of the inducing word, than there is to regard the sound and sight of the violin.

Second, the synesthete is entirely aware of the different provenances of her color experiences—surface colors by way of vision, synesthetic colors by way of audition. But, again, there are parallels in nonsynesthetic experience. With careful selection of the appropriate shades, a red after-image can be induced by a green color patch that is reported identical to a red patch directly presented. Yet the perceiving subject is in no doubt that one is an after-image and the other a color patch. From the latter fact, it is not inferred that the subject is in error in reporting the two experienced colors to be identical. By the same token, if the synesthete reports that a synesthetic and surface color are identical, the fact that she knows the different provenance of each should not count against the veridicality of that report.

Our synesthete subjects do, in fact, report that their synesthetic and "real" experiences are closely alike. However, to examine this issue in greater detail, we are working with a small number of colored-hearing synesthetes who have sufficient artistic talent to depict their color experiences in response to specific words. We are currently applying fMRI to these subjects to determine just how closely the activation patterns elicited in V4/V8 by a given word and its corresponding picture resemble one another. This is a difficult experiment that may lie beyond the technical limitations of current neuroimaging techniques. But it may provide a route by which to test objectively this key assumption in our argument: that, in colored-hearing synesthesia, similarity or even perhaps identity of qualia can occur despite disparate functional routes underlying them.

There is an apparent (but, as argued below, spurious) escape hatch for functionalism in the finding (Nunn et al., 2002) that, in colored-hearing synesthetes, left V4/V8 is devoted to synesthetic colors and right V4/V8 to visually detected colors. The sensitivity of fMRI does not allow us to assert that this observation represents complete lateralized separation between the two functions. Replication of this experiment is, therefore, a priority and will form part of our proposed research program. However, given that the different lateralizations were observed in the same subjects within a single scanning session, they cannot readily be dismissed as artifact. Thus, one might try to salvage the functionalist account of colored-hearing synesthesia by asserting that the two functions (elicited by spoken words or seen colors) do not in fact share qualia, since one is associated with qualia generated in left V4/V8 and the other with qualia generated in right V4/V8. However, this line of defense must take as axiomatic what ought to be an empirical hypothesis: namely, that different neural processing produces different qualia. Yet subjectively, to the synesthete, both are experienced as color. Indeed, one may also interpret the different lateralization of color produced visually and synesthetically as providing an even stronger counter-example to functionalism. For there is considerable evidence that, in normal subjects, activity in V4/V8 in either hemisphere is sufficient for the experience of color. Thus, an opponent of functionalism might argue that, in colored-hearing synesthetes, color experiences are produced by two routes that differ in all critical respects: input, output, and the site (left or right hemisphere) of the closest neural correlate of the consciousness of color.

There will perhaps be a temptation to dismiss current findings on the basis that they depend on "illusory" perception. I have myself, drawn a parallel between colored-hearing synesthesia and other illusory experiences of color and motion. In particular, they appear to rest upon the same neural foundation: activation of that part of the visual system responsible for the analysis of the visual feature (color, motion) concerned, without activation in earlier parts of the visual pathways. However, to dismiss findings on this basis would be to misunderstand how normal vision works. In a very real sense, vision, too, is illusory. Thus, for example, in the particular case of concern here, that of color vision, it is almost universally agreed that colors, as such, are not properties of the objects that we perceive as being colored. The basis that such objects provide for the brain's construction of colors lies in the light reflectances of their surfaces as a function of the wavelengths of light by which they are illuminated (Zeki, 1993). There is no known relationship (other than correlational) between these reflectances, whether measured on the surfaces themselves or as computed by the brain, and the qualia by which they emerge into conscious perception.

Note finally that the phenomenon of colored hearing provides a possible empirical basis upon which to ask an ancient philosophical question: Why should color qualia have not been used normally, as they are used unusually by colored-hearing synesthetes, to represent in consciousness auditory inputs (words) rather than visual inputs (reflectances)? Perhaps colored-hearing synesthetes are on the first step along an evolutionary pathway that could have led to the allocation of color qualia to words (were it not for the fact that this pathway has been preempted by the visual system). This type of question, of course, takes us to the heart of the hard problem of conscious experience. Until we can go beyond correlation to mechanism in understanding how qualia come to be allocated to function, that problem will remain. The considerations advanced above render it less likely that the allocation of qualia in colored-hearing synesthesia is determined solely or even at all by function as such. And, as noted earlier, even one such counter-instance to functionalism, if it can be firmly established, may be sufficient to overthrow it.

References

Barbur, J.L., Watson, J.D.G., Frackowiak, R.S.J., & Zeki, S. (1993). Conscious visual perception without V1. *Brain, 116,* 1293–1302.

Baron-Cohen, S,. Harrison, J., Goldstein, L.H., & Wyke, M. (1993). Colored speech perception: Is synesthesia what happens when modularity breaks down? *Perception, 22,* 419–426.

Chalmers, D.J. (1996). *The conscious mind: In search of a fundamental theory.* New York: Oxford University Press.

Crick, F.H.C. (1994). *The astonishing hypothesis: The scientific search for the soul.* New York: Scribner.

Cytowic, R.E. (2002). *Synesthesia: A union of the senses* (2nd ed). Cambridge, MA: MIT Press.

Dennett, D.C. (1991). *Consciousness explained.* Boston: Little, Brown.

Dehay, C., Bullier, J., & Kennedy, H. (1984). Transient projections from the fronto-parietal and temporal cortex to areas 17, 18 and 19 in the kitten. *Experimental Brain Research, 57,* 208–212.

ffytche, D.H. (2002). Neural codes for conscious vision. *Trends in Cognitive Science, 6,* 493–495.

ffytche, D.H., Guy, C.N., & Zeki, S. (1995). The parallel visual motion inputs into areas V1 and V5 of human cerebral cortex. *Brain, 118,* 1375–1394.

ffytche, D.H., Howard, R.J., Brammer, M.J., David, A., Woodruff, P., & Williams, S. (1998). The anatomy of conscious vision: an fMRI study of visual hallucinations. *Nature Neuroscience, 11,* 738–742.

Gray, J.A. (1995). The contents of consciousness: a neuropsychological conjecture. *Behaviour Brain Science, 18,* 659–702.

Gray, J. (2004). *Consciousness: Creeping up on the Hard Problem.* Oxford: Oxford University Press.

Gray, J.A. (1999). The hard question of consciousness: Information processing versus hard wiring. In C. Taddeo-Ferretto & C. Musio (Eds.), Neuronal bases and psychological aspects of consciousness, vol. 8. (pp. 450–457). Singapore: World Scientific.

Gray, J.A., Chopping, S., Nunn, J., Parslow, D., Gregory, L., Williams, S., Brammer, M.J., & Baron-Cohen, S. (2002). Implications of synesthesia for functionalism: theory and experiments. *Journal of Consciousness Studies, 9,* 5–31.

Grossenbacher, P.G., & Lovelace, C.T. (2001). Mechanisms of synesthesia: Cognitive and physiological constraints. *Trends in Cognitive Science, 5,* 36–41.

Hadjikhani, N., Liu, A.K., Dale, A.M., Cavanagh, P., & Tootell, R.B.H. (1998). Retinotopy and color sensitivity in human visual cortical area V8. *Nature Neuroscience, 1,* 235–241.

Howard, R.J., ffytche, D.H., Barnes, J., McKeefry, D., Ha, Y., Woodruff, P.W., Bullmore, E.T., Simmons, A., Williams, S.C., David, A.S., & Brammer, M. (1998). The functional anatomy of imagining and perceiving color. *NeuroReport, 9,* 1019–1023.

Hubbard, E.M., & Ramachandran, V.S. (2001). Cross wiring and the neural basis of synesthesia. *Investigations in Opthalmology and Visual Science, 42,* S438.

Jones, D.K., Williams, S.C., Gasston, D., Horsfield, M.A., Simmons, A., & Howard, R. (2002). Isotropic resolution diffusion tensor imaging with whole brain acquisition in a clinically acceptable time. *Human Brain Mapping, 15,* 216–230.

Luria, A.R. (1968). *The mind of a mnemonist.* New York: Basic Books.

Mattingley, J.B., Rich, A.N., Yelland, G., & Bradshaw, J.L. (2001). Unconscious priming eliminates automatic binding of color and alphanumeric form in synesthesia. *Nature 410,* 580–582.

Moutoussis, K., & Zeki, S. (2002). The relationship between cortical activation and perception investigated with invisible stimuli. *Proceedings of the National Academy of Sciences, USA, 99,* 9527–9532.

Nunn, J.A., Gregory, L.J., Brammer, M., Williams, S.C.R., Parslow, D.M., Morgan, M.J., Morris, R.G., Bullmore, E.T., Baron-Cohen, S., & Gray, J.A. (2002). Functional magnetic resonance imaging of synesthesia: Activation of V4/V8 by spoken words. *Nature Neuroscience, 5,* 371–375.

Paulesu, E., Harrison, J., Baron-Cohen, S., Watson, J.D.G., Goldstein, L., Heather, J., Frackowiak, R.S.J., & Frith, C.D. (1995). The physiology of colored-hearing: A PET activation study of colored-word synesthesia. *Brain, 118,* 661–676.

Ramachandran, V.S., & Hubbard, E.M. (2001a). Psychophysical investigations into the neural basis of synesthesia. *Proceedings of the Royal Society of London, B, 268,* 979–983.

Ramachandran, V.S., & Hubbard, E.M. (2001b). Synesthesia—a window into perception, thought and language. *Journal of Consciousness Studies, 8,* 3–34.

Rich, A.N., & Mattingley, J.B. (2002). Anomalous perception in synesthesia: A cognitive science perspective. *Nature Review Neuroscience, 3,* 43–52.

Tootell, R.B.H., Reppas, J.B., Dale, A.M., Look, R.B., Sereno, M.I., Malach, R., Brady, T.J., & Rosen, B.R. (1995). Visual motion aftereffect in human cortical area MT revealed by functional magnetic resonance imaging. *Nature, 375,* 139–141.

Velmans, M. (1991). Is human information processing conscious? *Behaviour Brain Science, 14,* 651–669.

Woolf, N., & Hameroff, S. (2001). A quantum approach to visual consciousness. *Trends in Cognitive Science, 5,* 472–478.

Zeki, S. (1993). *A vision of the brain.* Oxford: Blackwell.

Zeki, S., & Bartels, A. (1998). The asynchrony of consciousness. *Proceedings of the Royal Society of London, B, 265,* 1583–1585.

Zeki, S., Watson, J.D.G., Lueck, C.J., Friston, K.J., Kennard, C., & Frackowiak, R.S.J. (1991). A direct demonstration of functional specialization in human visual cortex. *Journal of Neuroscience, 11,* 641–649.

Zeki, S., Watson, J.D.G., & Frackowiak, R.S.J. (1993). Going beyond the information given: The relation of illusory visual motion to brain activity. *Proceedings of the Royal Society of London, B, 252,* 215–222.

9

The Emergence of the Human Mind: Some Clues from Synesthesia

V. S. Ramachandran and Edward M. Hubbard

You know my methods, my dear Watson. They are founded upon the observation of trifles.

—Sherlock Holmes

For a scientific phenomenon to gain wide acceptance, three different criteria must be fulfilled. First, the phenomenon must be real, in the sense of being reliably repeatable. Second, there should be at least some potential candidate explanations, and third, the phenomenon must have broad implications beyond the narrow confines of one specialty. Without all three in place, a phenomenon will be regarded as an anomaly (see Kuhn, 1962) and will not succeed in attracting the attention of the scientific community. For example, telepathy fulfills criterion three; it has vast implications *if* true. The problem is that it doesn't satisfy criterion one and certainly not two. Continental drift when it was discovered 70 years ago satisfied criterion one (many observations pointed to it, such as the distribution of fossils, the fit between continent outlines, and so on) and criterion three, but it was rejected because there was no mechanism that could account for it—that is, until plate tectonics was discovered. Chargaff's base-pairing rules satisfied one and two but not three (until Crick and Watson saw their true significance).

One of us (V.S.R.) considered many examples of such "anomalous" phenomena in *Phantoms in the Brain* (Ramachandran & Blakeslee, 1998), mostly from the older literature of neurology. In this chapter, we consider another example, synesthesia. Our goal is to inspire new interest in this topic, so that it gets the attention it deserves. We will try to do this by satisfying the three criteria spelled out above. First, we show that synesthesia is a genuine sensory effect. Second, we suggest what the underlying neural mechanisms might be. Third, we point out that, far from being just an oddity, synesthesia might help illuminate some of the most puzzling aspects of the mind such as the evolution of metaphor, language, and even abstract thought in humans. In addition, we discuss the philosophical riddle of qualia and point out how studying synesthesia can provide some hints about the evolution, functional significance, and neural correlates of qualia. These ideas are somewhat speculative, but our goal at this stage is simply to provide a starting point for thinking about these issues; not to provide final answers.

Is Synesthesia Real?

In the nineteenth century Francis Galton (1880/1997) noticed that certain otherwise normal individuals claimed to "see" specific colors when listening to musical notes (e.g., C-sharp might be red) or when looking at printed numbers (e.g., 5 might be red, 7 might be blue). The phenomenon runs in families, suggesting a genetic propensity (Bailey & Johnson, 1997). In our own informal samples, conducted by asking undergraduates at the University of California-San Diego whether they experience any form of synesthesia, we found that approximately 1 in 200 people is a synesthete, an incidence much higher than previously believed (see also Day, this volume). Synesthesia seems so outlandish that there has been a tendency to dismiss it as bogus, and it has been treated as an oddity by mainstream neuroscience (although there have been a few notable exceptions; see Baron-Cohen & Harrison, 1997; Gray, Williams, Nunn & Baron-Cohen, 1997). It is fair to say that the four standard explanations for the phenomenon have been:

- These people are just crazy
- They are "acid junkies" or "potheads" (and, sure enough, synesthesia is sometimes experienced by LSD users. But to us that makes the phenomenon more interesting, not less).
- They are just remembering early childhood memories (perhaps from having played with colored refrigerator magnets). However, this does not explain why it runs in families (unless the same magnets were passed on) nor why the rest of us nonsynesthetes do not have such experiences (you might think of cold when seeing ice, but you certainly don't feel cold).
- They are being "metaphorical" as when you or I say cheese is "sharp." Cheese is soft to touch, so why do we refer to the taste as sharp? You might respond that it is just a metaphor but why do you use a tactile adjective for a taste sensation? How do we know that synesthetes are not being equally metaphorical when they say, "C-sharp is red"? Perhaps synesthetes are just more gifted in this regard!

Aa Bb Cc Dd Ee Ff Gg Hh **Ii** Jj Kk Ll Mm Nn **Oo** Pp
Qq Rr Ss Tt Uu Vv Ww Xx Yy Zz

0 1 2 3 4 5 6 7 8 9

Plate 2.1. Findings for the most common synesthetic colors for each alphabet letter and numerical digit, based on my research sample of synesthetes; thus a typical synesthete's set.

This example has not been taken from any one case, but rather put together from many. Let us say that, for a given synesthete, whom I will name "Bob," 1 is black, 2 is sky blue, 3 is red, 4 is dark blue, 5 is light green, 6 is yellow, 7 is orange, 8 is dark green, 9 is purple, and 0 (zero) is white. Thus, we have the following:

$$3 + 4 = 7 \qquad\qquad 3 + 4 \neq 9 \qquad\qquad 3 \times 4 = 12.$$

Now, this means that, in math class, red plus blue equals orange (!), while in science and art classes — and most everywhere else — red plus blue equals purple. Likewise, in math, if you take red away from orange, you get blue, whereas, in art class, you get yellow.

How does one reconcile these differences? Consider that, in science class, you learn that, if you combine all colors, you get white — however, white is zero, which is nothing! On the other hand, in art class, if you melt all of your crayons from your box together, you get black — and, for Bob, black is one (1).

And it only becomes more complex when one begins algebra, because the letter 'X', for our synesthete, is also black, and 'Y' is yellow. Now, how can X and Y be "variables" if 'X = black = 1' and 'Y = yellow = 6'? It works just fine if we say

$$X + 4 = 5 \qquad \text{or} \qquad 9 - Y = 3;$$

however, it can become more confusing in an equation like

$$4 \times Y = 20,$$

as this could mistakenly become

$$4 \times 6 = 20.$$

Note that the yellow 'Y' has been replaced by the same-colored yellow '6'. However, also note that the white zero of '20' has not totally disappeared on the white page; nevertheless, because the zero is perceived to be white (or "clear"; or clear when on a white surface), the zero might frequently be ignored or overlooked.

Plate 2.2. A representation of a typical color-graphemic synesthete's letter and digit sets.

Plate 2.3. Colored letters and numbers with gender and personalities.

However, I do not wish to convey that these types of synesthesia always present a problem for the synesthete, nor that they cannot be overcome — often in amusing and enjoyable manners. Take the following example from one of my Synesthesia List members:

"Today, I wanted to remember '43.75', and couldn't write it down, so it was destined to be lost. Then I tried this new technique and it worked!

"4 is almost the same color as R.

3 and S are the only yellows.

I just picked a similar green in my alphabet for 7 — V.

And 5 is close to Es orange.

"So I came up with 'R S V E'. But, since P is also orange (though a touch darker than 5), I just changed the E to P and got 'RSVP'. I'm not sure how well it will work with a less memorable string of letters, of course, but its fun to play with, at least."

Plate 2.4. An attempt at imaging Feynman's perception of a basic Bessel function equation.

$$J_n(x)$$

Plate 2.5. How Feynman sees equations.

Plate 3.1. Kandinsky's "Yellow-Red-Blue" (1925) is from his period of totally nonrepresentational works, but this particular painting seems evocative of the concept of a person experiencing vivid synesthetic imagery. (Oil on canvas, Musee National d'Art Moderne, Centre Georges Pompidou. Reproduced with permission.)

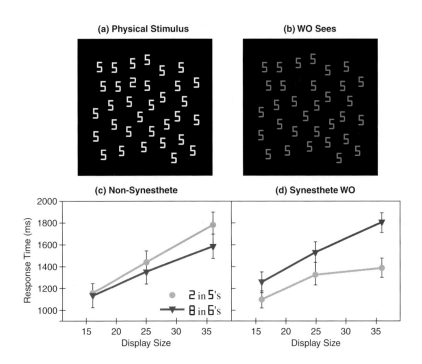

Plate 4.1. Visual search for synesthetically colored digits. (A) Schematic of target "present" display, (B) Schematic for synesthetically colored display, (C) Visual search results for nonsynesthetic observers and (D) synesthetic observer W.O. (Reproduced with permission from PNAS)

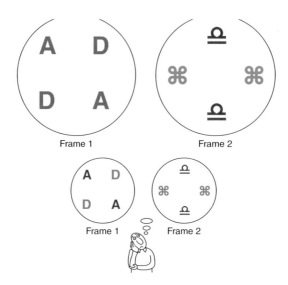

Plate 4.2. The two frames composing an apparent motion sequence in which the directions of motion are ambiguous. In frame 1, L.R. sees one of the achromatic characters as red and the other as green. In frame 2, the forms (non-alphabetic) are actually colored.

Trial Type

Different Background Trials

Same Background Trials

C's Perception

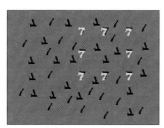

Plate 5.1. Examples of both the displays used in the perceptual grouping experiments and C.'s perception of these displays.

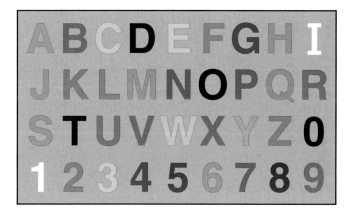

Plate 6.1. A.D.'s (top) and C.P.'s (bottom) letter-color and digit-color mapping.

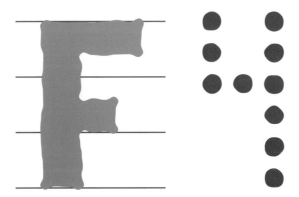

Plate 6.2. When A.D. was asked to color in an outline of an F and the circles making up a 4 to illustrate her color perception, she colored them as represented, reporting that the colors were "a property" of the letters.

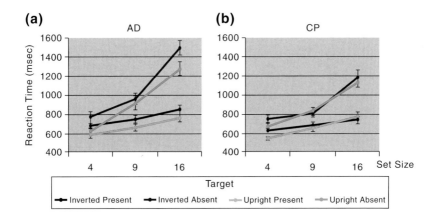

Plate 6.3. Mean reaction times (in milliseconds) as a function of set size for (a) A.D. and (b) C.P.

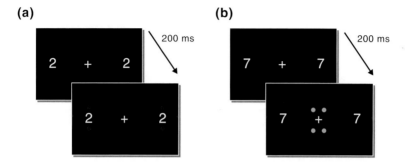

Plate 6.4. Sample displays used in experiment 2. Throughout each block, target colored dots appeared in positions that require motivated diffuse or focused attention, putting the previously presented digits either inside (a) or outside (b) the attentional window.

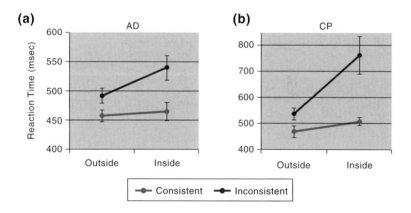

Plate 6.5. Mean reaction times (in milliseconds) for (a) A.D. and (b) C.P. in the inside and outside conditions for achromatic digits inducing either congruent or incongruent synesthetic colors.

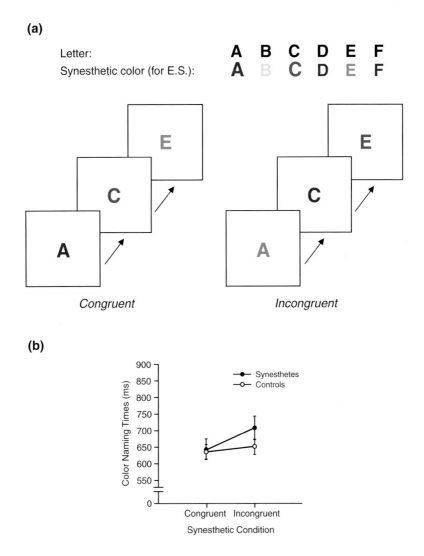

Plate 7.1. (a) E.S. experiences red when she sees an achromatic (gray) letter A. Presenting a green A creates competition between the display color (green) and the synesthetic color of the letter (red) and is therefore an incongruent stimulus for E.S. In contrast, a red A causes no competition and is therefore a congruent stimulus. (b) Group results for synesthetes and controls in the synesthetic Stroop task (Adapted from Mattingley et al., 2001b with permission of Nature Publishing Group.)

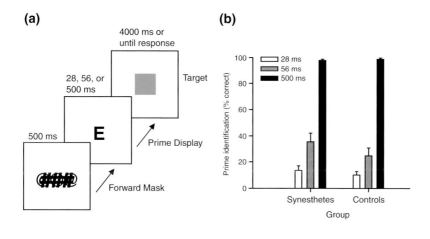

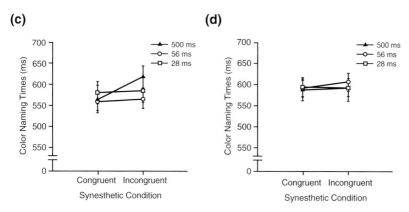

Plate 7.2. (a) Sequence of displays in a typical trial of the synesthetic priming task. The task was to name the target color as quickly as possible. (b) Verification in a separate block of trials where processing of primes was limited under masked conditions. Participants' ability to identify the primes was severely curtailed at 56 and 28 ms relative to the visible priming condition of 500 ms. (c) Synesthetes were significantly slower to name target colors when these were preceded by a visible (500 ms) incongruent versus congruent prime. Under masked conditions (28 and 56 ms) there were no such effects. (d) Controls showed no difference in naming target colors when these were preceded by an incongruent versus congruent prime at any prime duration. (Adapted from Mattingley et al., 2001b with permission of Nature Publishing Group.)

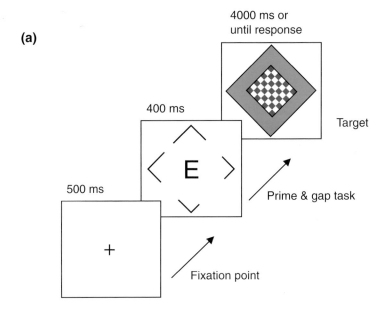

(a)

4000 ms or
until response

Target

400 ms

Prime & gap task

500 ms

Fixation point

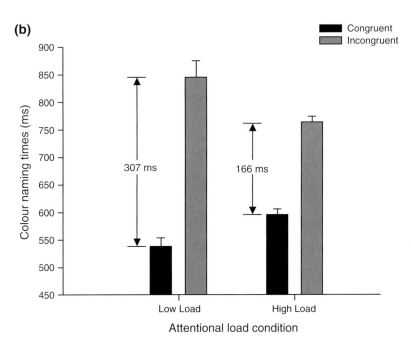

(b)

Congruent
Incongruent

Colour naming times (ms)

307 ms

166 ms

Low Load   High Load

Attentional load condition

Plate 7.3. (a) Sequence of displays in a typical trial of the synesthetic priming task with concurrent attentional load. The primary task was to name the target color as quickly as possible; the secondary task in the low- and high-load conditions was to discriminate the larger of two gaps in diagonally opposite sides of the diamond surrounding the prime letter. (b) Results from the low- and high load conditions for a single synesthete.

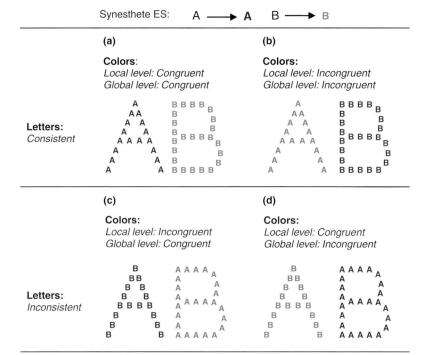

Plate 7.4. Examples of the local-global stimuli used to study the effect of competition between multiple synesthetic inducers. The task was to name the display color as quickly as possible. (a) Letters consistent; both levels colored congruently. (b) Letters consistent; both levels colored incongruently. (c) Letters inconsistent; local letters colored incongruently and global letter colored congruently. (d) Letters inconsistent; local letters colored congruently and global letter colored incongruently. (Adapted from Rich & Mattingley, 2003, with permission from Lippincott, Williams & Wilkins Publishers.)

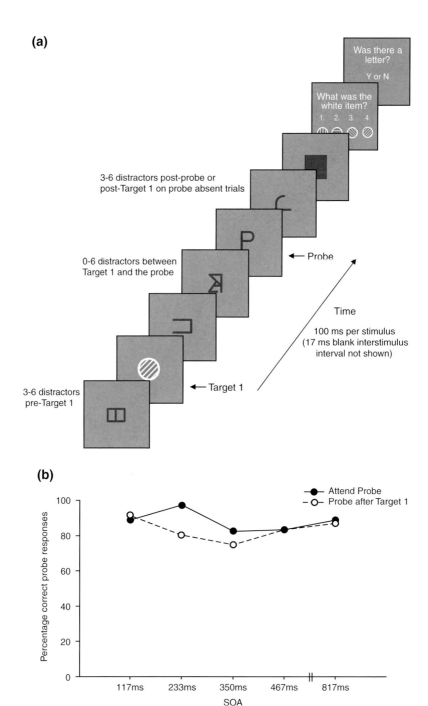

(a)

Was there a letter?
Y or N

What was the white item?
1.   2.   3.   4.

3-6 distractors post-probe or post-Target 1 on probe absent trials

◄— Probe

0-6 distractors between Target 1 and the probe

Time

100 ms per stimulus
(17 ms blank interstimulus interval not shown)

◄— Target 1

3-6 distractors pre-Target 1

(b)

● Attend Probe
○ Probe after Target 1

Percentage correct probe responses

SOA

Plate 7.5. (a) Sequence of events in a typical trial of the synesthetic attentional blink task. In the standard attentional blink (AB) participants were asked to identify the orientation of stripes in the white disk (Target 1) and then to discriminate the presence versus absence of a letter in the stream (the probe).

(c)

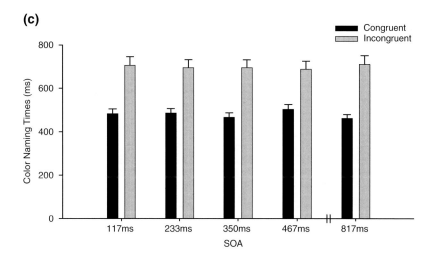

(d)

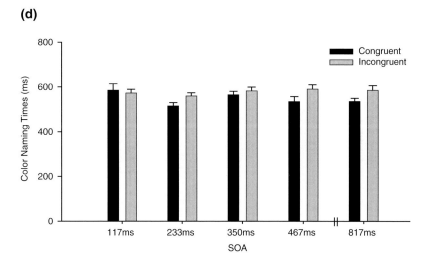

Plate 7.5 cont. In the attend probe task, participants first named the color at the end of the stream as quickly as possible and then gave an unspeeded probe response. In the critical task, participants first made a speeded color-naming response and then identified Target 1. (b) Accuracy of probe discrimination for N.W. (c) N.W.'s mean color-naming times in the attend probe task for trials in which she correctly discriminated the presence of a probe letter. (d) N.W.'s mean color-naming times in the critical task for trials in which she correctly identified Target 1.

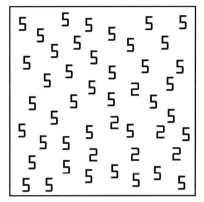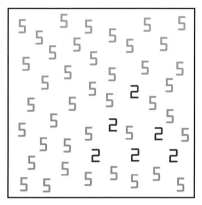

Plate 9.1. Schematic representation of displays used to test whether synesthetically induced colors lead to pop out. (a) When presented with a matrix of 5s with a triangle composed of 2s embedded in it, control subjects find it difficult to find the triangle. (b) However, because they see the 5s (say) green and the 2s as red, our synesthetic subjects were able to easily find the embedded shape.

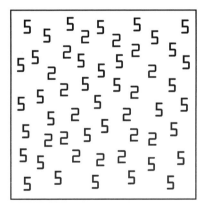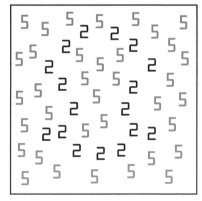

Plate 9.2. A demonstration of the effect of synesthetically induced colors on symmetry detection. (a) Control subjects find it hard to detect the butterflylike shape composed of 2s embedded in the display of 5s. (b) However, because he sees 5s and 2s as different colors, subject J.C. was immediately able to spot the symmetric shape in the display. This phenomenological observation needs fuller experimental confirmation.

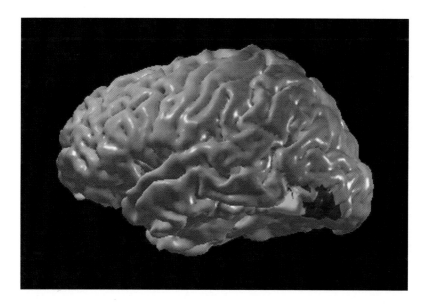

Plate 9.3. Schematic showing that cross-wiring in the fusiform gyrus might be the neural basis of color-graphemic synesthesia. Area V4 is indicated by red, and the number-grapheme area is indicated by green.

The last two explanations are the most viable, but there are problems with all of them. For example, the idea that synesthetes are crazy or simply trying to draw attention to themselves would predict that synesthetes should be telling everyone around them about how different they are. In our experience, it is usually quite the opposite. Synesthetes often think that everyone else experiences the world the same way they do, or else they have been ridiculed as children and have not told anyone about their synesthesia for years.

The idea that synesthesia is a result of drug use is only applicable to a few people, and seems to occur only during the "trip." One explanation of this is that certain drugs might pharmacologically mimic the same physiological mechanisms that underlie genetically based synesthesia. However, it may also be that pharmacologically induced synesthesia is not based on the same neural mechanisms as the congenital, lifelong experiences of true *synesthetes*, in spite of the superficial similarities. Additionally, not everyone who uses psychedelics experiences synesthesia; perhaps only those with a genetic predisposition will experience synesthesia under the influence of psychoactive drugs.

The memory hypothesis also fails as an explanation of synesthesia because it cannot address the questions of why only some individuals have these memories intact, why only specific classes of stimuli are able to induce synesthesia, and why there should be a genetic basis for synesthesia (see below). Additional data, such as that obtained on color-blind synesthetes and the phenomenon of "Martian colors" also argue against the idea that synesthesia is simply a result of memory associations (although learning and memory clearly play important roles in *which* specific associations are set up).

Finally, the idea that synesthetes are being metaphorical does not help much; it is an example of the classic blunder of trying to explain one mystery (synesthesia) with another (metaphor), and that strategy is rarely successful in science. No one has the foggiest idea of how metaphors are represented in the brain. In this chapter, we will turn this explanation upside down and suggest the exact opposite; synesthesia is a concrete sensory phenomenon whose neural basis can be pinned down and that in turn can provide a foothold—an experimental lever—for understanding the neural basis of metaphors.

Synesthesia: A Genuine Sensory Effect

Subjective reports of synesthetes vary enormously. However, carefully listening to their introspective reports, one finds strong hints that the phenomenon is probably genuine (and probably sensory, at least in one group of synesthetes whom we refer to as "lower synesthetes"; see below). For instance, the first two synesthetes we interviewed and tested, J.C. and E.R., made it clear that the colors were spatially localized on the number or letter; they claimed they were not just remembering the color. Indeed, the very opposite was true, the colors actually seemed to facilitate their memory (see also Dixon, Smilek & Merikle, this volume). We have encountered synesthetes who said they learned to type more quickly and learned musical scales more easily than their classmates because the letters (or musical notes) were "color coded."

We then made psychophysical measurements that provided additional evidence that synesthesia (at least in a subset of synesthetes) is a genuine sensory effect rather than a memory or a metaphor. In J.C., the saturation of induced color decreased monotonically with contrast, and the color vanished completely below about 8–9% contrast even when the number was still clearly visible. The color also vanished if two numbers (say 2 and 5) were alternated in time at 4–5 Hz—even though the alternation of the numbers themselves was clearly visible at rates up to 15 Hz (Ramachandran & Hubbard, 2001a). Such a high level of sensitivity to the elementary physical parameters defining the grapheme also supports our view that the effect is indeed sensory.

These findings suggest that synesthesia is sensory but do not completely rule out alternative, cognitively based explanations. To obtain clear-cut evidence that synesthesia is indeed a sensory phenomenon, we devised the stimulus shown in plate 9.1a, a matrix of randomly placed computer generated 5s with some 2s scattered among them. Indeed, one could even regard this as a clinical test for synesthesia.

Since the 5s and 2s are made up of identical features (three horizontal bars and two vertical ones), you cannot spot the 2s except by a detailed item-by-item inspection. Eventually you see that they are arranged to form a triangular shape (a nonsynesthetic subject typically takes a few seconds). Our two synesthetes, on the other hand, saw this display as colored (plate 9.1b), and the red 2s clearly "popped out" from the background; so they instantly saw a red triangle segregated from a green background (Ramachandran & Hubbard, 2001a).

This experiment shows two things. First, synesthetes are not "crazy" or "making up" this effect. If they were crazy, why are they actually much better at this task than normals? Second, the fact that synesthetes literally *see* a red triangle in plate 9.1a strongly suggests that the synesthetically induced colors are genuinely sensory, not some high-level memory association or metaphor. Treisman (1982) and others have shown that this type of segregation can occur only for elementary sensory features like motion, color, and depth, but not for more complex features like graphemes (unless the graphemes also happen to differ along some elementary dimension). Metaphors and memories don't pop out. These results provided the first clear-cut evidence, since the time of Galton, that synesthesia was an authentic effect—indeed, a genuine sensory phenomenon worthy of further study (Ramachandran and Hubbard, 2001a).

Another observation we made is also consistent with the claim that synesthesia is a sensory phenomenon. When we showed J.C. and E.R. Roman numerals (e.g., V instead of Arabic 5), they reported that they either saw no color (E.R.) or saw the color consistent with the letter, not the number (J.C.). This suggests that, at least in our first two "lower" synesthetes, it is not the numerical concept (e.g., of ordinality) that induced the color, but rather the actual physical appearance of the grapheme.

In the past, it has been claimed that Stroop interference shows that synesthesia is sensory. For example, if the number 5 is seen as red, but is presented in the wrong ink color (e.g., green), the synesthete is slower to name the ink color (i.e., her reaction time is slightly longer). But this effect merely demonstrates that synesthesia is automatic, not necessarily that it is sensory (MacLeod, 1991). Such a slowing can result from interference at almost any stage in processing from sensory input to motor output.

Synesthetically Evoked Colors Can Drive Apparent Motion

In addition to showing that synesthetically evoked colors can lead to pop-out and segregation, we have also found that the colors can drive apparent motion (Ramachandran & Hubbard, 2002). As in our first experiment, we began with a matrix of randomly placed 2s with a small cluster of 5s embedded near one corner of the display. This display was flashed briefly (350 ms) and replaced by a similar matrix of 2s that was uncorrelated with the first frame, and the cluster of 5s was now in the opposite corner. The two frames were cycled continuously. When nonsynesthetes see this display, they just see random apparent motion. But when J.C. looked at it, he said he saw the red cluster "jumping" or moving back and forth between the two displays. This observation suggests that just as real color can support long-range or form-based apparent motion (Ramachandran and Gregory, 1978), so can synesthetically induced colors. This observation is also consistent with our view that synesthesia is mediated relatively early in the sensory processing hierarchy; it may involve the activation of motion neurons in area MT by colors evoked in the fusiform gyrus.

More recently we constructed displays to show that even the detection of symmetry (normally thought to be preattentive) can be based on synesthetically induced splotches of color, even though the inducing graphemes are not symmetrical (so a nonsynesthete cannot perceive the symmetry; see plate 9.2b). Remarkably, the global symmetry of the induced colors overrides the asymmetry of local defining elements (Ramachandran and Hubbard, 2002).

What Causes Synesthesia?

Our evidence so far strongly supports the notion that synesthesia is a sensory phenomenon, but what causes it? We were struck by the fact that recognition of visual numbers (Pesenti, Thioux, Seron & De Volder, 2000; Rickard et al., 2000) and visual words (Cohen et al., 2000; Polk et al., 2002) depends on the fusiform gyrus (especially left) and that this visual "word-form area" (Cohen et al., 2000) lies directly adjacent to the "color area" (Leuck et al., 1989; Zeki & Marini, 1998). We realized it probably was not a mere coincidence that the most common type of synesthesia is the number (grapheme)-color type and that the areas for numbers and colors are next to each other in the brain. We therefore suggested that graphemic-color synesthesia is caused by a cross-activation of sensory brain maps between these adjacent brain regions (see plate 9.3). By this we mean that the presence of the inducing elements (e.g., numbers) not only evokes activity in the number/form area, as it should, but also automatically evokes activity in another sensory map (e.g., hV4 color area) in a manner analogous to the cross-activation between hand and face representations seen in phantom-limb patients (for a more detailed treatment of the analogy between phantom limbs and synesthesia, see Hubbard & Ramachandran, 2003; Hurley & Noë, 2003).

The idea that synesthesia is the result of some kind of "crossed wires" is hardly new; it is probably as old as the phenomenon itself. However, this idea is normally couched in vague terms. Until recently, our knowledge of the physiological mechanisms of sensory processing was not sophisticated enough to suggest anatomical hypotheses. However, taking advantage of developments in neuroscience over the past 30 years, we were able to develop more precise, testable formulation of this notion in terms of the known anatomy and physiology of brain areas. Specifically, we proposed that synesthesia results from cross-activation of color-selective regions in the fusiform gyrus via grapheme nodes in the same gyrus (Ramachandran and Hubbard, 2001a, 2001b). There is now evidence from functional imaging (Nunn et al., 2002) that such activation of V4 does indeed occur. Our own imaging studies, discussed below, have also shown evidence of V4 activation (Hubbard, Ramachandran & Boynton, 2003, 2004).

How might this cross-activation of sensory maps come about? Recall that synesthesia runs in families and may have a genetic basis. Perhaps some families have a gene mutation(s) that causes one of three changes: (1) actual "cross wiring" an excess of connections between brain modules that are ordinarily distinct, or a failure of pruning that is ordinarily produced by that gene (Ramachandran & Hubbard, 2001a, 2001b); (2) a cross-activation that results from excess activity (but no actual connections) or a disinhibition between brain modules that are ordinarily functionally insulated, which could account for drug-induced synesthesia; or (3) excess activation caused by disinhibition of back-projections from higher to lower visual areas in the hierarchy (Armel & Ramachandran, 1999; Grossenbacher & Lovelace, 2001; see also Smilek et al., 2001), of the kind we have found in a patient who began to experience tactile to visual synesthesia after blindness due to retinal degeneration (retinitis pigmentosa). If so, synesthesia might provide some clues to understanding visual imagery, which is also thought to require top-down activation through back-projections (see Ramachandran and Hubbard, 2001b).

We prefer the more neutral term "cross-activation" to "cross-wiring" because it covers all three potential mechanisms. But two additional questions emerge. First, if genetic differences are involved, why do they affect one brain area and not others? Second, does this mean we are implying that synesthesia can occur only between adjacent brain modules, and, if so, how can we account for more exotic variants like tasting shapes?

The answer to the first question is that the abnormal cross-activation gene may be selectively expressed in certain areas (e.g., fusiform for graphemic-color synesthesia or the temporal-parietal-occipital (TPO)/angular gyrus area for others) due to transcription factors. This would also explain why if you have one type of synesthesia you are also more likely to have another type; perhaps the gene is expressed in several locations in some synesthetes.

Turning to the second question, we have to bear in mind that while it is usually true that adjacent brain modules are more likely to be connected to begin with (and therefore more likely to be involved in cross-activation), even modules remote from each other often have some connections (e.g., Kennedy, Batardiere, De Lay & Barone, 1997, have shown a connection between primary auditory cortex and V4), and an enhancement of these through the three mechanisms suggested above could therefore mediate synesthesia. One would expect, however, that the likelihood of one map cross-activating another increases with the proximity between the two areas.

An example might be the celebrated case of the "man who tasted shapes" described by Cytowic (1993). M.W. would remark that most tastes evoked distinct shapes such as peppermint evoking the sensation of cool marble columns. Conversely, one of our subjects, M.B., reported that tactile sensations evoked specific tastes (Ramachandran & Hubbard, 2003a). We would suggest that this is because the gustatory (taste) cortex is in the insula very close to the hand area of the Penfield map in S1 (Ramachandran and Hubbard, 2001b). Similarly, Ward and Simner (2003) have recently proposed that tasting foods in response to hearing words may depend on cross-activation between brain regions involved in auditory word processing and brain regions involved in taste processing.

Another question is, if cross-activation of brain maps is the correct explanation, why is color the most commonly evoked sensory experience in synesthesia, and why is it much more often number to color rather than color to number? The answer may lie in the manner in which different complex dimensions (sensory or otherwise) are mapped in the brain—a topic about which very little is known. Perhaps the dimensions of color are represented in such a way that it is easier to map them onto other sensory inputs than is possible with, say, touch (Hubbard & Ramachandran, 2003; Ramachandran & Hubbard, 2003b). This hypothesis would also explain the preferred directionalities and pairings that we see in day-to-day cross-modal metaphors even in nonsynesthetes (see below).

Higher and Lower Synesthetes

When we began our research on synesthesia in late 1999, we were lucky to have discovered two subjects who showed all the effects described above: pop out (or, strictly speaking, segregation), reduction of color with lower contrast, high flicker rates, and so on. This provided, to our knowledge, the first unambiguous proof that synesthesia is a genuine sensory phenomenon. Recall also that these subjects saw colors only with Arabic numbers but not with Roman numerals, which implies it is the visual appearance of the grapheme, not the high level numerical concept (e.g., of sequence or ordinality) that drives the color. This observation is also consistent with the early sensory cross-activation model (since the fusiform gyrus represents the visual graphemes), not the numerical concept.

But later we came across synesthetes in whom this was not true; in them not just numbers but even days of the week or months of the year were colored (no wonder many scientists thought they were crazy). Monday might be blue, Tuesday red, and Wednesday brown (or December might be yellow and March blue). What all these have in common is the idea of numerical sequence or ordinality. This ability probably depends on the angular gyrus (it remains to be determined whether that structure mediates cardinality, ordinality, or both). It might be interesting to see if patients with lesions in the left angular gyrus have problems with calendars ("calendar agnosia" or "sequence agnosia"). Our basis for suggesting this is that patients with angular gyrus lesions often have problems with elementary arithmetic (dyscalculia).

We were struck by the fact that some of the higher color areas in the color-processing hierarchy, which receive their input from V4 in the fusiform, lie in the general vicinity of the angular gyrus. We therefore suggested that in these synesthetes, the colors are evoked as a result of cross-activation similar to that seen in graphemic-color synesthesia (Ramachandran & Hubbard, 2001b), except that, in this case, the cross-activation occurs, not in the fusiform gyrus, but in the region of the angular gyrus, an area known to be involved in the processing of numerical quantities (e.g., Gerstmann, 1940; Pesenti et al., 2000; Rickard et al., 2000) and abstract spatial maps (for a review, see Burgess, Jefferey & O'Keefe, 1999).

Additionally, as first reported by Galton (1880/1997), who documented cases of synesthesia involving number-forms or curvy number lines, we also find that many of these synesthetes experience curvy number-lines (see below). We propose that, in these number-form synesthetes, cross-activation occurs between representation of numerical sequence in the angular gyrus and representations of space in the posterior superior parietal lobe. Roughly speaking, depending on whether the gene is expressed mainly in the fusiform or angular gyri, you end up with two types of synesthetes whom we call "lower" and "higher" synesthetes. We are not implying that the distribution is bimodal—that remains to be seen. Indeed, there may be many complex mixed types depending on how widely the gene is expressed.

There are two (and only two as far as we know) cases in the literature of patients losing their synesthetically induced colors following brain lesions. Consistent with our higher–lower distinction, Spalding and Zangwill (1950) reported a patient with a gunshot wound, which entered near the right angular gyrus and lodged near the left temporal—parietal junction. Five years after injury he complained of spatial problems and showed difficulty in number tasks. In addition, the patient, who experienced synesthesia before the injury, complained that his "number plan," his forms for months, days of the week, and letters of the alphabet, was no longer distinct. In the second study, Sacks, Waserman, Zeki, and Siegel (1988) reported a 65-year-old male patient who became color-blind (probable cerebral achromatopsia) after his car was hit by a truck. Before the accident, the patient experienced colors when presented with musical tones. However, after the accident, he no longer experienced colors when listening to musical tones and reported a transient alexia. This would indicate that a brain region common to color vision, synesthetic colors, and reading might have been damaged in the accident. Although no anatomical localization was performed, we would predict that this region was in the fusiform gyrus, which has been shown to be critical for color perception in humans.

One prediction we made based on this model was that the psychophysical properties of the induced colors should be different in higher and lower synesthetes (Ramachandran and Hubbard, 2001a, 2001b) (e.g., in higher synesthetes the induced colors might not lead to pop out and perceptual segregation). Preliminary data supporting the distinction between these two types of synesthesia have recently been presented (Hubbard, Ramachandran & Boynton, 2003, 2004). We predicted that lower synesthetes should perform better than control participants on our perceptual tasks (described in Ramachandran & Hubbard, 2001a, 2001b) because their colors are elicited early in the perceptual pathway. In contrast, higher synesthetes should not show this effect because their colors are elicited later in the processing hierarchy. We reported behavioral data from six synesthetes, five of whom performed significantly better than controls on the embedded figures task (data from two participants were presented in Ramachandran & Hubbard, 2001a), and three of whom performed better on the crowding task (preliminary data presented in Ramachandran & Hubbard, 2001b). Additionally, we found that performance for the two tasks was positively correlated for synesthetes but not for matched control participants (who also took part in fMRI studies). In six synesthetes BOLD signal change measured with fMRI was greater than for controls in a predefined retinotopically organized region of the brain (hV4) that is known to be color responsive (Hadjikhani, Liu, Dale, Cavanagh & Tootell, 1998; Leuck et al., 1989; Wade, Brewer, Rieger & Wandell, 2002), but not in grapheme-selective regions anterior to these retinotopically defined regions. Finally, we found that behavioral performance correlated with percent BOLD signal change in V1, V2 and hV4, but not in grapheme-selective areas. These differences in behavioral performance and neural responses suggest that the synesthetes we tested may comprise two different subtypes of synesthesia (see Sagiv, Knight & Robertson, 2003, for converging ERP evidence).

After reviewing the phenomenological reports from these synesthetes, we find a clear correspondence between their phenomenological reports and their behavioral performance. The experiences of those synesthetes that do not perform differently from control subjects seem to be driven by the numerical concept (e.g., by Roman numerals or dot clusters) rather than the visual form. In addition, these higher synesthetes report that their colors appear in their mind's eye instead of being projected out into the world. They also report that abstract sequences, such as number lines and calendars (both months of the year, and days of the week) are represented as having a specific spatial form.

This convergence of phenomenological reports, behavioral data and neuro-imaging data suggests that it may be premature to perform group studies of the sort conducted by Mattingley, Rich, Yelland, and Bradshaw (2001). In our initial interviews, the synesthetes we tested seemed to represent a single group, with similar experiences. They all reported that they saw colors when viewing letters and numbers. However, closer inspection of their behavioral performance, neural responses, and phenomenology suggests that their experiences differed in important ways, despite the initial superficial similarity. If, as our data suggest, there are distinct groups of higher and lower synesthetes, then treating all color-grapheme synesthetes as a unitary group, as Mattingley et al. (2001; this volume) have done, may present a misleading picture. Specifically, we predict that an individual subject analysis of the Mattingley et al. data would demonstrate that some synesthetes did indeed show Stroop interference, while others did not. Lumping the data from these two groups together might therefore obscure a real effect that is present in only a subset of their subjects (the lower synesthetes).

Finally, we should point out that in some synesthetes it is the phoneme that seems to evoke the color, not the grapheme. It remains to be seen whether these overlap with the group that we refer to as "higher synesthetes." One possibility is that the phoneme-color synesthetes are the equivalent of the higher synesthetes for those lower synesthetes who see colors in printed visual letters, whereas the number concept/calendar synesthetes are higher synesthetes (as we already noted) for visual number graphemes. The cross-activation for lower synesthetes would be in the temporal lobe for both types of lower synesthetes and in the vicinity of the TPO junction for both types higher synesthetes (e.g., involving the angular gyrus for the calendar–spatial form ones and the superior temporal gyrus for phoneme–color ones).

Grossenbacher and Lovelace (2001) and Dixon et al. (this volume) have made similar distinctions. Grossenbacher and Lovelace distinguish between "perceptual" and "conceptual" synesthetes on the basis of differences in the stimuli that elicit synesthetic experiences, while Dixon et al. distinguish between "associator" and "projector" synesthetes on the basis of whether they report experiencing colors in the external world or in the mind's eye. Our proposal has the advantage of accounting for both sets of differences under a unified framework and tying these differences to the known anatomical localization of different stages of number and color processing.

The existence of reciprocal connections and cross-activation between the neural nodes that deal with related categories even in normal subjects probably complicates the picture and may account for the variability seen in synesthesia and the existence of mixed types (e.g., hearing the word five reminds even a nonsynesthete slightly of the grapheme 5, the written word five, as well as the concept of 5th of the month, producing a sort of penumbra of associated neural activation). One such synesthete we interviewed, A.C., reported such clusters of experience, in which, for example, (5, the letter E, the musical note E, and Wednesday, were all experienced as blue, while 1, the letter A, and Monday were all experienced as red, and 7, the letter F, Friday, and the notes G and F# were all experienced as green). Such reciprocal co-activation may be even more powerful in synesthetes, blurring the distinction between the node and its penumbra and between different types of synesthesia (and evoking different degrees of activation of the color nodes at different stages of color processing, depending on the particular synesthete you are studying.) The failure to recognize this co-activation has resulted in some of the controversy in the older literature about whether synesthetes are merely being metaphorical.

Objective Evidence of Convoluted Number Lines

Some synesthetes report that when they think about numbers, days of the week, or months of the year, each number (or day, or month) seems to always occupy a specific location in space. The numbers are represented sequentially along an imaginary line, called a "number-form" by Galton (1880/1997). The number form is often long and convoluted, sometimes even doubling back on itself, but is generally stable within an individual, even across trials separated by long periods.

Despite these suggestive introspective reports, no objective evidence confirming the existence of convoluted number lines has been obtained. To objectively demonstrate the existence of such convoluted number lines, we took advantage of the well-known numerical distance effect seen in all people (Dehaene, 1997; Dehaene, Depoux & Mehler, 1990; Moyer & Landauer, 1967). Magnitude comparison between two numbers suggests a linear mental representation of numbers in the brain. When numbers are numerically closer, it requires more time to determine which of the two is larger (Dehaene et al., 1990). We predicted that "higher" synesthetes, consistent with their reports of curvy number-lines, would show unusual patterns of response times. In accordance with Dehaene et al., nonsynesthetes should demonstrate a monotonic pattern of decreasing response times (RTs) as the distance between test and standard numbers increases. For instance, if we were to choose 55 as a standard, we would expect nonsynesthetes to respond more quickly to test numbers that were numerically "further" from the standard in either direction, such as 21 or 87. For the synesthetes with convoluted number lines, however, we expected their abnormal mental representations of numbers to create differences indicative of the nature of their specific representation.

First, we mapped out the specific spatial representation for synesthete V.L.V., as shown below:

...	41	42	43	44	45	46	47	48	49	50
	51	52	53	54	55	56	57	58	59	60
	61	62	63	64	65	66	67	68	69	70 ...

Instead of the monotonic decrease in response times as numerical distance increases, we predicted longer response times for synesthetes at points where the Cartesian distance between numbers is smaller within their mental representation. For example, a control participant would be quicker to respond that 45 is less than 55 than 49, but V.L.V. should show longer response times due to the smaller distance between 55 and 45 in her convoluted representation of numbers, thereby providing the first unambiguous empirical evidence to support the existence of convoluted number representations in synesthetes.

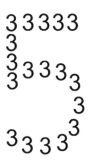

Figure 9.1. Hierarchical figure demonstrating top-down influences in synesthesia. When our synesthetic subjects attend to the global 5, they report the color appropriate for viewing a 5. However, when they shift their attention to the 3s that make up the 5, they report the color switching to the one they see for a 3.

Remarkably, the overall shape of the RT distribution for V.L.V., contains peaks closely corresponding to the reported shortest Cartesian distance along her mental number-line. To quantitatively test this, we developed two mathematical models, one for control subjects, and a second for V.L.V., based on her convoluted number line. V.L.V. fit the synesthete model significantly better than chance and better than the model developed for the control participants. Conversely, control participants fit the model developed for controls better than the model developed for V.L.V. Of particular interest is the fact that the only significant fit was between V.L.V. and the distribution modeled on her convoluted representation of numbers. These results suggest that V.L.V.'s convoluted spatial representation of numbers influences her ability to process numbers because of the shortened Cartesian distances between certain numbers.[2]

In sum, here we present the first evidence that not only do Cartesian and numerical representations interact, but that specific idiosyncratic features of these representations can be tested through behavioral methods. One wonders whether the remarkable abilities of certain savants may depend on a similar ability to form spatial representations of numbers, which may be especially fine grained in them. Indeed, in one of our subjects, the number line seemed to exist in "world-centered" coordinates; so he was able to inspect it from different angles as he wandered around his number landscape.

Top-Down Influences on Synesthesia

The fact that synesthesia is the result of cross-activation of sensory maps does not rule out the possibility that top-down influences, such as attention and

Figure 9.2. Ambiguous stimuli demonstrating further top-down influences in synesthesia. When presented with the ambiguous H/A form in "THE CAT," both of our synesthetes reported that they experienced different colors for the H and the A, even though the physical stimulus was identical in both cases.

visual imagery, can modulate the effect. The picture in figure 9.1 (a large 5 made up of little 3s) is ambiguous and can be seen as either the "forest" (the 5) or the "trees" (the 3s). When we showed this picture to our two synesthetes, they reported that they saw the color switch from red to green depending on whether they were attending to the forest or the trees (Ramachandran & Hubbard, 2001b; see also Rich and Mattingley, this volume, for Stroop experiments based on our observations). This observation implies that even though synesthesia is evoked by the visual appearance alone, not by the high level concept, the manner in which the visual input is categorized, based on attention, is also critical. Similarly, in figure 9.2, there is an ambiguous letter in the middle. On its own, it could depict either an H or an A. When flanked on either side by T and E (horizontally), it looks like H, whereas when flanked by C and T (vertically), it looks like an A (as in CAT). When our subject grouped the letters vertically, she saw the middle character as an A and saw blue, but when she grouped the letters horizontally, she saw the middle character as an H and saw pink (Ramachandran and Hubbard, 2002).

Some Additional Phenomenology and Questions

Thanks to the lingering and pernicious effects of behaviorism, it is unfashionable in psychophysics to ask people what they are actually experiencing, but common sense suggests that this might provide useful insights.

For example, despite the fact that Gestalt psychologists depended on "mere demonstrations" and asking subjects what they experienced, this method allowed them to explore fundamental questions in perceptual organization. With this view in mind, we present below tentative questions that remain to be answered, along with some preliminary observations we have made (Ramachandran & Hubbard, 2001a, 2001b, 2003b). Which of these apply only to lower synesthetes, only to higher, or to both remains to be studied carefully (bearing in mind, especially, that there may be more than just two types).

Color localization. Where exactly is the color perceived? In general, lower synesthetes say they see the color spatially localized on the printed number or letter. Sometimes the color is confined entirely within the margins of the number (or letter), at other times it bleeds, forming a slight halo around the number. Higher synesthetes, on the other hand, make remarks like "I see the color in my mind's eye." We must bear in mind that this is such an ineffable experience that the subject experiences the same frustration in trying to convey it to us as you might experience in describing colors to a rod-monochromat.

"Martian" colors. Some synesthetes describe seeing odd "Martian colors" in graphemes that they cannot see in the real world (see below); this has been noticed before, but no adequate explanation has been provided in the literature. We would explain it in terms of cross-activation that bypasses earlier stages of processing such as opponent processes in the retinal ganglion cells (see discussion of the color-anomalous synesthete below). Sometimes synesthetes see "mixed" colors in a number or letter. For example, one synesthete reported that she experienced the sound of a French tenor's voice as being simultaneously red and green, a color combination that is impossible to see in the real world due to the opponent processing in the retina. Another synesthete reported that the number 5 was blue but in a "patchy" manner, "like a Dalmatian dog." The Martian color effect and the Dalmatian effect are both hard to account for in terms of early memory associations: How can you remember something you have never seen in the real world (Ramachandran and Hubbard, 2001b)?

Memorability. Synesthetic colors are often used as a mnemonic device (see also Dixon et al., this volume). One of our subjects says she remembers phone numbers by color. When trying to recall the number she conjures up a spectrum—a visual image corresponding to the number in her mind's eye and then proceeds to "read off" the numbers. Another claimed he learned to type much faster than his classmates did because for him the keyboard was color-coded (Ramachandran & Hubbard, 2001b). A third subject found it easy to learn musical scales because the piano keys were colored. Each note had a unique color (she was a colored-hearing rather than grapheme-color synesthete). Merikle, Dixon, and Smilek (2002, this volume) recently reported an ingenious experiment. They showed a random matrix of numbers to a synesthete and found he could more readily memorize the numbers than nonsynesthetes because of the extra cue provided by the color.

Imagery. We found that in some synesthetes, when the subject visualized a number, the color was paradoxically more saturated than when actually seeing the number (Ramachandran and Hubbard, 2001b). It is as if when looking at a real black numeral the physical color interfered with or slightly reduced the vividness of the color evoked by cross-activation in the fusiform gyrus or higher up, whereas with top-down imagery-driven activation of the grapheme node, there is no bottom-up interference from the real color.

Spatial interactions. A double-digit number presented visually is usually seen as the corresponding two colors. If the numbers are too close spatially, in some subjects the colors clash and cancel each other out. Intriguingly, if the two different numbers or letters evoke the same color, the colors enhance each other (one synesthete said "Rama" was extremely red because both R and A were red for her). It remains to be seen whether this is true for grapheme-color synesthetes or only for phoneme-color synesthetes (or for both).

Graphemes within words. When a whole word is presented, some synesthetes report that all the letters are always tinged the same color as the first letter. It would be interesting to see if this is true for compound words or hyphenated words. Silent graphemes (e.g., k in "knock") are still seen vividly colored. It remains to be seen if this is only true for lower synesthetes.

Tactile graphemes. Numbers or letters drawn on the palm usually do not evoke colors unless the subject starts visualizing them.

Auditory presentation. If we say "five" to a grapheme-color synesthete, she experiences the color "in her head" (presumably only in higher synesthetes) or automatically imagines the number visually (in lower synesthetes?), and the corresponding color is spontaneously evoked. In two subjects we found that if we said "two, three, two, three, two, three." the subject reported seeing a sort of spatially spread out palette or "spectrum" of corresponding colors in front of her (Ramachandran and Hubbard, 2001b).

Bilingual synesthetes. In some bilingual synesthetes (e.g., Chinese and English) one language alone has colored graphemes, whereas the other does not. Remarkably, in one of our synesthetes, O.R., the colors were evoked only by her second language. Although she learned to read Hebrew graphemes first, she experienced colors for only her second language, English. This requires more intensive study on a larger population of bilingual synesthetes (see also Mills et al., 2002).

Different graphemes. In the native language (for example, English), letters (graphemes) are colored. But the graphemes of a second language learned in adulthood (for instance, Japanese) are *initially* not colored. After a few months to a year, the characters in the second language start assuming entirely sound-based colors; that is, the colors they would be if they were written in Roman letters (Ramachandran & Hubbard, 2003a). This is true for both of the Japanese syllabic alphabets, Hiragana and Katakana. However, letters that do not have English phoneme equivalents tend to assume either arbitrary colors or colors of graphemes that physically resemble the English writing. However, in Kanji, in which a symbol or grapheme stands for a whole word rather than a phoneme, or sound, the symbol takes on pronunciation-based colors. For example, the Kanji word for "love" is pronounced "ai." For one of our bilingual synesthetes, the English letters "A" and "I" are seen as red and black, respectively, and for her, this particular Kanji is therefore "red with a touch of black." But there are exceptions, where the meaning of the Kanji overrides the pronunciation, giving it the Kanji symbol the color of the word that represents the meaning in English. For example, the word for "west" in Kanji is "nishi"—which in Roman letters for our subject should have been purple, black, yellow, red-purple, and black. (The symbol is the same as for love but has a different meaning when used in a certain context with a different pronunciation.) But this Kanji always looked green because the word sound "west" in English letters would be green, orange, yellow, blue, and the concept of "west" dominates over the Kanji pronunciation at the level where the synesthetic color is evoked. Also, the colors of the Kanji symbol for numbers are the same as those for the corresponding Arabic numerals rather the colors of the Kanji sounds themselves. Effects of this sort may help us elucidate how sound, meaning, and symbols interact with each other in the human brain to generate more complex linguistic tokens and how different components of such tokens elicit synesthetic colors at different stages of the brain's processing systems.

Auditory-visual interactions. If a normal person sees your lips pronouncing one phoneme visually on a videotape but hears the wrong sound, he will hear what your lips are "saying" rather than what he is actually hearing—the McGurk effect. In two phoneme-color synesthetes we found that the color evoked corresponded to the perceived phoneme—influenced by visual capture—rather than the actual physical, auditorily presented sound. It remains to be seen if this is true of all synesthetes. (We have seen one exception in whom the color did not match the mouthed sound.)

Alphanumeric categorization. An O can be seen as one of two different colors depending on whether it was seen as the letter O or the number zero.

Occlusion. We presented partially occluded amodally completed letters and numbers (e.g., Bregman's Bs; Bs that are partially covered by an ink blot so only parts of it are visible; see figure 9.3). Without the occluder in place, the B fragments did not produce color, but as soon as the occluder was introduced (so the observer completed the Bs perceptually behind it), the color was clearly visible, although, oddly, it seemed to spread in front of the occluder (and after such priming, even the letter fragments started to evoke colors when the occluder was removed.).

Emotions. Anecdotal observations suggest that synesthetes have disproportionately strong emotional reactions to their color (or other) associations. For example, if a number is presented in the "right" color, it feels harmonious, whereas if presented in the wrong color it feels strongly aversive—like discordant notes or "nails scratching on a blackboard" as one synesthete told us. We have suggested (Ramachandran and Hubbard, 2001b) that this may occur in those synesthetes in whom the "hyperconnectivity" gene is expressed not only between sensory maps but also between sensory areas and areas that subserve emotions (e.g., between the inferior temporal lobe and the amygdala or nucleus accumbens). Such individuals may have a disproportionately large emotional reaction (and perhaps skin conductance response) to even trifling discord or harmony. Such heightened emotions could also provide a basis for learning and reinforcement to influence the development of synesthesia, because they would progressively amplify preexisting small biases (given the disproportionately large reinforcement).

Most of the observations on this list are very preliminary and need to be confirmed with additional subjects. We have to be especially wary of the brain's tendency to selectively attend to positive instances that confirm our hunches. It is hard to believe, though, that synesthesia research will not shed light on the basic mechanisms used by the brain to create perceptual categories of objects and events in the world.

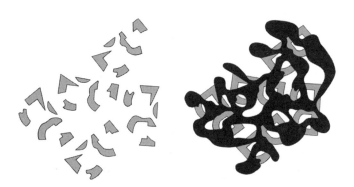

Figure 9.3. The Bregman Bs. When presented with the B fragments, our synesthete J.C. reported experiencing no colors. However, when presented with the Bs with the ink spot over them, J.C. reported experiencing the appropriate colors for the Bs. The color was clearly visible, although, oddly, it seemed to spread in front of the occluder (and after such priming, even the fragments started to evoke colors).

A Colorblind Synesthete

Colorblindness can occur when the color areas in the brain are damaged by a head injury, tumor, or stroke, but the most common cause is an inherited absence of, or deficiency in, one of the three cone pigments. Such a person is born with an inability to perceive the full range of colors that people with normal color vision can see. Depending on which cone pigment is lost and the extent of loss, he may either be partially or completely colorblind. This was the problem experienced by one of our synesthetes, S.S.; he had the inherited form of cone-pigment deficiency and experienced fewer colors in the world than most of us do.

The odd observation S.S. made was that he often saw numbers tinged with colors that he could otherwise never see in the real world. He referred to them, quite charmingly, as "Martian colors" that were "weird" and seemed quite "unreal." Ordinarily one would be tempted to ignore such remarks as being crazy, but in this case, the explanation was staring at us in the face: we realized that our theory about cross-activation of brain maps provides a neat explanation for this seemingly incomprehensible phenomenon.

Remember, S.S.'s cone receptors are deficient, so he cannot, under any circumstance, see the full range of colors by looking at anything in the real world. And yet, in all likelihood the cortical receiving centers in the brain concerned with colors (such as V4 in the fusiform gyrus) were probably programmed by a different set of genes that are not affected in his brain. But if S.S. looks at a number, the form of the number gets processed all the way up to the fusiform and produces cross-activation of cells in V4 much as they would for real colors in a normal person. It is as if the activation skips the retinal processing of color and directly accessess and stimulates the full range of color-coded cells in V4, depending on which number was presented. Since S.S. has never experienced (and can never experience) these colors in the real world and can do so only by looking at numbers, he sees them as strange and spooky—nothing like he can ordinarily see—so he calls them "Martian colors."

Synesthesia, Blindsight, and the Problem of Qualia

Consciousness is one of the unsolved riddles of science. It is so mysterious that it is not even clear whether it is a philosophical problem or a scientific one (recall that many so-called philosophical problems have been usurped by science during the last century). It is easy to fall into the trap of thinking we are conscious of everything that goes on in the brain (but not of, say, events in the liver or the kidney, which obviously have nothing to do with conscious awareness). Actually, the evidence suggests that we are not conscious of even most of what goes on in the brain. Thanks mainly to Freud, we know that most behavior is governed by a cauldron of emotions and motives of which we are completely unaware or only dimly aware and that what we call our conscious life may be no more than an elaborate post-hoc rationalization to justify actions. At a very mundane level, think of what happens when you drive a car while talking to a friend next to you. Unless something very salient and unexpected happens, (e.g., an actual zebra crosses at a zebra crossing), your consciousness is focused on the conversation, and you are largely unconscious of all the complex computations your visual pathways are engaged in while negotiating traffic and dodging trucks and pedestrians. We may conclude from this that routine activities like driving do not require consciousness, but the kind of "off-line" symbol manipulation involved in activity like conversation does require consciousness. Interestingly, it is hard to imagine the converse of this scenario, devoting all your attention to the driving while having a meaningful conversation unconsciously with your friend (see Ramachandran, 2004).

Saying that most events in our brains—and the corresponding behaviors —do not reach consciousness is easy, but this is surprisingly hard to prove scientifically. We realized that synesthesia might provide some clues because it provides a way of selectively activating a set of visual areas while bypassing others, something that cannot be done in non-synesthetes, except by direct brain stimulation. Instead of asking the somewhat nebulous questions, what is consciousness or what is the self, we can refine our approach to the problem by focusing on just one aspect of consciousness, our awareness of visual sensations, and ask, given our detailed knowledge of the anatomy and function of the more than 30 visual areas in the brain, how does the activity of neural circuits in these areas allow us to experience (say) a red sensation? (Crick & Koch, 1998; Ramachandran & Blakeslee, 1998; Ramachandran & Hirstein, 1997).

Does conscious awareness of red require activation of all or most of these areas, or only a small subset of them? What about the whole cascade of activity from the retina to the thalamus to the visual cortex (area 17) before the messages get relayed to the 30 areas? Is their activity also required, or can you skip them and directly activate V4 (the color area in the fusiform) and experience an equally vivid red? If you look at a red apple, you would ordinarily activate the visual area for both color (red) and form (applelike). But what if you artificially stimulate the color area without stimulating cells concerned with form (assuming that is even possible), would you then experience "disembodied" red color floating out there in front of you like a mass of amorphous ectoplasm? And finally, we know that there are many more projections going backward from each area in the hierarchy of visual processing to earlier areas than there are going forward; the function of these back-projections is completely unknown. Is their activity required for conscious awareness of red (Hochstein & Ahissar, 2002)? If you could selectively silence them with a chemical while you look at a red apple, would you lose awareness? These questions come perilously close to being the kind of impossible-to-do armchair thought experiments that philosophers revel in, but the key difference is that these experiments can be done not just in principle but also in practice—and maybe even within our lifetimes.

Let us return, now, to synesthesia to see how it may help us answer some of these seemingly intractable questions. To achieve this goal, we took advantage of a visual phenomenon known as crowding. If you fixate the small cross in figure 9.4, it is quite easy to discern the number 5 off to one side, even though you are not looking at it directly. But if we now add four other numbers (like 2s) all around it, then you can no longer identify the middle number (5); it looks out of focus. Normal volunteers are at chance level identifying this number. This is not due to reduced acuity in the periphery of vision; after all, the 5 can be seen perfectly clearly when 2s do not surround it. The reason the 5 cannot be identified is because of limited attentional resources; the flanking 2s somehow distract attention away from the central 5 and prevent you from seeing it.

The big surprise came when we showed the same display to our two synesthetes. Our question was, if they see the middle number as colored, would this somehow make it more conspicuous and thereby rescue it from the crowding effect? We found that synesthetes did indeed perform better than control subjects, but the really exciting part came when we asked subjects about their experience. Instead of saying that they saw the letter or number, and then the color, imagine our amazement when they looked at the display and made remarks like "I did not see the middle number—it was fuzzy. But it looked red so I guessed it must have been a 5." This is a remarkable observation, for it suggests that even though they were not consciously registering the middle

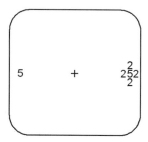

Figure 9.4. A demonstration of the crowding effect. A single grapheme presented in the periphery is easily identifiable. However, when it is flanked by other graphemes, the target grapheme becomes much harder to detect. Synesthetic colors are effective (as are real colors) in overcoming this effect.

number, it was nonetheless being processed somewhere in the brain at an unconscious level (see Dehaene et al., 2001) and evoking the appropriate color. And then they could use this color to intellectually deduce what the number was. If our theory is right, the implication would be that the number is processed in the fusiform gyrus and evokes the appropriate color before the stage at which the crowding effect occurs in the brain—indeed, even before the number is consciously perceived. This was strong evidence that we are dealing with cross-activation relatively early in sensory processing—not some high-level metaphorical association or memory. Just as you can drive a car negotiating traffic without even being conscious of it (because your attention is on a conversation), the number is registered unconsciously and evokes the appropriate color, even though you cannot see the number itself. We have seen this effect in two subjects, but we do not yet know whether it is true of all synesthetes or whether it is true only of the lower synesthetes.

At first, this finding may seem to be at odds with our claim that top-down imagery can influence the induced colors. However, on further reflection, there is really no contradiction. The crowded number is not ambiguous; it allows the full activation of the corresponding cells in the fusiform, and its lack of visibility is due to attentional limitations at some later stage. Consequently, the number activates corresponding color nodes in V4 even though it is ignored later. With the ambiguous display (like CAT), in contrast, the middle letter partially activates two grapheme nodes equally effectively until top-down context biases one of the two nodes, thereby allowing it to reach threshold and activate the corresponding color.

Finally, we should point out that the converse of the blindsight effect is also true. We found in two synesthetes that if the number is presented in peripheral vision and scaled for eccentricity, the evoked color vanishes even though the number is still clearly visible. This effect has since been confirmed by Noam Sagiv and Lynn Robertson (personal communication, 2002) although they found that the number getting close to the frame of the monitor seems to be critical—not just eccentricity. Whatever the ultimate interpretation of this effect, as we noted originally, it represents a double dissociation from the blindsight effect. In blindsight an invisible (or indiscernible) grapheme evokes color, whereas the fall off with eccentricity implies that the very opposite is true under other circumstances—a number that is clearly visible can fail to evoke color. Second, in what may be the first report of laterality effects in synesthesia, we found that in one of these subjects the graphemes were colored mainly in the right visual field but not in the left; implying asymmetric cross-activation in left versus right fusiform gyrus (see Ramachandran and Hubbard 2001a; see also recent imaging study by Nunn et al., 2002, which has revealed striking asymmetries). It is unclear, however, how much these laterality effects are specific to synesthesia per se and how much they relate to the linguistic nature of the forms of synesthesia investigated so far.

Why Is Synesthesia More Common in Artists, Poets, Novelists, and Composers?

We now turn to the question of why synesthesia is more common among "artsy" types, such as painters, poets, composers, and novelists, if, indeed, it is. According to one recent survey (Domino, 1989), as many as a third of all artists claim to have had synesthetic experiences of one sort or another. But is this simply because artists are often more prone to express themselves in vague metaphorical language, or maybe they are just less inhibited about admitting having had such experiences? Or is the incidence genuinely higher? And if so, why? Do artists and poets seem to have synesthesia because they have a vivid imagination and they are prone to talk as if they do? Or is their creativity linked in some deeper way to their synesthesia? Is synesthesia the result of a vivid imagination, or is a vivid imagination the result of synesthesia?

One thing that artists, poets, and novelists have in common is that they are especially good at using metaphor ("It is the East and Juliet is the sun"). It is as if their brains are set up to make links between seemingly unrelated domains, like the sun and a beautiful young woman. When you hear "Juliet is the sun" you don't say, "Does that mean she is an enormous glowing ball of fire?" (Actually, schizophrenics, who sometimes take metaphors literally, tend to do this.) You say, instead, "She is warm like the sun, nurturing like the sun, radiant like the sun," or "She rises from bed like the sun, dispelling the gloom of the night." Your brain instantly finds the right links highlighting the most salient and beautiful aspects of Juliet. In other words, just as synesthesia involves making arbitrary links between seemingly unrelated perceptual entities like colors and numbers, metaphor involves making links between seemingly unrelated conceptual realms. Perhaps this is not just a coincidence. Perhaps the reported higher incidence of synesthesia in artists is rooted deep in the architecture of their brains.

The key to this puzzle is the counterintuitive observation that at least some high-level concepts are probably anchored in specific brain regions. Numbers are among the most abstract of concepts (see, e.g., Dehaene, 1997). Warren McCullough, in emphasizing the very abstract nature of numbers, once asked the rhetorical question, "What is a number that Man may know it? And what is Man that he may know number?" (quoted in Dehaene, 1997). Yet even such an airy abstraction is represented, as we have seen, in a relatively small brain region—the angular gyrus. Indeed, if a stroke is small enough, it can even make a person lose the ability to name specific categories (e.g., tools but not fruits and vegetables). All of these entities are stored close to each other in the inferior temporal lobe, but they are sufficiently separated from each other that a small stroke can knock out one and not the other. It might be tempting to think of fruits and tools as perceptions rather than concepts. However, two tools (e.g., a hammer and saw) can be visually as dissimilar from each other as they are from a fruit (e.g., a banana). This suggests that it is the concept of use that is critical, not the visual appearance alone.

If even concepts exist in the form of brain maps, then perhaps we have the answer to our question about metaphor and creativity. If a mutation were to cause excess connections between different brain maps, then depending on where and how widely in the brain the trait was expressed, it could lead to both synesthesia and to a propensity toward linking seemingly unrelated concepts and ideas. This would explain the higher incidence, perhaps, of synesthesia among artists, poets, and creative people in general. Obviously, we are not saying that being a florid synesthete is sufficient or even necessary for poetry and metaphor, only that the same gene(s) predispose people to be more prone to creativity and that is why they survived (just as the sickle cell gene confers protection against sleeping sickness in recessive form but is fatal as a double recessive).

These ideas take us back full circle to where we started. Instead of saying synesthesia is more common among artists because they are being metaphorical, we should say they are better at metaphors because they are synesthetes (or have synesthetic propensities). Many scientists have argued in the past that synesthesia is a fundamentally different phenomenon from metaphors (e.g., Cytowic 1989/2002; Marks, 1975, 1982) but we disagree. If our reasoning so far is correct, then the two are closely related and may be based on a deep similarity of brain mechanisms.

Synesthesia and Metaphor: The Missing Link

The evidence we have considered so far suggests that some sort of glitch or minor flaw in brain circuits causes synesthesia. But we have also been trying to move away from this idea to the notion that the phenomenon is not just an odd quirk in some people, but that we are all synesthetes to some extent.

To appreciate this, look at the two forms in figure 9.5, one of which looks like an inkblot (right), and the other is a jagged piece of shattered glass (left). If we were to ask you, "Which of these is a *bouba* and which is a *kiki?*" You would pick the inkblot as bouba and the other one as kiki, even though you have never been told this before. We tried this in a large classroom recently and 98% of the students made this choice. One common criticism we have heard is that this might have something to do with the blob resembling the physical form of the alphabet B (for bouba) and the jagged thing resembling a K (as in kiki). However, Köhler (1929, 1947) conducted similar experiments on the island of Tenerife with prelinguistic peoples. The overwhelming majority of

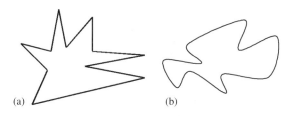

Figure 9.5. Demonstration of kiki and bouba. Because of the sharp inflection of the visual shape, subjects tend to map the name kiki onto the figure shown in panel a, while the rounded contours of the figure in panel b make it more like the rounded auditory inflection of bouba.

subjects assigned *maluma* to the rounded shape and *takete* to the angular one. His experiment has been repeated many times in many countries since then. The results have been equally striking and have been taken as demonstrating a so-far unexplained parallelism between visual and auditory structures. In his original experiments, Köhler (1929) called the stimuli *takete* and *baluma*. He later renamed the *baluma* stimulus *maluma* (Köhler, 1947). However, the results were essentially unchanged and "most people answer[ed] without hesitation" (p. 133; for further discussion, see Lindauer, 1990, Marks, 1996). Our results again confirm these findings with a different set of stimuli and different names.

Why does this happen? Our hypothesis is that the gentle curves and undulations of contour on the amoebalike figure metaphorically mimic (or have similar Fourier spectra) the gentle undulations of the sound "bouba" as represented in the hearing centers in the brain, and the gradual inflection of the lips producing the curved "booo baaa" sound. The waveform of the sound "ki ki" and the sharp inflection of the tongue on the palette likewise mimic the sudden changes in the jagged visual shape. This experiment suggests a deep connection between auditory and visual stimuli and suggests that these properties map in a nonarbitrary manner onto each other.

The angular gyrus of the brain receives signals from the spatial sense modalities (vision, touch, and hearing) and integrates these signals to create an abstract description of the world (see, e.g., Yeterian & Pandya, 1985). We have recently obtained some preliminary evidence that people with damage to this region no longer get the bouba–kiki effect; they are no longer able to match the shape with the "correct" sound; instead, they randomly match sounds with shapes. This observation gives us a clue to understanding how abstract thinking might have first evolved in our hominid ancestors.

To see how the bouba–kiki effect may help explain the evolution of abstract thinking, let us take another look at this effect. Clearly, the visual shape is conveyed by light reflected from the paper and making a spatial pattern of photons dancing on the retina. The auditory sound is conveyed by a time-varying pattern of hair cell movements in the ear. The two have absolutely nothing in common except for the single abstract property of "jaggedness" that is extracted somewhere in the parietal lobes—probably the angular gyrus. So you can think of this structure as performing a very elementary type of abstraction—extracting the common denominator from a set of seemingly dissimilar entities. We do not know how exactly the angular gyrus does this job, but once this ability to engage in cross-modal abstraction emerged, it might have paved the way for the more complex types of abstraction that humans excel at. This strategy, the opportunistic takeover of one function, for a different function, is very common in evolution.

One reason this formulation seems counterintuitive at first is that metaphorical associations in ordinary language seem so arbitrary (sharp cheese) but in fact this is not true. Lakoff, Johnson, and Turner have shown that there are strong directional constraints and that some pairings are much more common than others (Lakoff, 1987; Lakoff & Johnson, 1980, Lakoff & Turner, 1989). A large number of metaphors refer to the body, and many more are intersensory (or synesthetic). Furthermore, we have noticed that synesthetic metaphors (e.g., "loud shirt") also respect the directionality seen in synesthesia (Ullman, 1945; Williams, 1976; but see Day, 1996). That is, they are more frequent one direction than the other (e.g., from the auditory to the visual modality). We suggest that these rules are a result of strong anatomical constraints that permit certain types of cross-activation but not others. Indeed, the preferred directions and frequency of associations may be similar for both (Ramachandran and Hubbard, 2001b).

Consider that when confronted with a foul smell or taste we scrunch up our noses and raise our hand—palm facing out—and call it disgusting. Darwin showed that this disgust response occurs even in newborn infants and suggested that it might be hardwired. But why do we use the same word "disgust" and the same facial expression when referring to a morally disgusting person? Why not say, "he is painful" rather than "he is disgusting"? This is true not just in English but in a variety of other languages as well.

Again, we suggest that anatomy holds the key. The olfactory bulb projects to the orbito-frontal cortex, and olfactory and gustatory "disgust" is almost certainly mediated by this part of the frontal lobes. But why do we use the same word, "disgusting," and make the same face in response to someone whose behavior is morally disgusting? This is unlikely to be coincidence because it is cross-cultural: The Tamil phrase for moral disgust means "he smells bad" and the French word "dégoûtant(e)" (used for social situations) literally means, "bad tasting." We would argue that this usage emerged because moral and social disgust is also mediated by the orbito-frontal cortex (Lane, Reiman, Ahern & Schwartz 1997; Northoff et al., 2000). Early mammals may have used the orbito-frontal cortex exclusively for olfactory and gustatory disgust, but later, as mammals became more social, the same regions were taken over for mapping moral and social dimensions (which makes sense given the close link between territoriality, sexuality, aggression, and smell); hence the same facial expressions and the same terminology. Although this similarity between olfactory and social responses has been noticed before, no anatomical explanations have been put forward to account for it. The near-universal use of sexually loaded words for aggression may also be based similarly, on anatomy; why else would sexuality, which is pleasant and affiliative, be associated with aggression? We say "fuck you," not "bite you," even though bite you would be more appropriate.

These ideas support Freud's remark that "anatomy is destiny" but we must not get carried away. While some of our basic mental operations may be constrained by hard-wired anatomy, humans also excel at making arbitrary associations partially facilitated by Hebbian mechanisms. For example, French is considered "sexy" and "feminine" because the words un peu, je suis, monsieur, and so on, all involve pouting the lips, with obvious sexual connotations such as kissing, whereas German is considered "brusque" and "masculine." This is unlikely to be based on a genetic difference between the brains of the French and the Germans!

The Angular Gyrus, Multisensory Convergence, and the Evolution of Abstraction

Earlier we suggested that, depending on the stage at which cross-activation occurs, there might be "higher synesthetes" and "lower synesthetes" and that in the former the cross-talk might be in the general vicinity of the angular gyrus, which is known to be involved in high-level numerical concepts. The idea that some types of synesthesia might involve the angular gyrus is also consistent with the old clinical observation that this structure is involved in cross-modal synthesis; information from touch, hearing, and vision is thought to flow together in the angular gyrus to enable construction of high-level percepts. For example, a cat is fluffy (touch) and it meows (hearing) and has a certain appearance (vision) and odor (smell), all of which are evoked by the memory of a cat or the sound of the word "cat." No wonder patients with damage to the angular gyrus lose the ability to name things (anomia) even though they can recognize them. Additionally, these patients have difficulty with arithmetic, which also involves cross-modal integration; you learn to count with your fingers. (Indeed, if you touch the patient's finger and ask him which one it is, he often cannot tell you.) All of these bits of clinical evidence strongly suggest that the angular gyrus is a great center in the brain for cross-modal synthesis. So perhaps it is not so outlandish after all that a flaw in the circuitry could lead to colors being quite literally evoked by certain sounds.

We have noticed that patients with anomia caused by lesions of the left angular gyrus also have difficulty with metaphors, often taking them literally. One patient we saw recently incorrectly interpreted 14 out of 15 proverbs, even though he was mentally lucid and intelligent in other respects. Could it be that the angular gyrus, which is disproportionately larger in humans compared to apes and monkeys, originally evolved for cross-modal abstraction, but then became co-opted for other types of abstraction such as metaphors as well? (It would be interesting to see, though, whether these patients are even worse at cross-modal metaphors such as "loud shirt" than at other types of metaphors.)

Cross-modal abstraction became increasingly important in mammalian evolution, especially primate evolution. In the primate brain, visual cortical processing begins at the occipital pole (V1) and is elaborated in secondary visual areas, anterior to V1. Primary auditory cortex lies in the superior bank of the temporal lobe, while somatosensory processing begins in the post-central gyrus in the parietal lobe. Both audition and somatosensation have secondary areas dedicated to the processing of elaborated auditory and somatosensory percepts posterior to the primary areas. That is, while visual processing becomes more elaborated moving anteriorly from the occipital pole, auditory and somatosensory processing becomes more elaborated moving posteriorly from A1 and S1. These more and more elaborated streams of information come together in the TPO junction (Brodmann's areas 39 and 40), which includes the angular and supramarginal gyri. Wilkins and Wakefield (1995) summarize the data suggesting that the TPO junction is differentially enlarged in humans relative to nonhuman primates.

Strikingly, in nonhuman primates, such as the macaque, and even in the chimpanzee (referred to as the pongid brain plan), a clear lunate sulcus is evident in the posterior portion of the brain. In humans, the lunate sulcus is rarely if ever seen. This clear division demarcates V1 from the rest of the brain in pongid brains. The absence of the lunate sulcus in humans is consistent with an increased parietal volume and specifically suggests that the growth of the parietal cortex pushed the lunate to a more posterior and inferior position. Given the presence of the lunate in pongid brains, and its clear absence in humans, it is clear that at some point along the hominid lineage the parietal must have increased in size, and the absence of a lunate sulcus could be taken as evidence for this increase in the size of the parietal cortex.

Because we cannot directly study the brains of extinct species, we must infer their organization indirectly on the basis of endocasts. Dart (1925) described the organization of the lunate sulcus in *Australopithecus*, based on data from the first Tuang child and reported it to be fairly posterior, consistent with the proposal of a "general bulging of the parieto-temporal-occipital association areas" (pp. 197–198; cited in Wilkins & Wakefield, 1995, p. 170).

Holloway (1970, 1975) reported that the position of the lunate sulcus is indeterminate, but if the endocasts can be interpreted at all, the position is more posterior, consistent with Dart. Falk (1980) however, reported that a reexamination of the same endocast suggests an anterior position for the lunate sulcus. Others have reported that the position cannot be determined from the endocast. Based on these data, it is unclear whether *Australopithecus* (which lies between chimpanzees and humans, evolutionarily) had a pongid or hominid brain organization.

However, *H. habilis* clearly shows a pattern of hominid brain organization (Falk, 1983). The development of the inferior parietal lobule of *H. habilis* is much greater than that of the *Australopithecine*. There are clear supra-marginal and angular gyri, suggesting that the size of the inferior parietal has been expanded in *H. habilis* relative to *Australopithecus*.

Van Essen et al. (2001) conducted a comparative study not only of anatomical landmarks, like the lunate, but also of the organization of specific visual areas between the human and the macaque. The boundaries of macaque visual areas were obtained through a variety of different techniques and were then projected into a common polar coordinate system. With this common reference frame, it is possible not only to compare the position of visual areas, but also to warp the visual areas between individual macaques to identify common patterns of visual area organization. Van Essen et al. found that primary visual cortex is conserved across the species (Northcutt & Kaas, 1995). With increasing distance from V1, the fit between the two templates becomes less and less accurate, with the most significant differences between the macaque and the human atlas occurring in the parietal region. The deformed parietal visual areas are disproportionately expanded on the human map compared to the macaque map. For instance, deformed areas LIPd, LIPv, and the VIP complex collectively occupy both banks of the human intraparietal sulcus, whereas these areas occupy mainly the lateral bank of the intraparietal sulcus in the macaque.

In summary, there is a clear increase in the size of the parietal cortex in humans compared to our pongid ancestors. Comparisons between modern nonhuman primates and humans suggest significant physiological differences. Endocasts from nonhuman primates suggest that perhaps as early as *Australopithecus*, and definitely no later than *H. habilis*, the size of the parietal increased dramatically. These anatomical changes would set the stage for more complex types of cross-modal abstraction, as exemplified by the ability to say which of two irregular shapes you just felt with your hands is identical to the one you are seeing. (After all, the two have almost nothing in common; the touch receptors are stimulated serially, whereas the visual shape is apprehended in parallel.) From this to the kinds of cross-modal synesthesia involved in the bouba–kiki effect was but a short step. The result was the creation of more abstract tokens—the basis of symbol manipulation and thinking in general. Given the way evolution works, it is not inconceivable that the angular gyrus (and the TPO in general) evolved originally for cross-modal mappings but then became an exaptation for other types of abstraction as well (and perhaps for metaphorical thinking in general). There may be additional division of labor between left and right angular gyri—the former for language-related analogical reasoning, the latter for spatial and artistic metaphors, a hypothesis that can be tested in patients.

Geschwind (1965) highlights the potential significance for this area of the brain for the evolution of language. Specifically, as Geshwind notes, the TPO is the "association area of association areas." We suggest that the accelerated evolution of the TPO junction and, specifically, the multimodal integration that it permits, were critical for the development of abstraction and in turn for the evolution of language. We detail these points below.

Evolution of Language

The evolution of language is one of the oldest puzzles in psychology. It generated so much acrimonious and unproductive debate in the nineteenth century that the French Linguistics Society introduced a formal ban on all papers dealing with the topic. But problems cannot be removed by censorship. The question is still unanswered: How did an ability as sophisticated and complex as human language evolve in just 200,000 or 300,000 years, a mere blink in evolutionary time? How can the blind workings of chance—natural selection—transform the emotional grunts and howls of apelike ancestors to all the linguistic sophistication of Shakespeare or even George W. Bush? And even more puzzling, how did the hierarchical tree structure of syntax, which involves the embedding of clauses within clauses and rescursivity (e.g., "She hit the boy that kissed the girl that she disliked") evolve? Did Chomskyan deep structure of syntax (assuming there is such a thing as deep structure) evolve as a separate module out of the blue as Chomsky implies, or did it coevolve with semantics (or meaning)?

Classically, there have been two major schools of thought about how language could have evolved, the spandrel hypothesis (Gould, 1979, 1997) and the adaptationist hypothesis (Pinker, 1994). Although these are not the only authors who have defended either view, we take these as modal representatives of these two views. Gould argues that language was not specifically selected by natural selection for its function—open-ended communication. On the contrary, language is the specific deployment of a more general-purpose mechanism, thinking, which evolved for other purposes (just as our fingers evolved for climbing but can now be used for counting, which explains why most mathematical systems use base 10). Pinker, in contrast, argues that language is an "instinct" just like coughing or sneezing (albeit more sophisticated), which evolved through conventional Darwinian selection for the specific purpose of communication. The reason it seems so mysterious to us is because the intermediate steps are missing.

Gould's (1979, 1997) view of language evolution seems reasonable, but we are uncomfortable with it because it merely postpones the problem; it does not solve it. Saying language is simply a deployment of thinking does not tell us much because we have no idea how thinking evolved. If anything, thinking is even more complex. Pinker's (1994) view is correct, but only trivially so. Indeed how else could language have evolved other than through natural selection? But, in our view, Pinker does not go far enough; the idea is too general. It is a bit like answering the question, how does digestion work, with the answer, by obeying the laws of thermodynamics. Obviously, this must be true, but it does not tell us much about the precise mechanisms of digestion. In the case of language, what we would like to know is, what was the actual sequence of steps that culminated in language? What was its exact trajectory through the fitness landscape? For answering this question, Gould's idea of exaptations is much more useful, although he does not tell us what the exaptations might have been that resulted eventually in language. In biology, the devil is in the details.

Our proposal lies somewhere between these two extremes. We have proposed what we call the "synesthetic boot-strapping theory of language" (Ramachandran and Hubbard, 2001b). To understand this we need to go back to the bouba–kiki example. Why do most people who have never seen these shapes before automatically associate the jagged shape with the sound "ki-ki" and the undulating shape with "bouba"? We suggest that this is an example of a preexisting, universal cross-modal synesthesia that involves abstracting the property of "jaggedness" or "undulation" in the angular gyrus. Recall that we had seen a patient with a lesion in the angular gyrus who no longer made this sound–shape association.

This observation gives us the vital clue to understanding the emergence of words, of the lexicon of early hominids. It shows that there is a preexisting, nonarbitrary correspondence between word sound and object appearance. Observations of this sort have been made since the time of Aristotle (see *The Cratylus*), but have been scientifically studied only sporadically in linguistics under the name of "sound symbolism" (see, e.g., Bolinger, 1950; Jakobson & Waugh, 1979; Rhodes, 1994). The main point to be garnered from this research is that phoneme clusters sometimes carry a sort of meaning. Consider a set of unrelated words beginning with /gl-/: "glow, glitter, gleam, glare" (the words are all related to light) or beginning with /sl-/: "slide, slink, slip, sled" (the words relate to liquidity and little friction). Words that start with /tw-/ ("twist, twirl, twiddle, twine") are often related to a twisty motion, with one thing going around another, which, if you pronounce the words, you can feel your own mouth and lips doing.

We would suggest, contrary to the "arbitrariness of the sign" proposed by Ferdinand de Saussure (1910/1993), that there was a built-in bias to associate certain sounds with certain visual shapes, and this bias, however small, may have been important in setting in motion the beginnings of a shared vocabulary. This type of cross-modal, nonarbitrary mapping may be based on cross-activation between visual maps in the fusiform gyrus and auditory/phoneme maps in the superior temporal gyrus, although it may also require a translation mediated by the angular gyrus (figure 9.6).

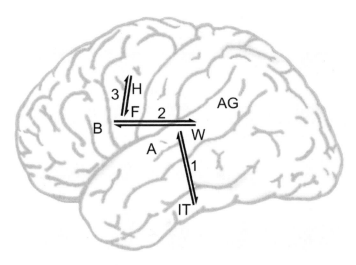

Figure 9.6. A new synaesthetic bootstrapping theory of language origins. Arrows depect cross-domain mapping of the kind we postulate for synesthesia in the fusiform gyrus. (1) A nonarbitrary synesthetic correspondence between visual object shape (as represented in IT and other visual centers) and sound contours represented in the auditory cortex (as in our bouba/kiki example). Such synesthetic correspondence could be based on either direct cross-activation or mediated by the angular gyrus—long known to be involved in intersensory transformations. (2) Cross-domain mapping (perhaps involving the arcuate fasiculus) between sound contours and motor maps in or close to Broca's area (mediated, perhaps, by mirror neurons). (3) Motor-to-motor mappings (synkinesia) caused by links between hand gestures and tongue, lip, and mouth movements in the Penfield motor homunculus (e.g., the oral gestures for "little" or "diminutive" or "teeny weeny" synkinetically mimic the small pincer gesture made by opposing thumb and index finger as opposed to "large" or "enormous"). The cross-wiring would necessarily require transforming a map of two-dimensional hand gestures into one-dimensional tongue and lip movements (e.g., the flexion of the fingers and palmar crease in "come hither" is mimicked by the manner in which the tongue goes back progressively on the palate). And you pout your lips to say "you," "vous," or "thoo" as if to mimic pointing outward, whereas "me," "mois," and "I" mimic pointing inward toward yourself.

But this is only one small step; there are also two other key steps required for this to be a viable theory of proto-language in particular and language evolution in general. In addition to the visual-to-auditory cross-activation (bouba–kiki), there is also a form of cross-activation between auditory–phoneme areas in the superior temporal gyrus and the visual areas on the one hand, and the motor–speech areas in the Broca's area in the frontal lobe, on the other. This latter area has maps of motor programs for moving tongue, lips, palate, larynx, and so on, for phonation and vocalization. Such a cross-activation may also occur between the visual appearance of the object and motor speech maps directly without auditory mediation. Three observations point toward this hypothesis.

First, consider the following experiment by Sapir (1929). He asked about 500 subjects of all ages 60 questions of the following type: "The word 'mal' and 'mil' both mean table in some language. Which type of table is bigger, 'mal' or 'mil'?" Sapir reports that 83% of children and 96% of adults consistently found the "mil" to be smaller and "mal" to be bigger. Newman (1933) showed that English vowels could be placed on a scale of small to large and that the size associated with each vowel reflected the size of the oral cavity during articulation. (It would be interesting to see if synesthetically induced color in higher synesthetes map on to this in some manner.)

Another observation that is consistent with our view comes from comparative linguistics. Berlin (1994) showed that if 50 bird names and 50 fish names from a South American Indian language are given to American college students to classify into fish and bird names, they do so significantly above chance, even though Indo-European languages do not share an ancestry with this language. We would regard this as an example of the bouba–kiki effect in action.

Second, even a newborn infant will stick its tongue out if he watches you doing it, so there seems to be a built-in visual appearance to oral movement translation. Since this occurs without the infant having had any experience of seeing him or herself, some sort of innate congruence must be in place between the visual representation and the somatosenory/kinesthetic sensations of sticking out the tongue.

Third, a class of neurons called mirror neurons, discovered in the homologue of the Broca's area in monkeys, will fire not only when the monkey performs a manual action, such as grabbing a peanut, but also when it watches another monkey performing the same action (di Pellegrino, Fadiga, Fogassi, Gallese & Rizzolatti, 1992; Fadiga, Fogassi, Gallese & Rizzolatti, 2000; Rizzolatti, Fogassi & Gallese, 2001). It seems likely that such neurons exist for vocal movements as well, making it easier for children to imitate parental sounds (partly as a result of the built-in translation from visual to motor and partly from auditory to motor maps). The extent to which such neurons are hard wired versus learned through Hebbian mechanisms remains to be investigated.

Another telling example is words like "fudge," "trudge," and "sludge," in which the movement of the tongue on the palette actually mimics the "stickiness" and viscosity of the seen or felt mud or chocolate (gradual adhesion followed by catastrophic release). We suggest that here, perhaps a nonarbitrary mapping between an abstract motor pattern used when interacting with these gooey substances and the motor pattern of the mouth mediates the choice of these phoneme clusters for these words. An effect first noticed by Darwin is quite consistent with this line of thinking and suggests a neural mechanism for this mediation. Darwin noted that when we cut a piece of paper with scissors our jaws clench and unclench unconsciously as if to echo the hand movements. Darwin could not have known this, but a sort of spillover of motor signals from the hand motor area to the mouth motor area that lies right below it in Penfield's motor homunculus in the precentral gyrus probably causes this effect, which we refer to as "synkinesia." That is, there appears to be a built-in translation between manual and oral gestures. Like synesthesia, this may rely on cross-activation of brain maps, in this case motor rather than sensory maps.

Many linguists do not like the theory that manual gesturing could have given rise to or at least set the stage for vocal language. Synkinesia, however, suggests that they may be wrong. When you want to depict something tiny you make a tiny pincerlike gesture opposing your thumb and forefinger and notice that your lips do the same when saying "teeny weeny" or "diminutive," synkinetically mimicking your fingers. Or when you beckon someone to come toward you, you stick your arm and hand out, palm up, and then flex your palm and fingers toward yourself, a gesture that the tongue mimics on the palette when it bends gradually backward before hitting the roof, while you make the sound "hither" ("ither" in Hindi). Similarly, you put your lips outward away from you for "go" and inward toward you when saying "come." If this were combined with guttural emotional cries emerging from the right hemisphere and anterior cingulate, it could lead to the first words (see more below).

Obviously, these anecdotal observations will need to be systematically studied, but the hypothesis that human vocal language evolved from a manual gestural system has a large (and growing) body of evidence to support it (for a recent review, see Corballis, 2002). One piece of evidence in favor of this view comes from recent work on mirror neurons and the suggestion that they may have played a critical role in the evolution of language (Arbib & Rizzolatti, 1996; Rizzolatti & Arbib, 1998). However, there is an important mismatch here. Mirror neurons in monkeys have been found to respond to manual actions, not orofacial actions. In contrast, in humans mirror-neuronlike activity overlaps with the frontal regions generally identified with

Broca's area (Iacoboni, Woods, Brass & Bekkering, 1999). One possible resolution to this dilemma would be to propose that, over the course of evolution, the mirror neuron system became specialized and segregated so that in humans there are two systems of neurons, premotor neurons, involved with manual gestures, and Broca's area neurons, involved with orofacial gestures (see also Arbib, in press). This proposed manual-to-orofacial split in the mirror neuron system neatly mimics the proposed transition between manual and verbal communication.

A second piece of evidence in favor of the gestural theory comes from the studies of Goldin-Meadow (2001), who notes that manual gestures still play a critical role in human communication, not simply mimicking verbal communication, but adding to it in a variety of ways. Even people who have been blind from birth gesture, suggesting that this behavior is not learned from others (Iverson & Goldin-Meadow, 1998). Additionally, it is well established that the same left-hemisphere brain mechanisms involved in processing verbal language in hearing adults are involved in processing language in deaf adults (Hickock, Bellugi & Klima, 1996, 1998), suggesting that there is no inherent modality specificity to the language system, although language is conventionally produced and understood through the auditory modality.

Assume our ancestral hominids communicated mainly through nonlinguistic emotional grunts, groans, howls, and shrieks produced by the right hemisphere and anterior cingulate. Later they evolved a rudimentary gestural system that became progressively more elaborate and sophisticated (this could have happened through a ritualization of real actions; e.g., "pulling" toward you became a sign for "come here"). If the gestures were then translated through synkinesia into oro-facial movements and if emotional guttural utterances were channeled through these mouth and tongue movements, you get the first spoken words. The last piece of the puzzle falls in place.

We therefore propose that language evolved through the synergistic bootstrapping of three effects (see figure 9.6): (1) visual to auditory mappings as in bouba–kiki mediated by visual-fusiform to auditory-superior temporal cross-activation (with possible angular gyrus mediation); (2) visual plus auditory representations in the back of the brain producing coactivation of corresponding Broca's motor mouth maps (e.g., "diminutive," "teeny weeny") most likely mediated by the arcuate fasiculus; and (3) synkinesia, the mouth mimicking hand gestures (as in teeny weeny, hither, etc.) which, in turn, evolved through conventionalization and ritualization of real actions.

Each of these biases might have been quite small to begin with—often this is all that is required to get a system started in evolution. Once the basic scaffolding was in place, however crude, further improvements were easy. Although the biases may have been small in our ancestors, given the arrangement we have proposed, they can progressively bootstrap each other, leading to a sort of avalanche effect culminating in modern language (especially with culture added to the equation).

One objection to this view might be that there are many objects for which words in modern languages are utterly dissimilar. For example, dog is "chien" in French, "kutta" in Hindi, and "nai" in Tamil. But this may be because once proto-language evolved in ancestral hominids, they could have diverged substantially; as noted above, it is the initial emergence of a trait that is often hard to explain in evolution.

We should also point out at this stage that our view is different from the now discredited onomatopoeic theory of language. The key difference is that in the latter theory words arose from using sounds that are arbitrarily associated with objects (e.g., "bow wow" for dog), whereas in our account the link between shape and sound (bouba–kiki) is not arbitrary; it involves a higher level of cross-modal abstraction.

An obvious advantage with our scheme is that we can now look at aphasias from this evolutionary framework instead of the classical black boxology that dominates cognitive science and artificial intelligence. (We have already noted that the bouba–kiki effect is compromised in patients with angular gyrus lesions.) Another prediction from our scheme is that if higher synesthetes have an inherited "flaw" in the angular gyrus region, some of them may exhibit the other components of the Gerstmann's syndrome (acquired angular gyrus lesions) such as dyscalculia, left–right confusion. We have recently found strong hints that this might indeed be true (in an informal survey we did of synesthetes attending the Second Annual Meeting of the American Synesthesia Association). Consistent with observations noted by Cytowic (1989/2002), we found that numerous synesthetes report left–right confusion, and dyscalculia, although Cytowic does not invoke the same arguments we do. Whether these reports reflect a genuine difference between synesthetes and nonsynesthetes will require a larger sample with more systematic testing, but they are suggestive.

What we have come up with so far is really a theory of proto-language including our vast lexicon and (to some extent) of semantics (as in the abstraction performed by the angular gyrus). But how would syntax be imported into this scheme, especially the hierarchical structure of the Chomskyan syntax? We would argue that once proto-language is in place, then, in conjunction with semantics, it becomes somewhat easier to make this transition than previously believed. But, more important, the evolution of tool use by hominids may have also played a major role in making this transition possible, culminating in full-fledged human language (as argued eloquently by Greenfield, 1991). In particular, there is a close operational analogy between the subassembly technique used by late (but not early) hominids and the hierarchical structure of syntax. For example, the sequence, (1) shape the ax's head, then (2) attach it to a handle, and then (3) chop the meat, bears a remarkable resemblance to the embedding of clauses within larger sentences (see also Ambrose, 2001). We suggest that this resemblance arises from an actual homology, rather than mere analogy or convergence. Frontal brain areas that originally evolved for subassembly in tool use may have been duplicated in evolution through gene duplication and then co-opted for a completely novel function—language. Linguists are forever complaining that not every subtle feature of modern language is explained by such schemes, but, surely, what we need is an initial framework or scaffolding to get things started because once this is available it is easier to account for the subsequent emergence of subtleties such as recursiveness.

Notice that this view differs from Gould's (1979, 1997) idea that language emerged from general-purpose mechanism such as thinking. We agree with Pinker (1994) that natural selection alone was the evolutionary force that resulted in language, but we do not agree that it evolved step by step for the specific purpose of communication. In particular, we suggest that the evolution of language resulted from an opportunistic co-opting of multiple exaptations that were previously selected for other functions altogether (e.g., cross-modal abstraction, synesthesia between vocal, visual, and auditory maps, synkinesia resulting from the fortuitous adjacency of mouth and hand cortex), subassembly in tool use, interactions with "world-based" constraints such as subject-verb-object sequence, and so on. Thus, in our scheme the fortuitous co-occurrence of multiple exaptations, and subsequent equally fortuitous interactions between them was absolutely critical in setting in motion the autocatalytic events that culminated in modern language. In this regard, we would agree with Gould in placing emphasis on exaptations, although not on the particular one—thinking—that he picked.

We should add that while some of the specific ideas on language we have put forth here are novel, most of them have been considered and debated extensively in one form or another by researchers outside the neuroscience community. Any novelty lies in our attempt to weave them into a comprehensible and coherent story that we hope will serve as catalyst to further thinking.

Conclusions

And yet there should be no combination of events for which the wit of man cannot conceive an explanation. Simply as a mental exercise, without any assertion that it is true, let me indicate a possible line of thought. It is, I admit, mere imagination; but how often is imagination the mother of truth?

—Sherlock Holmes

Synesthesia has been known for more than a century, but it has, by and large, been regarded as a curiosity. Only a couple pioneering researchers, Cytowic (1989/2002) and Marks (e.g., 1975, 1982) recognized its importance. But Cytowic was a prophet preaching in a wilderness, and the theories he proposed to explain synesthesia were a bit vague (in our view); he suggested that it was a "throwback" to an earlier stage in phylogeny when the nervous system was undifferentiated. There may be a grain of truth in this, but it does not explain the specificity of synesthetic experiences, which is one of its most striking characteristics. Fortunately, for the neuroscience and psychology community, synesthesia has finally been rescued from becoming a fringe phenomenon. Thanks to the research of several groups (Mattingley et al., 2001; Nunn et al., 2002; Palmeri, Blake, Marois, Flanery & Whetsell, 2002; Ramachandran and Hubbard, 2001a; Smilek, Dixon, Cudahy & Merikle, 2001) there has been a tremendous resurgence of interest in this topic in the last three years, and we can now move from an era of vague phenomenology to the era of experimental research. Such research promises to be exciting for two reasons. First, if a large enough family is identified, we may be able to identify the genetic factors that lead to synesthesia. From the gene we can go to the specific brain areas (e.g., fusiform gyrus in lower synesthetes and angular gyrus and TPO junction in higher synesthetes) to detailed psychophysics (e.g., pop out, blind sight, symmetry, apparent motion, etc), and perhaps all the way to metaphor and Shakespeare—in a single preparation. Second, the phenomenon may allow us to probe (through psychophysics, brain imaging, lesion studies, and modeling) the laws of interactions between brain maps (cross-activation). These laws, we believe, hold the key to understanding some of the most mysterious aspects of our minds, such as qualia, metaphor, analogy, and the emergence of abstract thought and language.

Acknowledgments   We thank Geoff Boynton, Patricia Churchland, Richard Cytowic, Francis Crick, Jeffrey Gray, Bill Hurlburt, George Lakoff, Oliver Sacks, and Mark Turner for discussions and the National Institute of Mental Health, Charlie Robins, and Richard Geckler for support.

Notes

1. We have been struck by the fact that even though schizophrenics are poor at interpreting metaphors and proverbs, they are very good at punning ("clang associations"). This seems like a paradox; why are they good with puns but poor with metaphor? The paradox is resolved when you realize that although puns and metaphors are superficially similar, they are the exact opposite of each other. A pun is a superficial or surface similarity masquerading as a deep insight (hence its comic appeal), whereas a metaphor involves illuminating a deep similarity despite surface differences. So perhaps it is not altogether surprising that the two

are dissociable and sometimes even inversely correlated in certain disease states. The matter deserves deeper study.

2. After this book had gone to press, we gave subject VLV a surprise one year retest (June 18, 2004); she reported that she no longer experienced her number line in the format described here. Instead she reported that she experienced numbers as a continuous line going from left to right. We are therefore skeptical about the reality of her synesthetic reports, and are uncertain how to best interpret these results. However, we still suggest this experimental logic as one way to test the reality of synesthetic number lines.

References

Ambrose, S.H. (2001). Paleolithic technology and human evolution. *Science, 291,* 1748–1753.

Arbib, M.A. (in press). From monkey-like action recognition to human language. *Behavioral & Brain Sciences.*

Arbib, M.A., & Rizzolatti, G. (1996). Neural expectations: A possible evolutionary path from manual skills to language. *Communication & Cognition, 29(3–4),* 393–424.

Armel, K.C., & Ramachandran, V.S. (1999). Acquired synesthesia in retinitis pigmentosa. *Neurocase, 5(4),* 293–296.

Bailey, M.E.S., & Johnson, K.J. (1997). Synesthesia: Is a genetic analysis feasible? In S. Baron-Cohen & J. E. Harrison (Eds.), *Synaesthesia: Classic and contemporary readings* (pp. 182–207). Oxford: Blackwell.

Baron-Cohen, S., & Harrison, J.E. (Eds.). (1997). *Synaesthesia: Classic and contemporary readings.* Oxford: Blackwell.

Berlin, B. (1994). Evidence for pervasive synthetic sound symbolism in ethnozoological nomenclature. In L. Hinton, J. Nichols, & J.J. Ohala (Eds.), *Sound symbolism.* New York: Cambridge University Press.

Bolinger, D. (1950). Rime, assonance, and morpheme analysis, *Word, 6,* 117–136.

Burgess, N., Jeffery, K.J., & O'Keefe, J. (Eds.). (1999). *The hippocampal and parietal foundations of spatial cognition.* New York: Oxford University Press.

Crick, F., & Koch, C. (1998). Consciousness and neuroscience. *Cerebral Cortex, 8(2),* 97–107.

Cohen, L., Dehaene, S., Naccache, L., Lehericy, S., Dehaene-Lambertz, G., Henaff M-A., & Michel, F. (2000). The visual word form area: Spatial and temporal characterization of an initial stage of reading in normal subjects and posterior split-brain patients. *Brain, 123,* 291–307.

Corballis, M.C. (2002). *From hand to mouth: The origins of language.* Princeton, NJ: Princeton University Press.

Cytowic, R.E. (1993). *The man who tasted shapes.* New York: G. P. Putnam's Sons.

Cytowic, R.E. (1989/2002). *Synesthesia: A union of the senses.* New York: Springer-Verlag.

Dart, R.A. (1925). *Australopithecus africanus*: The ape-man of South Africa. *Nature, 115,* 195–199.

Day, S. (1996). Synesthesia and synesthetic metaphors. *Psyche* [on-line], *2(32)*. Available: http://psyche.cs.monash.edu.au/v2/psyche-2-32-day.html

Dehaene, S. (1997). *The number sense: How the mind creates mathematics.* New York: Oxford University Press.

Dehaene, S., Dupoux, E., & Mehler, J. (1990). Is numerical comparison digital? Analogical and symbolic effects in two-digit number comparison. *Journal of Experimental Psychology: Human Perception & Performance, 16(3),* 626–664.

Dehaene, S., Naccache, L., Cohen, L., LeBihan, D., Mangin, J.F., Poline, J.B. Rivière, D. (2001). Cerebral mechanisms of word masking and unconscious repetition priming. *Nature Neuroscience, 4,* 752–758.

di Pellegrino G., Fadiga L., Fogassi L., Gallese V., & Rizzolatti G. (1992). Understanding motor events: A neurophysiological study. *Experimental Brain Research, 91(1),* 176–180.

Dixon, M.J., Smilek, D., Cudahy, C., & Merikle, P.M. (2000). Five plus two equals yellow: Mental arithmetic in people with synesthesia is not coloured by visual experience. *Nature, 406(6794),* 365.

Domino, G. (1989). Synesthesia and creativity in fine arts students: An empirical look. *Creativity Research Journal, 2(1–2),* 17–29.

Fadiga, L., Fogassi, L., Gallese, V., & Rizzolatti, G. (2000). Visuomotor neurons: Ambiguity of the discharge or "motor" perception? *International Journal of Psychophysiology, 35(2–3),* 165–177.

Falk, D. (1980). A re-analysis of the South African australopithecine natural endocasts. *American Journal of Physical Anthropology, 53,* 525–539.

Falk, D. (1983). Cerebral cortices of East African early hominids. *Science, 221,* 1072–1074.

Galton, F. (1880/1997). Colour associations. In S. Baron-Cohen & J. E. Harrison (Eds.), *Synesthesia: Classic and contemporary readings* (pp. 43–48). Oxford: Blackwell.

Gerstmann, J. (1940). Syndrome of finger agnosia, disorientation for right and left, agraphia, acalculia. *Archives of Neurology and Psychiatry, 44,* 398–408.

Geschwind, N. (1965). Disconnection syndromes in animals and man (Parts I, II). *Brain, 88,* 237–294, 585–644.

Goldin-Meadow, S. (2001). The role of gesture in communication and thinking. *Trends in Cognitive Sciences, 3(11),* 419–429.

Gould, S.J. (1979). The spandrels of San Marcos and the Panglossian paradigm: A critique of the adaptationist programme. *Proceedings of the Royal Society of London, B, 205,* 581–598.

Gould, S.J. (1997). The exaptive excellence of spandrels as a term and prototype. *Proceedings of the National Academy of Sciences, USA, 94,* 10750–10755.

Gray, J.A., Williams, S.C.R., Nunn, J., Baron-Cohen, S. (1997) Possible implications of synesthesia for the hard question of consciousness. In S. Baron-Cohen & J.E. Harrison (Eds.), *Synesthesia: Classic and contemporary readings* (pp. 173–181). Oxford: Blackwell.

Greenfield, P.M. (1991). Language, tools and brain: The ontogeny and phylogeny of hierarchically organized sequential behavior. *Behavioral & Brain Sciences, 4,* 531–595.

Grossenbacher, P.G., & Lovelace, C.T. (2001). Mechanisms of synesthesia: Cognitive and physiological constraints. *Trends in Cognitive Sciences, 5(1)*, 36–41.

Hadjikhani, N., Liu, A.K., Dale, A.M., Cavanagh, P., & Tootell, R.B.H. (1998). Retinotopy and color sensitivity in human visual cortical area V8. *Nature Neuroscience, 1(3)*, 235–241.

Hickok, G., Bellugi, U., & Klima, E.S. (1996). The neurobiology of sign language and its implications for the neural basis of language. *Nature, 381,* 699–702.

Hickok, G., Bellugi, U., & Klima, E.S. (1998). What's right about the neural organization of sign language? A perspective on recent neuroimaging results. *Trends in Cognitive Science, 2,* 465–468.

Hochstein, S., & Ahissar, M. (2002). View from the top: Hierarchies and reverse hierarchies in the visual system. *Neuron, 36(5),* 791–804.

Holloway, R.L. (1970). Neural parameters, hunting and the evolution of the human brain. In C.R. Noback & W. Montagna (Eds.), *Advances in Primatology.* New York: Appleton-Century-Crofts.

Holloway, R.L. (1975). Early hominid endocasts: Volumes morphology and significance for human evolution. In R.H. Tuttle (Ed.), *Primate functional morphology and evolution* (pp. 393–416). The Hague: Mouton de Gruyter.

Hubbard, E.M., & Ramachandran, V.S. (2003). Refining the experimental lever: A reply to Shannnon and Pribram. *Journal of Consciousness Studies, 9(3),* 77–84.

Hubbard, E.M., Ramachandran, V.S., & Boynton, G.M. (2003, May). Cortical cross-activation as the locus of grapheme-color synesthesia. Poster presented at the 3rd Annual Meeting of the Vision Sciences Society, Sarasota, FL.

Hubbard, E.M., Ramachandran, V.S., & Boynton, G.M. (2004). Synesthetic colors activate color selective visual areas (V4/V8/hV4). Manuscript in preparation.

Hurley, S., & Noë, A. (2003). Neural plasticity and consciousness. *Biology and Philosophy, 18,* 131–168.

Iacoboni, M., Woods, R. P., Brass, M., & Bekkering, H. (1999). Cortical mechanisms of human imitation. *Science, 286(5449),* 2526–2528.

Iverson, J.M., & Goldin-Meadow, S. (1998). Why people gesture as they speak. *Nature, 396,* 228.

Jakobson, R., & Waugh, L.R. (1979). *The Sound Shape of Language.* Bloomington: Indiana University Press.

Kennedy, H., Batardiere, A., Dehay, C., & Barone, P. (1997). Synesthesia: Implications for developmental neurobiology. In S. Baron-Cohen & J. E. Harrison (Eds.), *Synesthesia: Classic and contemporary readings* (pp. 243–256). Oxford: Blackwell.

Köhler, W. (1929). *Gestalt psychology.* New York: Liveright.

Köhler, W. (1947). *Gestalt psychology* (2nd edition). New York: Liveright.

Kuhn, T. (1962). *The structure of scientific revolutions.* Chicago: University of Chicago Press.

Lakoff, G. (1987). *Women, fire, and dangerous things: What categories reveal about the mind.* Chicago: University of Chicago Press.

Lakoff, G., & Johnson, M. (1980). *Metaphors we live by*. Chicago: University of Chicago Press.

Lakoff, G., & Turner, M. (1989). *More than cool reason: A field guide to poetic metaphor*. Chicago: University of Chicago Press.

Lane, R.D., Reiman, E.M., Ahern, G.L., & Schwartz, G.E. (1997). Neuroanatomical correlates of happiness, sadness, and disgust. *American Journal of Psychiatry, 154*, 926–933.

Lindauer, M.S. (1990). The meanings of the physiognomic stimuli taketa and maluma. *Bulletin of the Psychonomic Society, 28(1)*, 47–50.

Lueck, C.J., Zeki, S., Friston, K.J., Deiber, M.P., Cope, P., Cunningham, V.J., Lammertsma, A.A., Kennard, C., & Frackowiak, R.S. (1989). The colour centre in the cerebral cortex of man. *Nature, 340(6232)*, 386–389.

MacLeod, C.M. (1991). Half a century of research on the Stroop effect: An integrative review. *Psychological Bulletin, 109(2)*, 163–203.

Marks, L.E. (1975). On coloured-hearing synesthesia: Cross-modal translations of sensory dimensions. *Psychological Bulletin, 82(3)*, 303–331.

Marks, L.E. (1982). Bright sneezes and dark coughs, loud sunlight and soft moonlight. *Journal of Experimental Psychology: Human Perception & Performance, 8(2)*, 177–193.

Marks, L.E. (1996). On perceptual metaphors. *Metaphor & Symbol, 11(1)*, 39–66.

Mattingley, J.B., Rich, A.N., Yelland, G., & Bradshaw, J.L (2001). Unconscious priming eliminates automatic binding of colour and alphanumeric form in synesthesia. *Nature, 410(6828)*, 580–582.

Merikle, P., Dixon, M.J., & Smilek, D. (2002, April). The role of synesthetic photisms on perception, conception and memory. Lecture presented at the 12th Annual Meeting of the Cognitive Neuroscience Society, San Francisco, CA.

Mills, C.B., Viguers, M.L., Edelson, S.K., Thomas, A.T., Simon-Dackô, S.T., & Innis, J.A. (2002). The color of two alphabets for a multilingual synesthete. *Perception, 31(11)*, 1371–1394.

Moyer, R.S., & Landauer, T.K. (1967). Time required for judgments of numerical inequality. *Nature, 215*, 1519–1520.

Newman, S. (1933). Further experiments in phonetic symbolism. *American Journal of Psychology, 45*, 53.

Northcutt R.G., & Kaas J.H. (1995). The emergence and evolution of mammalian neocortex. *Trends in Neuroscience, 18(9)*, 373–379.

Northoff, G., Richter, A., Gessner, M., Schlagenhauf, F., Fell, J., Baumgart, F., Kaulisch, T., Kötter, R., Stephan, K.E., Leschinger, A., Hagner, T., Bargel, B., Witzel, T., Hinrichs, H., Bogerts, B., Scheich, H., & Heinze, H-J. (2000). Functional dissociation between medial and lateral prefrontal cortical spatiotemporal activation in negative and positive emotions: A combined fMRI/MEG study. *Cerebral Cortex, 10*, 93–107.

Nunn, J.A., Gregory, L.J., Brammer, M., Williams, S.C.R., Parslow, D.M., Morgan, M.J., Morris, R.G., Bullmore, E.T., Baron-Cohen, S., & Gray, J.A. (2002). Functional magnetic resonance imaging of synesthesia: Activation of V4/V8 by spoken words. *Nature Neuroscience, 5(4)*, 371–375.

Palmeri, T.J., Blake, R.B., Marois, R., Flanery, M.A., & Whetsell, W.O. (2002). The perceptual reality of synesthetic color. *Proceedings of the National Academy of Sciences, USA, 99,* 4127–4131

Pesenti, M., Thioux, M., Seron, X., & De Volder, A. (2000). Neuroanatomical substrates of Arabic number processing, numerical comparison, and simple addition: A PET study. *Journal of Cognitive Neuroscience, 12(3),* 461–479.

Pinker, S. (1994). *The language instinct.* New York: Willliam Morrow.

Polk, T.A., Stallcup, M., Aguirre, G.K., Alsop, D.C., D'Esposito, M., Detre, J.A., & Farah, M. J. (2002). Neural specialization for letter recognition. *Journal of Cognitive Neuroscience, 14(2),* 145–159.

Ramachandran, V.S. (2004). *The emerging mind.* London: Profile Books.

Ramachandran, V.S., & Blakeslee, S. (1998). *Phantoms in the Brain.* New York: William Morrow.

Ramachandran, V.S., & Gregory, R.L. (1978). Does colour provide an input to human motion perception? *Nature, 275(5675),* 55–56.

Ramachandran, V.S., & Hirstein, W. (1997). Three laws of qualia: What neurology tells us about the biological functions of consciousness. *Journal of Consciousness Studies, 4(5–6),* 429–457.

Ramachandran, V.S., & Hubbard, E.M. (2001a). Psychophysical investigations into the neural basis of synesthesia. *Proceedings of the Royal Society of London, B, 268,* 979–983.

Ramachandran, V.S. & Hubbard, E.M. (2001b) Synesthesia—a window into perception, thought and language. *Journal of Consciousness Studies, 8(12),* 3–34.

Ramachandran, V.S., & Hubbard, E.M. (2002, November). Synesthetic colors support symmetry perception, apparent motion, and ambiguous crowding. Lecture presented at the 43rd Annual Meeting of the Psychonomics Society. Kansas City, MO.

Ramachandran, V.S., & Hubbard, E.M. (2003a). Hearing colors, tasting shapes. *Scientific American, 288(5),* 52–59.

Ramachandran, V.S., & Hubbard, E.M. (2003b). The phenomenology of synaesthesia. *Journal of Consciousness Studies, 10(8),* 49–57.

Rickard, T. C., Romero, S. G., Basso, G., Wharton, C., Flitman, S., & Grafman, J. (2000). The calculating brain: An fMRI study. *Neuropsychologia, 38(3),* 325–335.

Rizzolatti, G., & Arbib, M.A. (1998), Language within our grasp. *Trends in Neurosciences, 21(5),* 188–194.

Rizzolatti, G., Fogassi, L., & Gallese, V. (2001). Neurophysiological mechanisms underlying the understanding and imitation of action. *Nature Reviews Neuroscience, 2(9),* 661–670.

Rhodes, R.A. (1994). Aural images. In J. Ohala, L. Hinton & J. Nichols (Eds.), *Sound symbolism.* (pp. 276–292). New York: Cambridge University Press.

Sacks, O., Wasserman, R.L., Zeki, S., & Siegel, R.M. (1988) Sudden color blindness of cerebral origin. *Society for Neuroscience Abstracts, 14,* 1251.

Sagiv, N., Knight, R.T., & Robertson, L.C. (March, 2003). Electrophysiological markers of synesthesia. Paper presented at the 10th Annual Meeting of the Cognitive Neuroscience Society, New York.

Sapir, E. (1929). The status of linguistics as a science. *Language, 5,* 207–214.

Saussure, F.D. (1910/1993). *Saussure's Third Course of Lectures on General Linguistics (1910–1911).* New York: Pergamon Press.

Smilek, D., Dixon, M.J., Cudahy, C., & Merikle, P.M. (2001). Synaesthetic photisms influence visual perception. *Journal of Cognitive Neuroscience, 13(7),* 930–936.

Spalding, J.M.K., & Zangwill, O. (1950). Disturbance of number-form in a case of brain injury. *Journal of Neurology, Neurosurgery, and Psychiatry, 12,* 24–29.

Treisman, A. (1982). Perceptual grouping and attention in visual search for features and for objects. *Journal of Experimental Psychology: Human Perception & Performance, 8(2),* 194–214.

Ullmann, S. (1945). Romanticism and synaesthesia: A comparative study of sense transfer in Keats and Byron. *Publications of the Modern Language Association of America, 60,* 811–827.

Van Essen, D.C., Lewis, J.W., Drury, H.A., Hadjikhani, N., Tootell, R.B., Bakircioglu, M., & Miller, M.I. (2001). Mapping visual cortex in monkeys and humans using surface-based atlases. *Vision Research, 41(10–11),* 1359–1378.

Wade, A.R., Brewer, A.A., Rieger, J.W., & Wandell, B.A. (2002). Functional measurements of human ventral occipital cortex: Retinotopy and colour. *Philosophical Transactions of the Royal Society of London, B, 357(1424),* 963–973.

Ward, J., & Simner, J. (2003). Lexical-gustatory synaesthesia: Linguistic and conceptual factors. *Cognition, 89,* 237–261.

Wilkins, W.K., & Wakefield, J. (1995). Brain evolution and neurolinguistic preconditions. *Behavioral & Brain Sciences, 18(1),* 161–226.

Williams, J.M. (1976). Synaesthetic adjectives: A possible law of semantic change. *Language, 32(2),* 461–478.

Yeterian, E.H., & Pandya, D.N. (1985). Corticothalamic connections of the posterior parietal cortex in the rhesus monkey. *Journal of Comparative Neurology, 237(3),* 408–426.

Zeki, S., & Marini, L. (1998). Three cortical stages of colour processing in the human brain. *Brain, 121(9),* 1669–1685.

Part IV

Development and Learning

10

Neonatal Synesthesia: A Reevaluation

Daphne Maurer and Catherine J. Mondloch

I n *The World of the Newborn,* Charles and Daphne Maurer (1988) proposed that the normal newborn is synesthetic. They argued that "the newborn does not keep sensations separate from one another, but rather "mixes sights, sounds, feelings, and smells into a sensual bouillabaisse" in which "sights have sounds, feelings have tastes," and smells can make the baby feel dizzy (p. 51). In later publications, D. Maurer and Mondloch provided additional evidence for this hypothesis (Maurer, 1993; Maurer & Mondloch, 1996) and distinguished strong and weak forms of it (Maurer & Mondloch, 1996). The purpose of this chapter is to review the basis for the original hypothesis and to reevaluate it in light of the evidence since 1996 on the neural basis of synesthesia, on developmental plasticity, and on cross-modal interactions in nonsynesthetic adults and children.

The Original Hypothesis

The hypothesis grew out of paradoxical evidence of U-shaped development of cross-modal perception: Babies demonstrated successful linking of information across sensory modalities near birth, failed at similar tasks later in infancy, and then appeared to gradually learn cross-modal links in the second half of the first year of life. For example, 1-month-olds who saw a patch of white light repeatedly for 20 trials showed evidence of habituation to that light and to a sound at a level identified by adults as best matching the intensity of the light. When another group was shown a more intense light, evidence of habituation shifted to a more intense sound (Lewkowicz & Turkewitz, 1980). Evidence of the young infant's ability to link auditory and visual information extends beyond intensity matching to synchrony—the synchrony of sound to the visual impact of a dropped object (Bahrick, 2001) and the synchrony of a spoken passage to lip movements of a stranger's face (Pickens et al., 1994). There is also evidence of links between touch and vision: After a familiarization period during which they mouthed a hard pacifier, 1-month-olds preferred to look at a novel, soft, deforming pacifier (and vice versa) (Gibson & Walker, 1984), and after tactual habituation to one object (e.g., a six-pointed star or a plain square), 2- to 3-month-olds demonstrated a similar preference to look at the novel shape (e.g., a six-pointed flower or a square with a central hole) (Steri, 1987). Apparent imitation of tongue protrusion also suggests integration between vision (e.g., the sight of a model sticking out his or her tongue or of any looming visual stimulus, Jacobson, 1979) and proprioception (i.e., the feeling of sticking out the tongue or of making similar movements with other appendages; Gardner & Gardner, 1970). (Note that some interpretations of the phenomenon do not involve cross-modal integration (e.g., the baby "reaches" with the tongue toward an interesting visual stimulus; Jones, 1996).

Despite such evidence of cross-modal integration near birth, there are surprising failures at later ages and evidence of the baby's subsequently learning to integrate differentiated senses. The most striking evidence comes from three studies that used the same procedure at different ages and found success at younger ages followed by failure later in infancy. For example, Pickens et al. (1994) found that 5- to 6-month-old full-term infants looked randomly at the adult reciting the passage they were hearing when that was paired with an adult reciting a different passage, while younger (3- to 4-month-old) and older (7- to 8-month-old) infants looked preferentially at the adult reciting the matching passage. Similarly, unlike younger infants (Steri, 1987), 4- to 5-month-olds fail to look differentially at two objects after tactile habituation to one of them (Steri & Pêcheux, 1986). The frequency with which babies stick out their tongue in response to a visual model also decreases systematically after the first month (Abravanel & Sigafoos, 1984; Fontaine, 1984; Heimann, Nelson & Schaller, 1989) and gradually reemerges later in infancy as the baby appears to learn the connection between movements of his or her own face and those of a visual model (e.g., Piaget, 1952).

Adultlike Synesthesia at Birth

We proposed that the apparent cross-modal integration in early infancy results from synesthetic perception. In one form of the hypothesis (which we originally called the "strong form"), young infants resemble synesthetic adults in whom stimulation of one sensory modality evokes a percept not only in that modality (such as hearing the presented sound or seeing the achromatic letter) but also a specific percept in a second modality (or along a second dimension, such as color). Thus, when the baby is habituated to an auditory stimulus, he or she simultaneously perceives and is habituated to the corresponding visual stimulus. This hypothesis is consistent with what is known about the brain basis of synesthesia and neural development during infancy. Colored word hearing (synesthesia in which specific sounds or letters evoke colored percepts) appears to be based on unusual connections between cortical areas. In such synesthetes, hearing words evokes evidence of neural activity not only in the auditory cortex but also in extrastriate visual cortex (Gray, Williams, Nunn & Baron-Cohen, 1997; Nunn et al., 2002), in a number of higher visual areas (Paulesu et al., 1995) and, in one study, even in the primary visual cortex (Aleman, Rutten, Sitskoorn, Dautzenberg & Ramsey, 2001). (Alternatively, such connections may exist in all adult brains but may be released from inhibition in synesthetes; Grossenbacher & Lovelace, 2001). In contrast, the synesthesia of one gustatory synesthete was correlated with cortical suppression. Synesthesia increased with cortical depressants like ethanol and amyl nitrate and decreased with cortical stimulants like amphetamines, nicotine, and caffeine. A PET scan confirmed a decrease in cortical blood flow through the parietal, frontal, and temporal cortices while the subject reported the synesthetic induction of tactile feeling (e.g., cold glass columns) by odorants (Cytowic, 1989). There is also evidence for suppression of some areas of sensory visual cortex during colored word hearing (Paulesu et al., 1995) and a pattern of event-related potentials during the induction of colored graphemes that is consistent with suppression of activity in the frontal cortex (Schiltz et al., 1999). Cytowic (1989) speculated that synesthesia is mediated by the limbic system, a speculation consistent with evidence that lesions of the monkey's amygdala abolish cross-modal matching between vision and touch while not interfering with matching within either modality (Murray & Mishkin, 1985). Thus, synesthesia might arise either from unusual connections between cortical areas or from cortical suppression.

There is ample anatomical evidence that young organisms have transient connections between cortical areas that will subsequently be pruned (DeHay, Bullier & Kennedy, 1984; DeHay, Kennedy & Bullier, 1988; Huttenlocher, 1994; Kennedy, Bullier & DeHay, 1989) and that the cortex of the human newborn is hardly functioning, as evidenced by anatomical immaturities, low levels of blood flow, and failure at behavioral marker tasks (reviewed in Atkinson & Braddick, 2003; Braddick, Atkinson & Hood, 1996; de Haan & Johnson, 2003). Moreover, there is anatomical evidence that the limbic system develops relatively early (reviewed in Benes, 1994) and behavioral evidence that it may be functional at birth (Pascalis & de Schonen, 1994). Thus, the newborn might have synesthetic perceptions because some of the transient connections are functional and/or because the limbic system is functioning with little specific input from the cortex. According to this form of the hypothesis, a stimulus such as a tone induces more than one percept for the baby—one in the inducing modality (hearing the tone) and one or more in other modalities (e.g., seeing a red color or tasting a sweet substance induced by the tone). In the strongest form of the hypothesis, unlike synesthetic adults, the baby is unable to differentiate real from synesthetically induced percepts (e.g., seeing a red object versus "seeing" a red-inducing tone; tasting sweet milk versus "tasting" a sweet-inducing tone). Of course, because of cortical immaturity, none of the baby's percepts is as richly differentiated as those of adults: red will not look as saturated and sweet will not taste as complex.

A Special Neonatal Form of Synesthesia

Another form of the hypothesis (which we originally called "weak form"; (Maurer & Mondloch, 1996) is that, largely because of an immature cortex, the baby does not differentiate stimuli from different modalities, but rather responds to the total amount of energy, summed across all modalities. The baby is aware of changes in the pattern of energy and recognizes some patterns that were experienced before, but is unaware of which modality produced the pattern. As a result, the baby will appear to detect cross-modal correspondences when stimuli from different modalities produce common patterns of energy change. When presented with a human voice, the baby may experience a pattern of changing oscillations and recognize their similarity to patterns experienced before from the same voice. Although aware of the oscillations, the baby does not yet perceive them as sound per se. As a result the baby may not differentiate between the pattern of oscillations created by the voice and by a stimulus from another modality—a bouncing ball or rhythmic stroking that creates the same frequency of oscillations. Additional evidence for this form of the hypothesis is that the newborn's visual preferences and sleeping patterns are related to total amount of stimulation, with equivalent effects of increasing stimulation within one modality and adding a moderate level of stimulation from another modality (e.g., Brackbill, 1970, 1971, 1973, 1975; Gardner, Lewkowicz, Rose & Karmel, 1986; Greenberg & Blue, 1977; Lewkowicz, 1991; Lewkowicz & Turkewitz, 1981; Turkewitz, Gardner, & Lewkowicz, 1984).

This form of the hypothesis resembles Zelazo's (1996) claim that the young infant has only first-level minimal consciousness in which the baby perceives objects but is unaware of whether he or she is seeing or feeling them. Newborns' perception may be analogous to the mandatory fusion of information from different visual cues that occurs in adults' perception of depth (Hillis, Ernst, Banks & Landy, 2002). Adults can perceive the slant of an object based on the changes in the texture on its surface or from binocular disparity and perceive it more accurately when those cues are consistent. However, when those cues are made inconsistent in the laboratory, adults' patterns of errors indicate that they cannot access information from the separate visual cues: they appear to perceive slant but not the visual cues specifying that slant. In adults, no such mandatory fusion occurs between visual and tactile cues to depth: performance is better if the cues are consistent, but it does not deteriorate if the cues are inconsistent, a pattern indicating fused cross-modal perception without loss of information from each modality. Unlike adults, a similar mandatory fusion may occur across modalities for infants, such that they perceive an object but lose access to information about the modality supplying the information.

Unlike synesthetic adults who experience two percepts—one in the inducing modality and a second in the synesthetic modality—the baby may experience just one percept for a given pattern of energy change, a percept that is the same whether the pattern is heard, seen, or tasted. Alternatively, the baby may experience different percepts when the energy change is heard rather than seen or tasted but may be less aware than adults of the modality of input and much more sensitive than adults to similarities across modalities in the pattern of energy change. This enhanced sensitivity will diminish as transient connections are pruned and as a more specialized cortex exerts more control. Thereafter the baby learns to interrelate differentiated senses, but remnants of the synesthesia persist in cross-modal influences (see "Synesthetic Correspondences in Children and Adults").

In the next section we explore evidence for transient connections between cortical areas during infancy. Such evidence comes from three sources: experimental studies with animals in which the sensory input to cortical regions is altered "natural" experiments involving deaf and blind humans, and neuroimaging and behavioral studies involving infants.

Evidence for Transient Connections during Infancy

Cortical Plasticity

Recent evidence on cross-modal plasticity suggests that the immature cortex is less specialized than it will be later in development. Altering the input to primary sensory cortices early in life is sufficient to change the nature of their specialization. The most striking examples come from studies in which retinal axons in the ferret are induced to replace the normal auditory innervation of the medial geniculate nucleus (MGN), where they establish an orderly visuospatial map. Neurons in the auditory cortex, to which the MGN projects, become sensitive to visual orientation, direction of motion, and velocity and mediate visual percepts (reviewed in Sur & Leamey, 2001).

These results suggest that the specialization of primary sensory cortex is largely determined by the nature of the inputs it receives. Studies in cats indicate that the mere absence of the normal sensory input (e.g., because of enucleation of the eyes at birth) is sufficient to induce responses to auditory stimuli in the primary visual cortex (Yaka, Yinon & Wollberg, 1999; reviewed in Bavelier & Neville, 2002). These effects are thought to reflect the stabilization of transient connections and/or the unmasking of silent inputs that would normally not be revealed or might even be inhibited (reviewed in Rauschecker, 1995; Bavelier & Neville, 2002). During normal development, these connections would be diminished through Hebbian competition in which the more frequent activation by input from the "correct" sensory modality increases the strength of the "correct" synaptic connections. Because such competitive effects have been demonstrated to operate within the visual modality over periods as short as 1 hr, they are unlikely to arise from the formation of new synaptic connections. Rather, they are likely to reflect competitive influences on preexisting connections (reviewed in Rauschecker, 1995). There is evidence of such competitive interactions in one fMRI study of synesthetes with colored hearing: in the control group, seeing colors activated an extrastriate visual cortical area called V4 in both hemispheres; in the synesthetes, hearing words activated that area in the left hemisphere and seeing colors did so only in the right hemisphere, as if the auditory input had captured V4 in the left hemisphere through Hebbian competition to the detriment of the normal visual input (Nunn et al., 2002).

Blind Adults

Human studies confirm that when the normal sensory input is missing (because of blindness or deafness), the primary visual and auditory cortices can become responsive to other sensory inputs. Neuroimaging studies using PET and fMRI have documented that, in adults blind from an early age, reading Braille activates the visual cortex, including much of extrastriate visual cortex and, in most studies, the primary visual cortex (Burton et al., 2002; Melzer et al., 2001; Sadato et al., 1998, but see Büchel, Price, Frackowiak & Friston, 1998). For example, in one study, while blind subjects read Braille, the increase in the fMRI signal over the baseline resting period was only 2% less from the primary visual cortex than it was from the sensorimotor cortex (Melzer et al., 2001). Because tactile input from feeling the Braille characters would be routed only to the hemisphere contralateral to the hand, yet the activation of visual cortex by Braille was bilateral, the reorganization is likely to reflect changes in cortical connections rather than in subcortical inputs to the visual cortex (Sadato et al., 1996). The functional importance of the visual cortical activity is indicated by the disruptive effect of transcranial magnetic stimulation placed so as to temporarily deactivate the visual cortex.

Adults blind from an early age reported that Braille dots did not make sense, that some were missing, and that extraneous phantom dots appeared, and their error rates increased significantly (Cohen et al., 1997; Cohen et al., 1999). No such disruption occurred when TMS deactivated other cortical areas. Additional evidence that the visual cortex plays a functional role in the ability to read Braille comes from a congenitally blind woman who lost that ability suddenly when she suffered a bilateral occipital stroke at age 63, despite intact peripheral sensitivity (Hamilton, Keenan, Catala & Pascual-Leone, 2000).

The visual cortex of congenitally blind persons is also responsive to sound. In a recent fMRI study (Röder, Sock, Bien, Neville & Rösler, 2002), spoken sentences activated left auditory cortical areas in both sighted and blind subjects, but in blind subjects, spoken sentences also activated primary and extrastriate visual areas, with a pattern that was related to syntactic and semantic difficulty: The harder the task, the greater the activation of visual cortex. Researchers using magnetoencephalography and event-related potentials (ERPs) have also noted that responses to oddball stimuli (an infrequent auditory frequency or location or incongruent word) are recorded from electrodes over the visual cortex only from people blind from an early age (Kujala et al., 1995; Leclerc, Saint-Amour, Lavoie, Lassonde & Lepore, 2000; Liotti, Ryder & Waldoff, 1998; Röder, Rösler & Neville, 2000; Röder et al., 1999), although not while the subjects are reading Braille (Kujala et al., 1995), as would be expected from the evidence presented above that the visual cortex plays an active role in decoding Braille. Overall, the evoked responses are more sharply tuned to variations in the auditory stimulus in blind subjects than in sighted subjects, and, correspondingly, blind subjects localize peripheral auditory sounds more precisely (Leclerc et al., 2000; Lessard, Paré, Lepove & Lassonde, 1998; Röder et al., 1999). The pattern of lateralization is also unusual, with more bilateral responses to language than in sighted adults (Röder et al., 2000, 2002), as is true in young infants, a pattern suggesting that transient connections for language in the right hemisphere have become stabilized.

The increased activation in visual cortex revealed by PET and fMRI when congenitally blind subjects process tactile or auditory information contrasts with decreased activation in some of these same areas in normally sighted subjects doing the same tasks (Sadato et al., 1998; Weeks et al., 2000). Although the decreased activation in normally sighted subjects could reflect merely a shift of attention away from vision when processing information from other modalities, the pattern is consistent with models postulating that synesthetic visual percepts reflect the activation of intercortical connections that are normally suppressed (e.g., Grossenbacher & Lovelace, 2001). Visual stimuli deactivate the auditory cortex (and vice versa), but only when presented alone (Laurienti et al., 2002). When a multimodal stimulus is presented, activation levels in the visual (or auditory) cortex are equivalent to the level of activation seen when only a visual (or auditory) stimulus is presented. That interpretation—that many intracortical connections are present but suppressed in the adult brain—is also consistent with evidence that the visual cortex of the blind is active during Braille reading, even when the onset of blindness was as late as 13 years of age, and there are some, albeit smaller, changes when the onset of blindness was even later (e.g., Burton et al., 2002; Cohen et al., 1999) or when normally sighted adults learn to be better at discriminating Braille characters during 5 days of training while blindfolded (Kauffman, Théoret & Pascual-Leone, 2002). In any event, studies of congenitally blind persons document that the visual cortex, including the primary visual cortex, can be made to respond to auditory and tactile input. The evidence from TMS, stroke patients, and animal models suggest that the responses in visual cortex contribute to somatosenory and auditory percepts.

Deaf Adults

Similar effects to those found for blind subjects have been documented for the congenitally deaf. Visual presentation of moving dots or sign language activates auditory cortical areas, including primary auditory cortex, based on position emission tomography (PET) and functional magnetic resonance imaging (fMRI) measurements (Finney, Fine & Dobkins, 2001; Nishimura et al., 1999, 2000; see Neville, 1995, for ERP evidence), and so does vibrotactile stimulation produced by resonances in a tube the subject is holding (Levänen, Jousmåaki & Hari, 1998). Combined with the evidence from congenitally blind persons, these studies suggest that the transient connections between cortical areas present in early infancy are modified postnatally by the type of input received. Input arriving from the "wrong" modality can stabilize the connection if the "right" input is missing, presumably through Hebbian competition, and/or such input can prevent normal inhibitory mechanisms from developing.

Neuroimaging Studies with Infants

Evidence using neuroimaging techniques with infants indicates that the transient connections may be functional and supports at least a special form of neonatal synesthesia. There is evidence for the influence of auditory input on the infants' somatosensory and visual cortices and for the influence of visual input on the infants' auditory cortex. For example, stimulation of the wrist elicits a somatosensory evoked response in both newborns and adults, but only in newborns is its magnitude enhanced when wrist stimulation is accompanied by white noise (Wolff, Matsumiya, Abrohms, van Velzer & Lombroso, 1974). Spoken language elicits large ERP responses over temporal regions in both adults and infants, but only in infants does it also elicit a large response over visual cortex (Neville, 1995), much as it does in blind adults (Leclerc et al., 2000; Liotti et al., 1998; Röder et al., 2000). fMRI studies show that spoken words also elicit activity over both temporal and visual cortices in synesthetes (e.g., Aleman et al., 2001; Nunn et al., 2002; Paulesu et al., 1995). Finally, at 2 months of age, PET activation in response to faces, relative to illuminated diodes, includes areas that will be differentially activated by faces in adults: an area within the right inferior temporal gyrus that is homologous to the adult fusiform face area and bilateral activation of inferior occipital cortex (Tzourio-Mazoyer et al., 2002; but see Dehaene-Lambertz, Dehaene & Hertz-Pannier, 2002). In addition, in infants faces activate the left inferior frontal and superior temporal gyri—areas that later become associated with language. Collectively, these results suggest less specificity of cortical areas during early infancy. Specificity increases during the first three years of life. For example, by 36 months the ERP response over the visual cortex in response to spoken language has declined to adultlike levels (Neville, 1995).

Behavioral Evidence

Recent behavioral studies that explore cross-modal correspondences during infancy are also consistent with the hypothesis that senses are not separate from one another in newborns. Molina and Jouen (2001) measured the frequency with which newborns squeezed smooth and granular objects and found that they squeezed smooth stimuli more frequently than granular stimuli. During the test period, the newborns were presented with the same tactile stimulus and a visual stimulus. The visual stimulus either matched (e.g., smooth–smooth) or did not match (e.g., smooth–granular) the tactile stimulus. Frequency of squeezing did not change when a matching visual stimulus was presented. However, frequency of squeezing increased when the granular tactile stimulus was accompanied by the smooth visual stimulus and decreased when the smooth tactile stimulus was accompanied by the granular visual stimulus. Molina and Jouen concluded that newborns are able "to compare texture density information across modalities" (p. 123). It is our contention that these results indicate a merging of the senses; newborns' handling of the tactile stimulus varies with the overall pattern of energy rather than with the texture of the tactile stimulus per se. Thus, the smooth–smooth and granular–granular combinations simply supply reflections of the same pattern of energy experienced in the first part of the study. The combined pattern of energy evoked by the smooth tactile–granular visual combination represents an increase in energy over smooth tactile alone and evokes the same frequency of squeezing as a granular texture. The combination of granular texture with a smooth visual pattern represents a reduction in energy in the synesthetic compound and hence yields the increased frequency of squeezing evoked by a smooth texture alone. Indeed, similar changes in frequency of squeezing might be observed if the tactile stimulus were accompanied by a pulsating versus a continuous tone.

Newborns do show evidence of learning some cross-modal correspondences that are not arbitrary—learning that is consistent with the neonatal synesthesia hypothesis because it may be based on similar patterns of neural firing in two sensory areas that are not yet differentiated. For example, after being habituated to a single toy that was both colocated and synchronous with a sound, newborns' looking time increased (i.e., they showed a novelty response) when the toy was presented on the opposite side of the midline from the sound (Morrongiello, Fenwick & Chance, 1998). Furthermore, after habituation to two objects, only one of which was colocated with sound, newborns looked longer when the sound was located with the other toy. Likewise, Bahrick (2001) showed that 4-week-old infants are sensitive to synchrony: they dishabituate when they see an asynchronous auditory–visual event after being habituated to a synchronous event. By 7 weeks of age, infants also show sensitivity to composition—another amodal relationship. After being habituated to a single object that was synchronous with a single-impact sound and to a cluster of objects that was synchronous with a multiple-impact sound, 7-week-olds looked longer when the sound–object pairings were reversed. Sensitivity to amodal correspondences may be based on shared patterns of neural stimulation (e.g., timing, spatial representation, proportion of fibres activated, Cytowic, 2002; Marks, 1987) and facilitate the infant's learning of more arbitrary relations (Bahrick, 2001). Sensitivity to arbitrary sound–object pairings (e.g., shape–pitch) emerges much later (Bahrick, 1994; Fernandez & Bahrick, 1994; see also Reardon & Bushnell, 1988).

Synesthetic Correspondences in Children and Adults

Although young children and adults with normal perception do not experience visual percepts in response to auditory stimuli, under a variety of conditions they appear to experience cross-modal interactions that parallel those experienced by synesthetes. This is evident in tasks involving sensory matching, perceptual judgments, and language.

Sensory Matching

Nonsynesthetic adults match higher-pitched tones with smaller, brighter lights (Marks, Hammael & Bornstein, 1987) and the lighter of two gray squares (Marks, 1974). They also match louder tones with brighter lights (Marks et al., 1987) and with larger objects (Smith & Sera, 1992). Some of these cross-modal correspondences can be attributed to intensity matching. This explanation can be invoked whenever subjects are asked to match stimuli that vary along dimensions we describe in more-end terms (i.e., "prothetic" dimensions), such as size, loudness, and brightness (Smith & Sera, 1992; Stevens, 1957): "big," "loud," and "bright" are more than "small," "quiet," and "dim," respectively. Thus, a match of the bigger of two objects or the brighter of two lights to the louder of two sounds could be based on intensity matching. However, intensity matching cannot be invoked if one of the dimensions is "metathetic" and cannot be described in more-end terms. Although "loud" is more than "quiet," and "bright" is more than "dim," adults do not describe either achromatic color (surface lightness) or pitch in more-end terms. Dark gray, for example, is not more than light gray, and "treble tones" are not more than bass tones." Thus, although adults match "large" with "bright" (Marks et al., 1987), they do not match "large" with either dark or light gray (Smith & Sera, 1992). Thus, the correspondences that both synesthetes and nonsynesthetic adults report between pitch and surface lightness and between pitch and size cannot be attributed to intensity matching.

Some correspondences may be learned (e.g., larger objects do make louder sounds than smaller objects when dropped, and smaller musical instruments, such as a violin, do make higher-frequency sounds than larger musical instruments, such as a cello). These learned correspondences are slow to develop. Unlike adults, two-year-olds do not match size and loudness; it is not until 3 years of age that children match the larger of two objects with the louder sound (Smith & Sera, 1992). Likewise, the correspondence between pitch and size is not adultlike in young children. Although adults match a higher pitch with a smaller light in a perceptual matching task, 9-year-olds do not; nor do they understand cross-modal metaphors involving pitch and size (Marks et al., 1987; but see below for evidence of pitch–size matching in 3-year-olds when tested with a more child-friendly procedure).

Other correspondences are not learned through experience. It is hard to imagine a learned basis for the correspondence between surface lightness and pitch—lighter objects do not make higher-pitched sounds in the real world. We hypothesize that unlearned correspondences that cannot be based on intensity matching are remnants of neonatal synesthesia. Consequently, they ought to be present throughout development. We have tested correspondences between pitch and both size and surface lightness in young children (Mondloch & Maurer, in press). We showed 30- to 36-month-olds a movie of two balls bouncing in synchrony with each other and with a central sound that varied in frequency. The balls differed in size and/or surface lightness. Each child was asked to point to the ball that was making the sound. Based on previous research (Marks et al., 1987), we predicted that the pitch–size correspondence, which may be learned, would be either absent or weak. In contrast, if the correspondence between pitch and surface lightness reported by both synesthetes and nonsynesthetes is a remnant of neonatal synesthesia, then young children ought to associate the lighter ball with the higher-pitched sound. In experiment 1, the balls differed in both size and surface lightness. Eleven of the twelve children said that the smaller, white ball was making the higher-pitched sound or that the larger, gray ball was making the lower-pitched sound ($p < .01$). In experiment 2 both balls were the same size, but they differed in surface lightness. Every child ($n = 12$) said that the white ball was making the higher-pitched sound. In experiment 3, both balls were white, but they differed in size. Only 9 of the 12 children matched the smaller ball with the higher-pitched sound ($p = .07$). We tested an additional 12 children; 10 of these children matched in the expected direction ($p < .05$).

Thus, when a child-friendly procedure is used, children as young as 30–36 months tend to match higher-pitched sounds with smaller objects, perhaps as a result of learning. However, this correspondence may be weaker than that between pitch and surface lightness. Because both pitch and surface lightness are metathetic, the pitch–surface lightness correspondence cannot be attributed to intensity matching. Furthermore, pitch and surface lightness are not reliably related in the real world, so this correspondence cannot be attributed to learning. Rather, our results support the hypothesis that some cross-modal correspondences have their origin in neonatal synesthesia.

Cross-modal influences on perceptual judgments. Adults' perceptual judgments are influenced by seemingly irrelevant input from other sensory modalities, with a pattern of correspondences similar to those reported by synesthetic adults. For example, adults are more accurate at identifying the odor of solutions that have the appropriate color (e.g., red–cherry) than an inappropriate color (e.g., red–lemon; Zellner, Bartoli & Eckard, 1991). In addition, they report that odors presented in colored solutions smell stronger than odors presented in colorless solutions (Zellner & Kautz, 1990), and the more saturated the color, the stronger the effect, regardless of whether the color is appropriate; red mint smells stronger than pink mint. Similarly, adults' discrimination of visual stimuli is influenced by auditory distractors: their performance is better if there is a synesthetic match (bright light/high pitch) than if the match is opposite (Marks, 1987; Melara, 1989). We contend that such cross-modal influences in adults arise from remnants of neonatal synesthesia.

Language

Additional evidence of natural correspondences in nonsynesthetic adults abounds in human language, as evidenced by the preponderance of cross-modal metaphors, such as "soft light" and "loud colours." Not only do adults match brighter lights with louder tones, they also rate sunlight as louder than moonlight (Marks et al., 1987). Furthermore, metaphors in which a visual noun is modified by an auditory word (e.g., "a loud tie") are much more common both in English and German literature than are metaphors in which an auditory noun is modified by a visual word (e.g., "bright thunder"; Day, 1996)—a pattern that parallels synesthesia.

Systematic investigations of the role of language in cross-modal correspondences have demonstrated that words denoting loudness, brightness, pitch, and surface lightness act in much the same way as sensory stimuli that vary on these dimensions. Adults rate "bright coughs" as louder than "dim coughs," and "loud sunlight" as brighter than "quiet sunlight" (Marks, 1982), just as they match brighter lights with louder tones (Marks et al., 1987). Likewise, they rate "bright" sneezes as higher pitched than "dim" sneezes and violins as brighter than thunder (Marks, 1982), just as they match higher pitched tones with lighter and brighter visual stimuli (Marks, 1974; Marks et al., 1987). Not only are sensory dimensions that adults match in laboratory studies mirrored in metaphors, but sensory dimensions that adults fail to match in laboratory tasks are not related metaphorically. Dark squares are not consistently matched with louder/quieter tones (Marks, 1974) and dark piano notes are not rated as much louder than bright piano notes (Marks, 1982).

Ramachandran and Hubbard (2001) suggest that synesthetic correspondences between sensory dimensions have not simply facilitated the production and understanding of cross-modal metaphors, but may have "boot-strapped" the very evolution of language. Adults rate angular nonsense figures as more aggressive, more tense, stronger, and noisier than rounded shapes (Marks, 1996); they also are more likely to label angular shapes "takete" or "kiki" and rounded shapes "maluma" or "bouba"—perhaps because there is a correspondence between the visual percept, the phonemic inflections, and the movement of the tongue on the pallete that results from the same cortical connections among contiguous cortical areas that underlie synesthesia (Ramachandran & Hubbard, 2001). Ramachandran and Hubbard also point out that the movements made to produce words conveying large objects frequently involve widening the vocal tract (e.g., large, huge), whereas words describing small objects often involve narrowing the vocal tracts (e.g., teeny, tiny). This tendency may be the result of natural constraints on sensory and motor maps, which are in turn linked in nonarbitrary ways to an object's appearance. Additional evidence reviewed by Ramachandran and Hubbard consists of mirror neurons (neurons that fire not only when a complex manual task is performed but also when a monkey watches a conspecific perform a complex task), and synkinesia (cross-activation of motor maps; e.g., the tendency to point both lips and fingers when referring to someone else).

Although cross-modal correspondences may have boot-strapped the evolution of language, Martino and Marks (1999) argue that language now plays a central role in mediating cross-modal correspondences in adults. According to their model, information from multiple sources (e.g., vision, audition, touch) "converges on a shared, abstract, semantic representation" (p. 921; see also Martino & Marks, 2001). When asked to classify stimuli (e.g., nonsense figures as angular/rounded; tones as high/low pitched), adults perform better when the stimulus is accompanied by a stimulus from another modality that is congruent, rather than incongruent (Marks, 1987). For example, adults' reaction time is faster when classifying tones as high/low pitched if the lower pitched tone is accompanied by a black square or a word printed in black ink, and if the higher pitched tone is accompanied by a white square or a word printed in white ink. That semantic codes may come to mediate these effects is evident in two findings: (1) Similar results are obtained when adjectives (e.g., SHARP, DULL, BLUNT) are accompanied by congruent (e.g., SHARP by a higher tone) versus incongruent (e.g., DULL by a higher tone) stimuli (Walker & Smith, 1984), and (2) the presentation of words (e.g., WHITE, DAY) influences the strength of the congruency effect between sensory stimuli (e.g., pitch–lightness; Martino & Marks, 1999). For example, adults classify a high-pitched tone faster if presented with the words WHITE or DAY printed in white ink than if presented with the words BLACK or NIGHT printed in white ink.

The interplay between language and perception is illustrated in a study conducted by Smith and Sera (1992) in which preschoolers (2–5 years) and undergraduate students were asked to match stimuli varying in size, loudness, or surface lightness to a perceptual or verbal model that represented an extreme value on one of the other dimensions. For example, after being presented with a large mouse or the word BIG, children would be asked which of two mice—one emitting a quiet noise, one a louder noise—was most like the model stimulus. Two-year-olds did not match "loud" with "big"; loudness–size matching became consistent by 3 years of age, just when children showed comprehension of the four relevant adjectives: big, little, loud, quiet. Thus, verbal comprehension may play a role in perceptual organization of polar dimensions. In contrast, only 2-year-olds matched darker gray with the bigger of two objects (i.e., indicated that the larger of two mice was most like the dark gray model mouse). Comprehension of the four relevant adjectives (dark, light, big, little) resulted in perceptual disorganization such that older children failed to match these two dimensions consistently. Individual adults were consistent; however, some matched dark gray with "big" and others matched dark gray with "little." Thus, cross-modal perception represents a complex interplay between language and the physiological response to sensory stimuli.

Summary

Our current knowledge of infant behavior, cortical plasticity, cross-modal matching, language, and synesthesia suggests that connections—either direct (e.g., Ramachandran & Hubbard, 2001) or indirect (e.g., Cytowic, 2002)—between brain regions typically associated with distinct modalities may underlie each of these phenomena and thus that knowledge of any one topic can inform us about the others. According to the neonatal synesthesia model, newborns fail to differentiate input from different senses—either because of connections between cortical areas that are pruned or inhibited later in development or because of the multimodal limbic system being more mature than the cortex. Because of more widespread cortical activation and/or multimodal limbic activity, newborns nevertheless sometimes behave as if they are able to relate input between distinct modalities. The remnants of this unspecialized cortex are most clearly evident in synesthetic adults who experience, for example, visual percepts in response to sound and in adults with abnormal sensory experiences, such as the congenitally blind or deaf who have unusual patterns of activation in cortical areas deprived of typical input. However, remnants also are observed in normal children and adults in their ability to match dimensions from different modalities (e.g., pitch and size) and in the prevalence of cross-modal metaphors (e.g., 'loud colours') in everyday speech. Fostering cross-talk among researchers from these distinct fields should facilitate our understanding of the normal development of cross-modal perception and language as well as our understanding of the roots of synesthesia.

References

Abravanel, E., & Sigafoos, A.D. (1984). Exploring the presence of imitation during early infancy. *Child Development, 55*, 381–392.

Aleman A., Rutten G.J., Sitskoorn M.M., Dautzenberg G., & Ramsey N.F. (2001). Activation of striate cortex in the absence of visual stimulation: An fMRI study of synesthesia. *Neuroreport, 12*, 2827–2830.

Atkinson, J., & Braddick, O. (2003). Neurobiological models of normal and abnormal visual development. In M de Haan & M. Johnson (Eds.), *The cognitive neuroscience of development* (pp. 43–71). East Sussex: Psychology Press.

Bahrick, L. (1994). The development of infants' sensitivity to arbitrary intermodal relations. *Ecological Psychology, 6*, 111–123.

Bahrick, L. (2001). Increasing specificity in perceptual development: Infants' detection of nested levels of multimodal stimulation. *Journal of Experimental Child Psychology, 79*, 253–270.

Bavelier, D., & Neville, H. (2002). Cross-modal plasticity: Where and how? *Nature Reviews Neuroscience, 3*, 443–452.

Benes, F. (1994). Development of the corticolimbic system. In G. Dawson & K. Fischer (Eds.), *Human behavior and the developing brain* (pp. 176–206). New York: Guilford.

Brackbill, Y. (1970). Acoustic variation and arousal level in infants. *Psychophysiology, 6,* 517–525.

Brackbill, Y. (1971). Cumulative effects of continuous stimulation on arousal level in infants. *Child Development, 42,* 17–26.

Brackbill, Y. (1973). Continuous stimulation and arousal level: Stability of the effect over time. *Child Development, 44,* 43–46.

Brackbill, Y. (1975). Continuous stimulation and arousal level in infancy: Effects of stimulus intensity and stress. *Child Development, 46,* 364–369.

Braddick, O., Atkinson, J., & Hood, B. (1996). Striate cortex, extrastriate cortex, and colliculus: Some new approaches. In F. Vital-Durand, J. Atkinson, & O. Braddick (Eds.), *Infant vision* (pp. 203–220). Oxford: Oxford University Press.

Büchel, C., Price, C., Frackowiak, R., & Friston, K. (1998). Different activation patterns in the visual cortex of late and congenitally blind subject. *Brain, 121,* 409–411.

Burton, H., Snyder, A., Conturo, T., Akbudak, E., Ollinger, J., & Raichle, M. (2002). Adaptive changes in early and late blind: a fMRI study of Braille reading. *Journal of Neurophysiology, 87,* 589–607.

Cohen, L.G., Celnik, P., Pascual-Leone, A., Corwell, B., Faiz, L., Dambrosia, J., Honda, M., Sadato, N., Gerloff, C., Catalá, M., & Hallett, M. (1997). Functional relevance of cross-modal plasticity in blind humans. *Nature, 389,* 180–183.

Cohen, L., Weeks, R., Sadato, N., Celnik, P., Ishii, K., & Hallett, M. (1999). Period of susceptibility for cross-modal plasticity in the blind. *Annals of Neurology, 45,* 451–460.

Cytowic, R.E. (1989). *Synesthesia: A union of the senses.* New York: Springer Verlag.

Cytowic, R.E. (2002). *Synesthesia: A union of the senses.* (2nd edition). New York: MIT Press.

Day, S. (1996). Synaesthesia and synaesthetic metaphor. *Psyche: An Interdisciplinary Journal of Research on Consciousness, 2.* Available at http://psyche.cs.monash.edu.ou/v2/psyche-2-32-day.html

de Haan, M., & Johnson, M. (2003). Mechanisms and theories of brain development. In M. de Haan & M. Johnson (Eds.), *The Cognitive Neuroscience of Development* (pp. 1–18). East Sussex: Psychology Press.

Dehaene-Lambertz, G., Dehaene, S., & Hertz-Pannier, L. (2002). Functional neuroimaging of speech perception in infants. *Science, 298,* 2013–2015.

DeHay, C., Bullier, J., & Kennedy, H. (1984). Transient projections from the fronto-parietal and temporal cortex to areas 17, 18, and 19 in the kitten. *Experimental Brain Research, 57,* 208–212.

DeHay, C., Kennedy, H., & Bullier, J. (1988). Characterization of transient cortical projections from auditory, somatosensory and motor cortices to visual areas 17, 18, and 19 in the kitten. *Journal of Comparative Neurology, 230,* 576–592.

Fernandez, M., & Bahrick, L.E. (1994). Infants' sensitivity to arbitrary object-odor pairings. *Infant Behavior and Development, 21*, 745–760.

Finney, E., Fine, I., & Dobkins, K. (2001). Visual stimuli activate auditory cortex in the deaf. *Nature Neuroscience, 4*, 1171–1173.

Fontaine, R. (1984). Imitative skills between birth and six months. *Infant Behavior and Development, 7*, 323–333.

Gardner, J., & Gardner, H. (1970). A note on selective imitation by a six-week old human infant. *Child Development, 41*, 1209–1213.

Gardner, J., Lewkowicz, D., Rose, S., & Karmel, B. (1986). Effects of visual and auditory stimulation on subsequent visual preferences in neonates. *International Journal of Behavioural Development, 9*, 251–263.

Gibson, E.J., & Walker, A.S. (1984). Development of knowledge of visual-tactual affordances of substance. *Child Development, 55*, 453–460.

Gray, J., Williams, S., Nunn, J., & Baron-Cohen, S. (1997). Possible implications of synaesthesia for the hard question of consciousness. In S. Baron-Cohen & J. Harrison (Eds.), *Synaesthesia: Classic and contemporary readings* (pp. 173–181). Oxford: Blackwell.

Greenberg, D.J., & Blue, S.Z. (1977). The visual preference technique in infancy: Effect of number of stimuli presented upon experimental outcome. *Child Development, 48*, 131–137.

Grossenbacher, P., & Lovelace, G. (2001). Mechanisms of synesthesia: Cognitive and physiological constraints. *Trends in Cognitive Sciences, 5*, 36–41.

Hamilton, R., Keenan, J., Catala, M., & Pascual-Leone, A. (2000). Alexia for Braille following bilateral occipital stroke in an early blind woman. *Neuroreport, 11*, 37–240.

Heimann, M., Nelson, K.E., & Schaller, J. (1989). Neonatal imitation of tongue protrusion and mouth opening: Methodological aspects and evidence of early individual differences. *Scandinavian Journal of Psychology, 30*, 90–101.

Hillis, J.M., Ernst, M.O., Banks, M.S., & Landy, M.S. (2002). Combining sensory information: Mandatory fusion within, but not between, senses. *Science, 298*, 1627–1630.

Huttenlocher, P. (1994). Synaptogenesis in human cerebral cortex. In G. Dawson & K. Fischer (Eds.), *Human behaviour and the developing brain* (pp. 137–152). New York: Guildford.

Jacobson, S.W. (1979). Matching behavior in the young infant. *Child Development, 50*, 425–430.

Jones, S. (1996). Imitation or exploration? Young infants' matching of adults' oral gestures. *Child Development, 67*, 1952–1969.

Kauffman, T., Théoret, H., & Pascual-Leone, A. (2002). Braille character discrimination in blindfolded human subjects. *NeuroReport, 13*, 571–574.

Kennedy, H., Bullier, J., & DeHay, C. (1989). Transient projection from the superior temporal sulcus to area 17 in the newborn macaque monkey. *Proceedings of the New York Academy of Sciences, 86*, 8093–8097.

Kujala, T., Huotilainen, M., Sinkkonen, J., Ahonen, A., Alho, K., Hämäläinen, M., Ilmoniemi, R., Kajola,M., Knuutila, J., Lavikainen, J., Salonen, O., Simola,J., Standertskjöld-Nordenstam, C-G., Tiitinen, H., Tissari, S., & Näätänen, R.

(1995). Visual cortex activation in blind humans during sound discrimination. *Neuroscience Letters, 183,* 143–146.

Laurienti, P., Burdette, J., Wallace, M., Yen, Y.F., Field, A., & Stein, B. (2002). Deactivation of sensory-specific cortex by cross-modal stimuli. *Journal of Cognitive Neuroscience, 14,* 420–429.

Leclerc, C., Saint-Amour, D., Lavoie, M., Lassonde, M., & Lepore, F. (2000). Brain functional reorganization in early blind humans revealed by auditory event-related potentials. *Neuroreport, 11,* 545–550.

Lessard, N., Paré, M., Lepore, F. & Lassonde, M. (1998). Early-blind human subjects localize sound sources better than sighted subjects. *Nature, 395,* 278–280.

Levänen, S., Jousmäaki, V., & Hari, R. (1998). Vibration-induced auditory-cortex activation in a congenitally deaf adult. *Current Biology, 8,* 869–872.

Lewkowicz, D.J. (1991). Development of intersensory functions in human infancy: Auditory/visual interactions. In M.J. Weiss & P.R. Zelazo (Eds.), *Newborn attention* (pp. 308–338). Norwood, NJ: Ablex.

Lewkowicz, D., & Turkewitz, G. (1980). Cross-modal equivalence in early infancy: Auditory-visual intensity matching. *Developmental Psychology, 16,* 597–607.

Lewkowicz, D.J., & Turkewitz, G. (1981). Intersensory interaction in newborns: Modification of visual preferences following exposure to sound. *Child Development, 52,* 827–832.

Liotti, M., Ryder, K., & Woldoff, M. (1998). Auditory attention in the congenitally blind: Where, when, and what gets recognized. *Neuroreport, 9,* 1007–1012.

Marks, L.E. (1974). On associations of light and sound: The mediation of brightness, pitch, and loudness. *American Journal of Psychology, 87,* 173–188.

Marks, L.E. (1982). Bright sneezes and dark coughs, loud sunlight and soft moonlight. *Journal of Experimental Psychology: Human Perception and Performance, 8,* 177–193.

Marks, L. (1987). Auditory-visual interactions in speeded discrimination. *Journal of Experimental Psychology: Human Perception and Performance, 13,* 384–394.

Marks, L.E. (1996). On perceptual metaphors. *Metaphor and Symbolic Activity, 11,* 39–66.

Marks, L., Hammel, R., & Bornstein, M. (1987). Perceiving similarity and comprehending metaphor. *Monographs of the Society for Research in Child Development, 52,* (serial no. 215).

Martino, G., & Marks, L.E. (1999). Perceptual and linguistic interactions in speeded classification: Tests of the semantic coding hypothesis. *Perception, 28,* 903–923.

Martino, G., & Marks, L.E. (2001). Synesthesia: Strong and weak. *Current Directions in Psychological Science, 10,* 61–65.

Maurer, D. (1993). Neonatal synesthesia: Implications for the processing of speech and faces. In B. Boysson-Bardies, S. de Schonen, P. Jusczyk, P. McNeilage, & J. Morton (Eds.), *Developmental neurocognition: Speech and face processing in the first year of life* (pp. 109–124). Dordrecht: Kluwer.

Maurer, D., & Maurer, C. (1988). *The world of the newborn.* New York: Basic Books.

Maurer, D., & Mondloch, C. (1996, October). Synesthesia: A stage of normal infancy? In S. Masin (Ed.), *Proceedings of the 12th meeting of the International Society for Psychophysics* (pp. 107–112), Padua.

Melara, R.D. (1989). Dimensional interactions between color and pitch. *Journal of Experimental Psychology: Human Perception and Performance, 15,* 69–79.

Melzer, P., Morgan, V., Pickens, D., Price, R., Wall, R., & Ebner, F. (2001). Cortical activation during Braille reading is influenced by early visual experience in subjects with severe visual disability: A correlational fMRI study. *Human Brain Mapping, 87,* 589–607.

Molina, M., & Jouen, F. (2001). Modulation of manual activity by vision in human newborns. *Development Psychobiology, 38,* 123–132.

Mondloch, C., & Maurer, D. (in press). Do small balls squeak? Pitch-object correspondence in young children. *Cognitive, Affective, & Behavioral Neuroscience.*

Morrongiello, B., Fenwick, K.D., & Chance, G. (1998). Cross-modal learning in newborn infants: Inferences about properties of auditory-visual events. *Infant Behaviour & Development, 21,* 543–554

Murray, E.A., & Mishkin, M. (1985). Amygdalectomy impairs crossmodal association in monkeys. *Science, 228,* 604–606.

Neville, H. (1995). Developmental specificity in neurocognitive development in humans. In M. Gazzaniga (Ed.), *The cognitive neurosciences* (pp. 219–231). Cambridge, MA: Bradford.

Nishimura, H., Doi, K., Iwuki, T., Hashikawa, K., Nishimura, T., & Kubo, T. (2000). Sign language activated the auditory cortex of a congenitally deaf subject revealed by positron emission tomography. In C. Kim, S. Chang, & D. Lim (Eds.), *Updates in cochlear implantation. Advances in otorhinolaryngology,* Vol. 57 (pp. 60–62). Basel: Karger.

Nishimura, H., Hashikawa, K., Doi, K., Iwaki, T., Watanabe, Y., Kusuoka, H., Nishimura, T., & Kubo, T. (1999). Sign language 'heard' in the auditory cortex. *Nature, 367,* 116.

Nunn, J.A., Gregory, L.J., Brammer, M., Williams, S., Parslow, D., Morgan, M., Morris, R., Bullmore, E., Baron-Cohen, S., & Gray, J. (2002). Functional magnetic resonance imaging of synesthesia: Activation of V4/V8 by spoken words. *Nature Neuroscience, 5,* 371–375.

Pascalis, O., & de Schonen, S. (1994). Recognition memory in 3–4 day old human neonates. *Neuroreport, 5,* 1721–1724.

Paulesu, E., Harrison, J., Baron-Cohen, S., Watson, J., Goldstein, L., Heather, J., Frackowiak, R., & Frith, C. (1995). The physiology of coloured-hearing: A PET activation study of colour-word synesthesia. *Brain, 118,* 661–676.

Piaget, J. (1952). *The origins of intelligence in children.* New York: International University Press.

Pickens, J., Field, T., Nawrocki, T., Martinez, A., Soutollo, D., & Gonzalez, J. (1994). Full-term and preterm infants' perception of face-voice synchrony. *Infant Behavior and Development, 17,* 447–455.

Ramachandran, V.S., & Hubbard, E.M. (2001). Synaesthesia—A window into perception, thought and language. *Journal of Consciousness Studies, 8,* 3–34.

Rauschecker, J. (1995). Compensatory plasticity and sensory substitution in the cerebral cortex. *Trends in Neuroscience, 18*, 36–43.

Reardon, P., & Bushnell, E. W. (1988). Infants' sensitivity to arbitrary pairings of color and taste. *Infant Behavior and Development, 11*, 245–250.

Röder, B., Rösler, F., & Neville, H. (2000). Event-related potentials during auditory language processing in congenitally blind and sighted people. *Neuropsychologia, 38*, 1482–1502.

Röder, B., Sock, O., Bien, S., Neville, H., & Rösler, F. (2002). Speech processing activates visual cortex in congenitally blind humans. *European Journal of Neuroscience, 16*, 930–936.

Röder, B., Teder-Sälejärvi, W., Sterr, A., Rösler, F., Hillyard, S., & Neville, H. (1999). Improved auditory spatial tuning in blind humans. *Nature, 400*, 162–166.

Sadato, N., Pascual-Leone, A., Grafman, J., Deiber, M-P., Ibañez, V., & Hallett, M. (1998). Neural networks for Braille reading by the blind. *Brain, 121*, 1213–1229.

Sadato, N., Pascual-Leone, A., Grafman, J., Ibañez, V., Deiber, M., Dold, G., & Hallett, M. (1996). Activation of the primary visual cortex by Braille reading in blind subjects. *Nature, 380*, 526–528.

Schiltz, K., Trocha, K., Wieringa, B.M., Emrich, H.M., Johannes, S., & Münte, T. (1999). Neurophysiological aspects of synesthetic experience. *Journal of Neuropsychiatry and Clinical Neurosciences, 11*, 58–65.

Smith, L. B., & Sera, M.D. (1992). A developmental analysis of the polar structure of dimensions. *Cognitive Psychology, 24*, 99–142.

Steri, A. (1987). Tactile discrimination of shape and intermodal transfer in 2- to 3-month-old infants. *British Journal of Developmental Psychology, 5*, 213–220.

Steri, A., & Pêcheux, M.G. (1986). Vision-to-touch and touch-to-vision transfer of form in 5-month-old infants. *British Journal of Developmental Psychology, 4*, 161–167.

Stevens, S.S. (1957). On the psychophysical law. *Psychological Review, 64*, 153–181.

Sur, M., & Leamey, C. (2001). Development and plasticity of cortical areas and networks. *Nature Reviews Neuroscience, 2*, 251–262.

Turkewitz, G., Gardner, J., & Lewkowicz, D.J. (1984). Sensory/perceptual functioning during early infancy: The implications of a quantitative basis for responding. In G. Greenberg & E. Tobach (Eds.), *Behavioral evolution and integrative levels* (pp.167–195). Hillsdale, NJ: Erlbaum.

Tzourio-Mazoyer, N., de Schonen, S., Crivello, F., Reutter, B., Aujard, Y., & Mazoyer, B. (2002). Neural correlates of woman face processing by 2-month-old infants. *NeuroImage, 15*, 454–461.

Walker, P., & Smith, S. (1984). Stroop interference based on the synaesthetic qualities of auditory pitch. *Perception, 13*, 75–81.

Weeks, R., Horwitz, B., Aziz-Sultan, A., Tian, B., Wessinger, C., Cohen, L., Hallett, M., & Rauschecker, J. (2000). *Journal of Neuroscience, 20*, 2664–2672.

Wolff, P., Matsumiya, Y., Abrohms, I.F., van Velzer, C., & Lombroso, C.T. (1974). The effect of white noise on the somatosensory evoked responses in sleeping newborn infants. *Electroencephalography and Clinical Neurophysiology, 37,* 269–274.

Yaka, R., Yinon, U., & Wollberg, Z. (1999). Auditory activation of cortical visual areas in cats after early visual deprivation. *European Journal of Neuroscience, 11,* 1301–1312.

Zelazo, P.D. (1996). Towards a characterization of minimal consciousness. *New Ideas in Psychology, 14,* 63–80.

Zellner, D.A., Bartoli, A.M., & Eckard, R. (1991). Influence of color on odor identification and liking ratings. *American Journal of Psychology, 104,* 547–561.

Zellner, D.A., & Kautz, M.A. (1990). Color affects perceived odor intensity. *Journal of Experimental Psychology: Human Perception and Performance, 16,* 391–397.

11

Developmental Constraints on Theories of Synesthesia

Lawrence E. Marks and Eric C. Odgaard

W riting a chapter on the development of synesthesia poses a special difficulty. The difficulty stems largely from the paucity of scientific evidence that speaks directly to the origins and developmental time-course of synesthesia. To be sure, our understanding of basic processes in sensation and perception is substantial and continues to grow, and research in recent decades has considerably advanced our understanding of developmental processes in perception. Nevertheless, our understanding of sensory and perceptual development is incomplete, and, to the best of our knowledge, direct evidence about the development of synesthesia simply does not exist.

Given this absence of direct evidence, the central question we pose in this chapter is not what do we know of developmental processes in synesthesia, but instead, given what we do know about synesthesia and what has been surmised about the underlying mechanisms, how does this knowledge and how do these suppositions delimit the possible mechanisms and processes of its development? Given what we know about the neural, perceptual, and cognitive mechanisms of synesthesia, it is possible to assess the plausibility of several potential theories. And for each of these theories, it is possible in turn to determine the constraints on developmental processes imposed by the hypothesized neural, perceptual, and cognitive mechanisms, as well as the constraints that developmental processes impose on possible mechanisms of synesthesia.

Consequently, in the present chapter we use the following strategy. We start with several psychological and neurophysiological theories of synesthesia that have already been proposed and, using these theories as stepping stones, generate a set of plausible hypotheses about the development of synesthesia. We take this step because any theory of synesthesia must, explicitly or implicitly, entail a trajectory of developmental phenomena and processes. We also classify each theory of synesthesia by two criteria: (1) whether the theory posits the existence of a special mechanism, absent in nonsynesthetes, through which the synesthesia operates and (2) whether the theory is couched primarily in psychological, neuroanatomical, or neurophysiological terms.

Psychological theories of synesthesia operate on one of two principles: associative learning or failure of differentiation. Theories of associative learning try to explain synesthesia as the result of overlearned pairings of stimuli and the corresponding sensations. The theory essentially denies the uniqueness of synesthetic experiences by proposing that synesthesia derives from the same mechanisms of association that govern many other aspects of behavior, in nonsynesthetes as well as synesthetes. In its purely psychological form, associative theory postulates no special mechanism for synesthesia. Other chapters of this volume, however, outline a wealth of recent behavioral and neuroimaging data that contradict simple associative theories.

Theories of synesthesia that posit failure of differentiation stake a more serious claim, especially in light of the behavioral and neural evidence suggesting the uniqueness of synesthesia. Failure-of-differentiation theories propose that the syncretism characteristic of perception in infants and young children typically disappears with development, resulting in nonsynesthetic adolescents and adults, but fails to disappear in synesthetes (see Werner, 1940). In its modern form, failure of differentiation arises neuroanatomically. Maurer (1993; see Maurer & Mondloch, this volume) has proposed a strong version of this theory by suggesting that all infants may be synesthetic. All of the versions of failure-of-differentiation theories suffer, however, from a common problem: They fail to distinguish between the arousal of a concurrent sensory experience, which is the defining property of synesthetic perception, and the lack of, or breakdown in, modality-specific mechanisms for processing sensory information, which is quite a different matter. The activation of nonspecific neural mechanisms proposed to be typical of infants in their first months of life, for instance, could lead to strict monesthesia, a set of qualitatively singular perceptual experiences that would fail to specify the modality of the actual stimulus, rather than to synesthesia, the binding of an atypical stimulus dimension (or dimensions) to the perception of some class of stimuli.

Considerations of neural coactivation lead us to consider neurophysiological theories of synesthesia, some of which may entail special neuroanatomical structures. Each of the neurophysiological theories proposes a process through which different neural regions or loci, typically operating independently of one another in nonsynesthetes, actually communicate in synesthetes. Theories of leakage and cross-talk suggest that neural loci fail to segregate fully in synesthetes. To the extent that the failure of segregation results from the presence in synesthetes, but not in nonsynesthetes, of interneurons connecting these loci, the theory is neuroanatomical as well as neurophysiological. On the other hand, disinhibition theory, an alternative, suggests that such neural interconnections between disparate loci (or modules) that process information in different modalities or that process information about different dimensions of a single modality are present in everyone. In those of us who do not experience synesthesia, cross-talk between loci is inhibited. But in those who experience synesthesia, inhibition is suppressed or absent.

Thus, both classes of neural theories propose failures in the development of a sensory mechanism. One explicitly proposes that modalities fail to develop their normal specificity in response to particular stimuli; the other implicitly proposes that the brain fails to develop normal mechanisms for inhibiting intersensory interactions. Both classes of theory are best suited for a subset of types of synesthesia—specifically, for those kinds of synesthesia that involve coactivation of perceptual dimensions known to arise from activity in adjacent sites of neural processing, as, for example, in colored-digit synesthesia; both color and number shapes are processed in the fusiform gyrus. Unfortunately, these theories, as they have been elaborated so far, fail to account for, or even consider, the learning that must underlie the development of any sort of synesthesia that involves culturally specific artifacts, such as digits and letters. It is a truism that one cannot develop digit-color synesthesia without learning, first or concurrently, one's own culture's system of numerals. Further, these neural theories do not so plausibly explain other kinds of synesthesia, kinds that link sensations associated with inducers and concurrents that are processed in nonadjacent regions of the cortex. As the main body of this chapter makes clear, each of the existing theories suffers from considerable limits in its ability to explain all of the kinds of synesthesia observed. Below we summarize the main issues.

1. Associative learning in and of itself cannot explain synesthesia. The preponderance of evidence calls for explanations in terms of specific neuroanatomical structures and/or neurophysiological processes in synesthetes.

2. The current neuroanatomical and neurophysiological theories of synesthesia are incomplete to the extent that they fail to consider the role of learning in the development of synesthesia. Consider those kinds of synesthesia in which the inducers and concurrents are relatively simple—for instance, synesthesia in which the inducers are sounds whose critical parameters are such properties as frequency and intensity, and in which the concurrents are visual sensations varying in color. In these instances, the synesthesia might appear (though it need not appear) early in infancy, when processing of dimensions such as pitch, loudness, brightness, and color is already reasonably well established.

But when the inducers are cultural artifacts, such as letters, words, and numbers, the synesthesia obviously requires considerable learning implying that the synesthesia either develops in late infancy or early childhood or that synesthesia changes its phenomenal characteristics with development.

3. None of the anatomical or physiological theories adequately specifies the mechanism by which synesthesia arises. Assuming that the development of synesthesia rests on the presence of a special mechanism that primes the development of intramodal or intermodal connections, we need to ask, where in the nervous system does the mechanism reside, and how does it operate? If synesthesia reflects normal variations in neuroanatomy and/or neurophysiology, how do these variations come about? The absence of such critical components to these theories suggests just how much we have yet to learn.

4. Synesthesia comes in a great variety of types, when defined in terms of the stimuli that serve both as inducers (e.g., speech sounds, visual shapes) and the sensations that serve as concurrents (e.g., colors). Theories of synesthesia need to explain why, for example, inducers are so rarely tastes or smells or touches, and why concurrents are so often colors.

5. Synesthesia can vary enormously with regard to the intensity and complexity of the concurrents: Visual concurrents, for example, can range in intensity and specificity from a "sense" of a particular color to a kaleidoscopic montage of shifting forms, colors, and textures. Although the former might be explained in terms of relatively low-level processes, the very nature of the latter suggests that these synesthetic experiences are, in at least some instances, elaborated neurophysiologically through relatively high-level perceptual processes.

6. Finally, there is a distinction, often overlooked but likely crucial, between two kinds of synesthesia: intramodal or cross-dimensional synesthesia, where the inducer and concurrent belong to different dimensions of the same modality, and intermodal or cross-modal synesthesia, where the inducer and concurrent belong to different modalities. It is likely, or at least plausible, that intramodal synesthesia represents the outcome of processes that are specific to neural regions commonly coactivated in nonsynesthetic perception, with the perceptual attributes often colocated in time and space. By way of contrast, it is also plausible that different processes underlie intermodal synesthesia, where neural regions mediating the inducers and concurrents are less often coactivated, and when they are coactivated, are nevertheless spatially discontinuous.

To the extent that the phenomenological differences revealed in various types of synesthetic perception are correlated with differences in neuroanatomy and neurophysiology, these phenomenological differences may well reflect fundamental differences in the underlying mechanisms. To the extent this is so, current theories of synesthesia, and the processes of synesthetic development that these theories imply, will be inadequate. The theories are inadequate because they do not yet fully address the possibility, occasionally suggested in the past (e.g., Harrison, 2001; Mattingley, Rich, Yelland & Bradshaw, 2001) that synesthesia is not a singular entity. Instead, in our view, the realm of synesthesia probably constitutes a cluster of phenomenologically related but perhaps neurologically distinct phenomena.

Theories of Associative Learning

Although mechanisms of associative learning could plausibly account for synesthesia when learning is conjoined to specialized physiological mechanisms, in and of itself associative learning cannot. Consequently, our review of the pertinent evidence will be relatively brief. Some of the relevant evidence, reviewed in subsequent sections of this chapter and considered thoroughly in other chapters of this volume, implicates the presence in synesthetes of special anatomical structures and/or physiological processes that are absent in nonsynesthetes.

Associative theories of synesthesia first appeared more than a century ago (e.g., Calkins, 1893; Claparède, 1903), and, subsequently, several researchers sought to show, experimentally, the plausibility of association as a generative mechanism. It is notable, however, that most of the experimental studies date back half a century and more. The paucity of modern studies seeking to induce synesthesia through associative learning probably reflects the common view that associative theories are inadequate.[1]

Several experiments have used paradigms resembling those of Pavlovian conditioning to try to teach synesthesia to adults. Presumably, positive results would mean that synesthesia could result from processes of association, although positive results would not necessarily mean that synesthesia typically does. In any case, the issue is moot, to the extent that these attempts have been largely unsuccessful. In a typical study, a participant is exposed over and over to pairs of stimuli, each taken from a different sense modality. The question is whether, after thousands of such pairings, the presentation of one of the stimuli elicits a conditioned sensation associated with the other. In perhaps the first such study, Kelly (1934) paired colors with musical notes. Extensive experience on the part of 18 participants with several color–note combinations led the participants to learn the associations, but with no evidence that the participants actually saw colors in the presence of the notes.

A similar conclusion may be drawn from results of an experimentally more elegant study by Howells (1944), in which repeated conjunctions of colors with musical notes affected color responses to the notes, but again without clear evidence that the notes induced color sensations (as opposed, say, to inducing conditioned or cued verbal responses). In related studies of conditioned hallucinations (Ellson, 1941a, 1941b) and imagery (Leuba, 1940; Leuba & Dunlap, 1951), participants did report sensory experiences, but the characteristics of the resulting experiences were not those of synesthesia. The same can be said of more recent efforts (Stevenson, Boakes & Prescott, 1998) in which participants learned to associate taste qualities to certain odorants, but (despite the authors' claims of success) without clearly demonstrating any synesthesia.

Aside from occasional instances in which it arises as a result of neural insult or injury, there is general consensus that synesthesia arises spontaneously in childhood (e.g., Cytowic, 2002; Harrison & Baron-Cohen, 1997; Marks, 1975). To the best of our knowledge, however, there is no evidence that most synesthetes, as infants or young children, are exposed on hundreds or thousands of occasions to the same pairs of stimuli in different modalities, or to the same paired attributes of stimuli in different dimensions of the same modality. Perhaps some children can learn to associate disparate sensations exceedingly rapidly, but there is no evidence that this is characteristic of all children. This may be true of that small fraction of infants or children who develop synesthesia, but then we need to ask, what is special about these infants or children that allows them to develop synesthesia? The answer to this question leads, in turn, to the speculation that a specific anatomical or physiological condition early in life directs a small fraction of the population to develop synesthesia. If so, then the specific characteristics of each synesthete's typically idiosyncratic experiences presumably depend nevertheless on some kinds of experience and perhaps on experienced associations. This is to say that, in addition to the appropriate mechanisms of association or learning, it is necessary to postulate a special anatomical mechanism or physiological process, possibly with a critical time period for the development of synesthesia.

Theories of Failed Differentiation

Where theories of associative learning claim that the mechanism underlying synesthesia is not unique to synesthetes, the preponderance of evidence supports just the opposite contention: that synesthesia, in most if not all cases, results from the presence of specialized neural structures or processes that are different from the structures or processes found in individuals lacking synesthesia. A neuroanatomical theory, and an explicitly developmental one at that, has been offered by Maurer (1993; see also Maurer & Mondloch, this volume). This theory casts in modern terms the suggestion, made earlier by Werner (1940), that synesthesia is an early, ontogenetically primitive form of perception. Maurer speculates that the perceptual world of infants (of all infants), is synesthetic—that convergent pathways in the sensory nervous system are responsible for producing an early state or stage of synesthesia, one that, in most people, disappears subsequently with development, as the nervous system prunes away those neurons responsible for multisensory convergence (see Edelman, 1987). With this pruning, individual modalities develop their specificity, and as specificity increases, synesthesia disappears. In a small number of infants, however, pruning is incomplete, and the synesthetic state, though perhaps reduced over time in prominence, continues nevertheless into childhood and adulthood.

Maurer's (1993) theory has a couple of clear strengths: For one, it posits an explicit process for the development of synesthesia (or, more precisely, for the development of nonsynesthesia), as the theory directly explains why most people lose the synesthesia of their infancy, and only indirectly if at all why a few maintain it. For another, Maurer's theory recognizes the need for an explanation that is explicitly neural to account for the difference between normal perception and synesthetic perception. Nonetheless, the theory suffers from three important limitations, a couple of which it shares with other current neuroanatomical and neurophysiological theories.

First, and unique to this theory, is its implication that synesthesia represents the basic state of infant perception, a state that results from convergence of inputs originating in receptors of different modalities. In support of this view, besides neurophysiological evidence of convergence (see Hoffman, 1978; Wolff, Matsumiya, Abrohms, van Velzer & Lombroso, 1974), is the behavioral evidence that young infants can respond similarly to stimuli in different modalities (e.g., to increases in the brightness of lights and the loudness of sounds; Lewkowicz & Turkewitz, 1980), a finding that could be explained by assuming neural units that receive multisensory inputs. Unfortunately, such a mechanism does not necessarily predict synesthesia—the evocation of concurrent sensations characteristic of another modality, in addition to the sensations appropriate to the stimulated modality.

The hypothesis of complete convergence of sensory inputs would predict one or another kind of monesthesia, where stimuli presented to different modalities would be confused because the stimuli all produced a common sensory response. This could happen either because stimulation of different modalities produced the same (singular) sensory experience or because it produced the same melange of qualities representing all modalities. An analogue to the former is found in the phenomenon of cone monochromacy, a condition of total color blindness in which different cone receptors are present, but their outputs converge onto a single channel that provides information about luminosity, or differences in light intensity, but provide no usable information about color *per se* or differences in wavelength. Similarly, neural units responding willy-nilly to sounds and lights would signal the presence of a stimulus, either a sound or a light, but need not confer visual attributes to auditory sensations or vice versa.

To maintain the two main tenets of the theory of failed differentiation—first, the notion that synesthesia characterizes the perceptual experiences of young infants, and second, the notion that most infants cast off their synesthesia in development, although a few maintain it—a more plausible version would graft multisensory coactivation onto modality-specific processing. That is, the theory could posit that early infancy is marked by a combination of specificity and lack of differentiation (consistent with the range of observations suggesting that infants sometimes do but other times do not seem to respond to modality-specific attributes of stimuli). Thus, the existence of modality-specific systems would permit the infant to perceive the unique qualities of each sense modality, while multisensory convergence might produce a melange of somewhat weaker sensory qualities appropriate to all the other modalities (the second version of monesthesia). In this fashion, infants would experience synesthesia, although their synesthesia would not necessarily resemble the various kinds of synesthesia observed in older children or adults.

Even if a theory of failed differentiation could account for synesthesia, it would still suffer from two weaknesses (although it should be noted that other neuroanatomical and neurophysiological theories fare no better in these respects). For one, the theory of failed differentiation needs to explain, as do other theories, why synesthesia takes on the particular forms that it does. As already indicated, certain kinds of synesthesia, such as visual hearing and colored words, letters, and numerals, occur relatively often (that is, relative to other types of synesthesia), though no kind occurs often in the population at large (see Day, this volume). Synesthesia involving taste, smell, and touch, however, is relatively uncommon. Still lacking is a cogent explanation as to why this should be so.

Second, and in our view of even greater theoretical importance, the theory of failed differentiation, like other theories, does not explain why synesthesia often involves stimuli whose properties are learned, and often learned rather slowly at that. For example, a common form of intermodal synesthesia involves visual hearing, in which acoustic stimuli (acoustic inducers) produce visual sensations (or concurrents) as well as auditory sensations. In many auditory–visual synesthetes, sounds of speech or of music produce characteristic colors or visual shapes (see Baron-Cohen, Wyke & Binnie, 1987; Carroll & Greenberg, 1961; Harrison & Baron-Cohen, 1995; Nunn et al., 2002; Podoll & Robinson, 2002). Yet the attribution of individual colors to phonemes or words or notes of the modern Western musical scale must follow, or coincide with, learning the language or the musical scale. The most that can be said is that the anatomical structures connecting regions processing information in different modalities must be capable of supporting the particular, often idiosyncratic, patterns of association between inducers and concurrents. Even granting that all young infants are synesthetic, and granting further that some of them remain synesthetic into childhood and beyond, then, in many cases, the nature of their synesthesia must change over time. That is, the synesthesia of adults would often differ markedly from the putative synesthesia of infancy.

A similar weakness characterizes explanations of intramodal synesthesia, for example, forms of synesthesia in which visually presented words, letters, or numbers elicit specific and often unique colors (see Dixon, Smilek, Cudahy & Merikle, 2000; Mattingley et al., 2001; Odgaard, Flowers & Bradman, 1999; Palmeri, Blake, Marois, Flanery & Whetsell, 2002; Ramachandran & Hubbard, 2001). The reading of words, letters, and numbers develops even more slowly, in general, than does aural language.

In this context, it is important to distinguish those cases of synesthesia that depend on the particular perceptual characteristics of an inducing stimulus (e.g., the printed Arabic numeral 7) and the meaning or conception of the stimulus (e.g., the concept of "seven"-ness; see Grossenbacher & Lovelace, 2001, for a distinction between perceptual and conceptual synesthesia). In the case of perceptual letter–color or number–color synesthesia, induction might perhaps arise through the activation of neurons that process elementary properties of the numbers or letters, such as their shape or contour, independent of the meaning of the stimuli (in adults, contours are processed in layers of the striate cortex that seem not to depend on the symbolic meanings of the stimuli).

It is conceivable, though to us implausible, that this kind of perceptual synesthesia is present before the age of 2 years or so—that is, before the age at which few children, even precocious ones, identify very many letters and numbers. For letter–color or number–color synesthesia to arise much earlier than this, infants would either be born with well-developed regions of visual cortex dedicated to identifying numbers and letters or a propensity for these regions to develop rapidly postpartum. To be sure, even very young infants and children may be exposed to blocks or mobiles, which could provide a basis for learning to identify letters or numbers. Yet it is also the case that much of what is called early reading (identification) is contextual, and even at 4 years of age, the ability to identify letters or match letters to their names is far from perfect (Share & Gur, 1999).

Theories of Sensory Cross-talk or Leakage

Central to theories of failed differentiation is the notion that synesthesia is characteristic of perception early in infancy. Subsequently, this early synesthesia disappears in most infants as individual sensory modalities complete their functional differentiation. Theories that seek to explain synesthesia in terms of neural cross-talk or leakage, in contrast, do not make these assertions (although a variant of cross-talk theory makes a related claim). Nevertheless, every theory of synesthesia entails or implies a developmental mechanism or process in perception that differs in synesthetes and nonsynesthetes. Unlike the theory of failed differentiation, theories of cross-talk maintain that individual sensory and perceptual modalities have substantially normal developmental courses in everyone, synesthetes and nonsynesthetes alike. What distinguishes synesthetes from nonsynesthetes, according to cross-talk theories, is the presence in synesthetes of an additional neural mechanism, or a change in the operation of a mechanism that is present in nonsynesthetes, too (although advocates of cross-talk theories have yet to specify just what this mechanism is, or how it operates).

Theories of sensory cross-talk assert that synesthesia results when inducing stimuli activate not only the neural system primarily associated with those stimuli but also, secondarily, through cross-talk or leakage, a neural system that typically processes qualities of another modality (or another dimension of the same modality). In colored-hearing synesthesia, for example, a spoken word not only activates all of the usual mechanisms of hearing but also visual subsystems involved in color perception. In colored-digit synesthesia, an achromatic visual stimulus presented in the form of a numeral activates not only the visual mechanisms involved in shape perception, and perhaps conceptual systems of the meanings of numbers, but also a numeral-specific chromatic mechanism. We consider here three cross-talk theories, each of which asserts that synesthesia results from a physiological process unique to this small fraction of the population.

Theories of Neuroanatomical Linkage

The first cross-talk theory has been offered most recently by Ramachandran and Hubbard (2001), and it postulates the presence, unique in synesthetes, of a neural structure or neural structures responsible for cross-talk. According to this anatomical–physiological theory, synesthetes possess neural pathways absent in nonsynesthetes, through which excitatory signals produced by inducers ultimately lead to concurrent sensations.

This idea has been conceptualized somewhat differently in a second theory, offered by Grossenbacher (1997; Grossenbacher & Lovelace, 2001). Grossenbacher proposes that synesthesia may arise in one of three different ways within his model of perceptual processing, characterized by feedforward and feedback connections in a set of hierarchical stages (e.g., Fellerman & Van Essen, 1991). Visual stimuli, for example, are first processed in terms of rudimentary attributes of stimulus dimensions, with signals flowing from converging receptive fields in the eyes to discrete regions of the striate cortex.

After these relatively direct processes of feature detection and delimitation, information about the stimulus is fed forward to progressively higher visual centers responsible for object recognition and more complex scene analysis. Concurrent with forward transmission is feedback activation, which serves as a kind of redundancy check on the system (and, presumably, as a way to explain phenomena such as priming). Grossenbacher suggests that synesthesia may occur as the result of what he calls "horizontal" transmission within this hierarchy, at one of three points: directly from the point at which the inducer is identified to the point at which the concurrent is aroused (e.g., a tone is identified as middle C, but also shifts to the visual channel and activates "green"); by feedforward activation (as middle C, once identified, is added to auditory scene analysis, signals also feed forward to the scene-level stage of color processing); or by additional feedback (in the example, signals from the musical scene analysis feed back to the stage of pitch identification). Undecided as to exactly how the cross-talk occurs, Grossenbacher is also noncommittal thus far whether the synesthetic signal constitutes the addition of coactivation (essentially, the neuroanatomical theory) or a failure of inhibition (disinhibition theory, as described below).

Theories of Disinhibition

A third cross-talk theory asserts that the nervous system of everyone contains interneurons or other pathways connecting neural regions that normally process information in distinct modalities (and in separate dimensions within modalities). In nonsynesthetes, any neural activity in these pathways is normally inhibited. In synesthetes, however, there is disinhibition (the usual inhibition is inhibited or eliminated), leading to coactivation of concurrents in a secondary modality or dimension. Thus, theories of disinhibition postulate no special neural hardware in synesthetes; instead, the theory claims that cross-talk would otherwise take place in the cortex of everyone, but is actively inhibited in the vast majority of the population (i.e., in nonsynesthetes). Under this hypothesis, synesthesia arises from failure or suppression of the inhibitory mechanism. Ramachandran and Hubbard (2003; see also this volume) have recently updated their theory to suggest disinhibition as a possible mechanism of synesthesia.

Note that it is possible to wed disinhibition theory to the theory of failed differentiation. In this amalgam, infancy would be characterized by synesthetic perception because of the presence of intermodal or interdimensional neural pathways whose activation induces synesthesia; this synesthesia would add to modality-specific perception. Under this premise, synesthesia disappears from infant perception not because of pruning of multisensory neurons but because of the development of inhibitory processes that come to suppress the cross-talk and hence the synesthesia. The theory of developmental disinhibition fares better than the theory of failed differentiation in that disinhibition theory directly predicts synesthesia rather than variants of monesthesia. Further, the development of inhibitory processes might go hand in glove with processes involved in learning cultural artifacts (words, letters, numbers). To the best of our knowledge, however, no one has attempted to elaborate a theory of this sort.

As we suggested earlier, all theories of synesthesia, including cross-talk theory, ultimately need to say something about development. Given the reasonable assumption that the putative neural pathways that connect modalities (or dimensions of a modality) and thereby subserve synesthesia do not sprout during development, these pathways must be present at birth or soon thereafter, though perhaps not functionally. This consideration constrains possible developmental trajectories of synesthesia. (1) According to the anatomical–physiological cross-talk theory, the pathways in question may be present at or near birth in those individuals destined to become synesthetic, but do not begin to operate until later in development—perhaps when appropriate mechanisms of associative learning operate. (2) According to disinhibition theory, the pathways are present perinatally in everyone and, according to the developmental variant of the theory, are also functional perinatally in everyone; eventually, these pathways become inactive (inhibited) in most older infants, but they continue to be active and functional in that small proportion who remain synesthetic. (3) Alternatively, although perhaps implausibly, the pathways hypothesized to be responsible for synesthesia might be largely inhibited (inactive) early in development in everyone, but for some unknown reason become disinhibited (and thus active) later in those who become synesthetic. Unfortunately, there are no data to shed direct light on any of these conjectures.

Strengths and Weaknesses

All the versions of cross-talk theory are consistent with two pieces of evidence. First, like other theories that seek to explain synesthesia neurophysiologically, these theories treat it as a real perceptual phenomenon. In doing this, cross-talk theories are compatible with findings from a growing body of carefully crafted studies using sophisticated behavioral paradigms and methods of neuroimaging. These studies (considered extensively throughout this volume, and sketched below) indicate that synesthesia in fact represents more than just the outcome of associative learning. Second, these theories are especially cogent in those cases of synesthesia in which the coactivated neural regions are physically contiguous. For example, because adjacent neural regions of visual cortex are activated during the processing of numbers and colors (both located in the fusiform gyrus), it is plausible that color–digit synesthesia arises from cross-talk between these two regions (Ramachandran & Hubbard, 2001).

Disinhibition theories have an additional strength: Disinhibition is uniquely suited to account for examples of adventitious synesthesia—that is, synesthesia that arises late in development, either as a result of brain injury or from ingesting psychotropic substances (see Bors, 1979; Goldenberg, Mullbacher & Nowak, 1995; Jacobs, Karpik, Bozian & Gothgen, 1981; Jacome, 1999; Vike, Jabbari & Maitland, 1984). None of the physiological theories that hinges on an anatomical difference between the brains of synesthetes and nonsynesthetes (i.e., neither the theory of failed differentiation nor the theory of unique anatomical pathways) can account for the sudden appearance of synesthesia in individuals who previously lacked it. Theories that account for synesthesia in terms of failure, via suppression or injury, of inhibitory processes, in contrast, could account for both developmental and adventitious synesthesia, although these theories would still have to explain functional differences, such as the tendency of percepts in adventitious synesthesia to be less consistent over time.

Despite the strengths of cross-talk theories, however, these theories also have their limitations and weaknesses. For one, much of the pertinent evidence comes from neuroimaging, and although this evidence supports the perceptual reality of synesthesia and suggests the possibility of coactivation, it sheds no direct light on the underlying processes. Evidence of actual cross-talk is still lacking. Second, cross-talk theories lend themselves most readily to explaining intramodal synesthesia, as in the induction of colors by numerals, when the dimensions are processed in neurally adjacent sites. But the theories become less cogent when trying to account for synesthesia involving inducers and concurrents that are processed in physically noncontiguous, and distant, regions of the cortex. Though cross-talk might apply in these cases, too, it seems less plausible to assume interconnections between, say, regions processing vocal speech, touch, and color (to explain such examples as the "crumbly yellow voice" reported in the synesthete S. by Luria, 1968) or between regions processing taste and geometrical shape (Cytowic & Wood, 1982). Examples such as these might lend themselves better to accounts of synesthesia couched in terms of network processes, rather than explicit connections between quasi-modular neural entities.

A notable property of synesthesia is that it is typically unidirectional (e.g., numbers may elicit colors, but colors do not elicit numbers), yet none of the theories explains very well, if at all, why this should be so. If numbers synesthetically induce sensations of colors by way of cross-talk between regions in the cortex, for example, then why do colors not also induce synesthetic sensations of number? Grossenbacher (1997; Grossenbacher & Lovelace, 2001) argues that the model of feedforward and feedback pathways can account for unidirectionality, but this account only restates the issue (if stages of hierarchical processing are connected through both feedforward and feedback channels, then there seems little reason not to predict bidirectionality in synesthesia). If synesthesia results from a mechanism that permits communication between two (or more) neural sites, we still do not know what properties of the mechanism are responsible for the one-way traffic, or how specific inducers connect to specific concurrents (e.g., a given numeral to a given color).

When color is induced synesthetically by an achromatically presented numeral, such as 2, it is often the case that many different exemplars of the numeral suffice. That is, concurrent color sensations may be evoked by numerals printed in various sizes and styles. What seems to matter is not the particular size or shape of a visual feature, but the appropriate categorization of the visual stimulus. This implicit reliance on categorization holds even if the inducers of the synesthesia are limited to Arabic printed numerals presented visually, as reported by Ramachandran and Hubbard (2001). In some instances, however, the categories that serve as effective inducers of synesthetic colors are much broader than this, consisting of Roman as well as Arabic numerals—indeed, even of numbers simply imagined or computed (Dixon et al., 2000). In the latter circumstances, the cortical processes that underlie the perception, or conception, of the inducers might be widespread or multifarious, making cross-talk rather awkward as an explanatory mechanism. In this regard, note that many of the cases of synesthesia studied in recent years, perhaps the majority of them, have used inducing stimuli that we term "cultural artifacts"—stimuli such as numerals, letters, and words. Stimuli of this sort are perceived and comprehended only after extensive learning and experience, and, implicitly or explicitly, learning their meanings often reflects the imposition of categorical structures on a variety of sensory inputs. Not only learning but concept formation undoubtedly plays a signal role in the development of many cases of synesthesia.

Constraints on Future Theories

In this review of theories of synesthesia, we have tried to make one central point: To be comprehensive as well as coherent, a theory of synesthesia needs to address two main issues: (1) the range and characteristics of intermodal and intramodal synesthesia, including the modalities and dimensions involved, as well as the specificity and unidirectionality, (2) the processes that lead to synesthesia's development, including the role of learning. No theory of synesthesia is yet sufficiently detailed to address these issues.

No theory sufficiently accounts for all the varieties of synesthesia; synesthesia may involve different modalities (often hearing and vision, but sometimes taste, smell, touch, or pain) or different dimensions of the same modality (in vision, letters, words, or numerals and colors). Further, none is sufficiently elaborated that it can account for the developmental processes that lead to these varieties of synesthesia. Associative learning theories are clearly inadequate to the extent that they deny the considerable evidence indicating that synesthesia rests on the presence of some kind of special physiological mechanism. Theories of failed differentiation and cross-talk suffer from several deficiencies, but share two major weaknesses. Both fail to account for the specificity and unidirectionality of inducer-concurrent relations (why inducers produce the specific concurrent sensations that they do and why, in a given individual, the synesthesia operates in one direction but not in the reverse). And both theories are incomplete, lacking a fundamental mechanism—in the case of failed differentiation, a mechanism explaining why synesthesia is maintained beyond early infancy, and in the case of cross-talk, a mechanism explaining how synesthesia develops.

It may very well be (indeed, it seems likely) that all these issues are ultimately related, that the mechanisms underlying the range of synesthesia, as well as its specificity, directionality, and development, are linked to synesthesia's unique anatomical structures or physiological processes. In the face of these considerations, we do not offer a theory of our own. Indeed, we would like to suggest, following others (Harrison, 2001; Marks, 2000; Mattingley et al., 2001) that synesthesia simply may not lend itself to a single, unified and unifying, theoretical conceptualization. It seems to us likely that several theoretical frameworks will be required to encompass all of the kinds of synesthesia. In short, synesthesia may dull Occam's razor.

Synesthesia: Simple and Complex

Although, as should be clear, synesthesia can take on diverse forms, a good deal of recent research on synesthesia has focused on cases that, for lack of a better word, may be described as "simple." That is, recent studies have generally applied behavioral paradigms or methods of neuroimaging to synesthetes who report either sensing or experiencing relatively formless percepts of color, usually in response to a sound, a digit, or a letter. As Grossenbacher (1997) has noted, however, these kinds of simple inducer-concurrent relations hardly suffice to characterize the full range of synesthesia. Synesthetes commonly report relations between many sets of inducers and concurrents. An example appears in Luria's (1968) account of the synesthestic experiences of the mnemonist S. V. Sherashevsky, who reported inducers and concurrents in all modalities. Further, the concurrent experiences were not always simple ones—as when he reported that a loud tone produced the taste of a 'briny pickle.' It is not uncommon among synesthetes to experience, for example, both sound–color and digit–color synesthesia.

Even in those individuals who experience only a single kind of synesthesia, say, where auditory inducers produce visual concurrents, the concurrents can vary considerably in perceptual complexity. Theories of synesthesia have given short shrift to the implications of this variety. Where one synesthete may experience rather undifferentiated colors when she hears a name spoken, another may report complex patterns of shape, color, and form. One might speculate, for example, that the experience of undifferentiated color in response to a word, digit, or letter may result from relatively low-level sensory processes (e.g., Ramachandran & Hubbard, 2001). Low-level sensory processes seem inadequate to account for the ways that a simple musical melody may induce a montage of visual forms, forms that change their color, size, and shape over time. Complex patterns of synesthetic concurrents, in our view, call for an even richer explanatory scheme, presumably one involving sequences of events in higher level regions of sensory and perceptual processing.

Modalities and Dimensions of Synesthesia

One of the most striking aspects of synesthesia is its diversity. Not only is synesthesia diverse in the exact pairings of inducers and concurrents (to a given synesthete, the numeral 2 may be red, to another green, and to still another brown), but synesthesia is also diverse with regard to modalities. Nevertheless, not all possible kinds of synesthesia occur equally often. First, in the great majority of cases the inducing stimuli are visual or auditory. Speech, other acoustic stimuli such as music, and various visual stimuli serve far more often as inducers than do tastes or smells or touches. This imbalance is at least as great if not greater in the distribution of concurrents. With colored hearing, colored words, colored letters, colored graphemes, and colored digits accounting for the lion's share of cases, colors make up by far the most common perceptual concurrent. Thus, the visual modality is implicated most often in synesthesia, with hearing next (see Day, this volume). We still lack cogent explanations why this should be so.

Synesthesia is also notable with regard to the combinations of inducers and concurrents that appear only rarely or not at all. To be sure, some combinations of modalities are especially rare (for instance, touch stimuli virtually never produce concurrents of smell). But even more striking are the limited kinds of intramodal synesthesia, in which both the inducer and the concurrent are characteristic of the same sensory modality. Two garden types of synesthesia, colored digits (where the inducer may be a numeral) and colored language (where the inducer may be a grapheme or a word) highlight this sort of intramodal activation, in that a visually presented stimulus induces a concurrent in another visual dimension. In the next section we address the matter of intramodal versus intermodal synesthesia. Here, the question of interest is why intramodal synesthesia seems absent from modalities other than vision. Why, for example, do we not find cases of synesthesia in which tones induce auditory concurrents that vary in timbre, or speech sounds induce auditory concurrents that vary in pitch? Or, to put it another way, why should visual dimensions be uniquely amenable to intramodal synesthesia?[2]

Intramodal versus Intermodal Synesthesia

On several occasions in this chapter, we subdivided synesthesia into intramodal and intermodal—distinguishing forms of synesthesia in which the inducers and concurrents reflect different dimensions of a single modality from those in which inducers and concurrents reflect different modalities entirely. In this section, we focus on the implications of this distinction for the mechanisms of synesthesia.

Speaking most broadly, intramodal synesthesia and intermodal synesthesia are similar on a basic, phenomenological level; in both, an inducing stimulus produces concurrents, either in a different dimension of the same modality or in another modality. Further, the evidence at hand suggests that, in both types of synesthesia, the induction of concurrents occurs through coactivation of neural regions that normally process the concurrents. Despite this broad commonality, there is a curious difference, perhaps theoretically significant, between the two kinds of synesthesia, a difference that is related to what we may loosely call the "binding" between the dimensions or modalities.

To start, we note that intermodal synesthesia is, ipso facto, a kind of multisensory perception—but very different from the kind of multisensory perception that goes on much of the time in normal (nonsynesthetic) experience. When we see and hear a person speaking, for instance, the nervous system normally integrates or binds the visual perception of movements of the lips with the auditory perception of phonetic and acoustic structure, such that mismatches may lead to multisensory integration, as in the McGurk effect (McGurk and MacDonald 1976). Spatial and temporal congruities seem requisite to this binding; certainly, many auditory and visual signals that we experience in daily life are not bound and integrated but sorted out and distinguished. In much of day-to-day multisensory perception, binding occurs when stimuli activating different modalities provide information about common stimulus events or objects. Intermodal synesthesia also involves binding, here of concurrents to inducers, but in most cases there is no environmental connection between the concurrents and inducers. Certainly, one is hard pressed to find the ecological commonality between tones or spoken words and colors. On the physiological side of this coin, intermodal synesthesia presumably occurs when an inducer produces coactivation in neural regions processing stimulus dimensions that are not frequently bound in normal multisensory perception.

The situation is rather different in the case of intramodal synesthesia. Although individual graphemes or digits are not generally associated with unique colors in the world, the dimensions of shape and color co-occur consistently. Objects in visual experiences have shapes, and colors inhere in these shapes (even the achromatic series contains colors, which run from black through gray to white). In this sense, intramodal synesthesia typically involves the activation of sensory or perceptual qualities in dimensions that are bound in space and time far more regularly than are the corresponding dimensions of intermodal synesthesia. Shape and color are spatially and temporally bound far more consistently, for instance, than are pitch and color. So theories of intermodal synesthesia may need to explain communication between neural mechanisms that only occasionally produce binding, whereas theories of intramodal synesthesia need to explain communication between neural mechanisms that typically do.[3]

Role of Learning

We began this review of synesthesia with evidence contravening the hypothesis that its source lies solely in associative learning. It is therefore perhaps fitting that, as we near the end, by a commodius vicus of recirculation, we return to the topic of learning. We do this to point out the necessary role that learning must play in any theory of synesthesia if the theory is to be successful. Despite the telling evidence against theories of associative learning per se, it strikes us as axiomatic that learning must play a prominent role in any theory of synesthesia, given how often synesthetic inducers consist of cultural artifacts such as words, names, letters, digits, units of time, or days of the week.

The learning of these cultural artifacts, as we term them, comes primarily, indeed, virtually exclusively, through language. This is not at all to say that linguistic mechanisms themselves mediate synesthesia. To the contrary, studies using neuroimaging show no clear evidence of linguistic mediation (see Aleman, Rutten Stiskoorn, Dautzenberg & Ramsey, 2001; Nunn et al., 2002; Paulesu et al., 1995), whereas, on the other hand, there is good reason to believe that perceptual mechanisms are responsible (Dixon et al., 2000;

Odgaard et al., 1999), at least, for those kinds of synesthesia that arise when the inducer is an external stimulus event (we remain agnostic regarding the mechanisms that underlie synesthesia when, say, a synesthete merely thinks about a word or letter or digit). Nevertheless, the organizational properties of synesthesia arise through early experiences, for it is these experiences that make it possible for the young child to learn, identify, and categorize words, letters, and numbers. Two points are important. First, these experiences presumably interact with whatever anatomical or physiological propensity may exist for synesthesia, and this interaction in turn lies at the heart of synesthesia's developmental time course. Language skills most likely begin to develop at some point in the first year of life (see Dehaene-Lambertz, Dehaene & Hertz-Pannier, 2002), early but well after the initial postnatal period of sensory confusion suggested as a period of synesthesia by Maurer (1993).

Reading, of course, generally comes much later, even in precocious youngsters, with the visual identification of letters, words, and numbers developing over a period of years, leading to our second point: that the developmental time course of language skills is substantial. These points imply that synesthesia may itself develop rather slowly, over a period of years, concurrently with acquisition of the necessary cultural artifacts. Alternatively, if synesthesia develops rapidly, then it may not come on stage until later in childhood, perhaps in the third, fourth, or fifth year of life, after the synesthetic child has acquired at least a basic mastery of the pertinent letters, words, numbers, and so on. Finally, synesthesia might make its first appearance very early, within the first year postpartum, but change its properties or characteristics as the young child comes into increasing contact with the rich world of stimulus events around her. This last explanation leaves open the possibility that synesthesia is indeed a typical state of infant perception, but at the cost of raising the questions as to how the senses remain linked to one another prior to and through the course of transformation and what mechanisms bring about the changes.

Acknowledgment   Preparation of this chapter was supported in part by National Institutes of Health (NIH) grant R01 DC00271-17 to L.E.M. and NIH postdoctoral fellowship F32 DC00463-03 to E.C.D.

Notes

1. Several examples of what has been termed "weak synesthesia" (Martino & Marks, 2001) probably do arise from learned associations. Weak synesthesia refers to the appreciation, evident in most people, of similarities between qualities of experience in different modalities. A well-known example is the attribution of warmth to red, orange, and brown colors and coolness to blue and green. Another example is the association of high-pitched sounds with small visual stimuli and low-pitched sounds with large ones. Although widely acknowledged

by adults, children do not spontaneously associate lower pitch with larger size (Marks, Hammeal & Bornstein, 1987) or red and orange versus blue and green colors with warm and cool sensations (Morgan, Goodson & Jones, 1975). Color–temperature and pitch–size associations appear to come from experience (with objects that glow when heated and with objects that resonate at lower frequencies the larger their size). The developmental time-course of these examples of weak synesthesia differs markedly from the time-course of strong perceptual synesthesia considered in this chapter.

2. It is important to distinguish synesthesia (where an inducer automatically produces the experience of a qualitatively different concurrent) from other phenomena that may seem perceptually akin to synesthesia but likely depend on rather different underlying neural mechanisms. Two examples are strong imagery, which occurs much more voluntarily than synesthesia, and phantom limb experiences, which involve mislocalized percepts of touch, pain, or position, presumably resulting from neural reorganization in the wake of the loss of the limb.

3. In this regard, we note that the visual dimensions found in cross-dimensional synesthesia are generally "separable" ones, in Garner's (1974) terms. Although the features of shape (or the meaning of the shape) and color are typically linked physically in a unitary visual stimulus, one can process the shape or grapheme or numeral more or less independently of its color, and vice versa. Some dimensions, such as the hue, saturation, and brightness of colors, however, cannot be processed independently of one another; these dimensions, said by Garner to be integral, are bound perceptually each to each in yet another way. But intramodal synesthesia does not seem to rely on color dimensions as both inducers and concurrents: We know of no cases of synesthesia in which, for instance, different colors induce different brightnesses.

References

Aleman, A., Rutten, G., Stiskoorn, M.M., Dautzenberg, G., & Ramsey, N.F. (2001). Activation of striate cortex in the absence of visual stimulation: an fMRI study of synesthesia. *NeuroReport, 12,* 2827–2830.

Baron-Cohen, S., Wyke, M.A., & Binnie, C. (1987). Hearing words and seeing colours: An experimental investigation of a case of synaesthesia. *Perception, 16,* 761–767.

Bors, E. (1979). Extinction and synesthesia in patients with spinal cord injuries. *Paraplegia, 17,* 21–31.

Calkins, M.W. (1893). A statistical study of pseudo-chromesthesia and of mental forms. *American Journal of Psychology, 5,* 439–464.

Carroll, J.B., & Greenberg, J.H. (1961). Two cases of synesthesia for color and musical tonality associated with absolute pitch ability. *Perceptual and Motor Skills, 13,* 48.

Claparède, E. (1903). Persistance de l'audition colorée. *Compte Rendus de la Société de Biologie, 55,* 1257–1259.

Cytowic, R.E. (2002). *Synesthesia: A union of the senses.* Cambridge, MA: MIT Press.

Cytowic, R.E., & Wood, F.B. (1982). Synesthesia II: Psychophysical relations in the synesthesia of geometrically shaped taste and colored hearing. *Brain and Cognition, 1,* 36–49.

Dehaene-Lambertz, G., Dehaene, S., & Hertz-Pannier, L. (2002). Functional neuroimaging of speech perception in infants. *Science, 298,* 2013–2015.

Dixon, M.J., Smilek, D., Cudahy, C., & Merikle, P.M. (2000). Five plus two equals yellow. *Nature, 406,* 365.

Edelman, G.M. (1987). *Neural Darwinism: The theory of neuronal group selection.* New York: Basic Books.

Ellson, D.G. (1941a). Experimental extinction of an hallucination produced by sensory conditioning. *Journal of Experimental Psychology, 28,* 350–361.

Ellson, D.G. (1941b). Hallucinations produced by sensory conditioning. *Journal of Experimental Psychology, 28,* 1–20.

Fellerman, D.J., & Van Essen, D.C. (1991). Distributed hierarchical processing in the primate cerebral cortex. *Cerebral Cortex, 1,* 1–47.

Garner, W.R. (1974). *The processing of information and structure.* Potomac, MD: Erlbaum.

Goldenberg, G., Mullbacher, W., & Nowak, A. (1995). Imagery without perception —A case study of anosognosia for cortical blindness. *Neuropsychologia, 33,* 1373–1382.

Grossenbacher, P. (1997). Perception and sensory information in synaesthetic experience. In S. Baron-Cohen & J. Harrison (Eds.), *Synaesthesia: Classic and contemporary readings* (pp. 148–172). Oxford: Blackwell.

Grossenbacher, P., & Lovelace, C.T. (2001). Mechanisms of synesthesia: Cognitive and physiological constraints. *Trends in Cognitive Sciences, 5,* 36–41.

Harrison, J. (2001). *Synaesthesia: The strangest thing.* New York: Oxford.

Harrison, J., & Baron-Cohen, S. (1995). Synaesthesia: Reconciling the subjective with the objective. *Endeavour, 19,* 157–160.

Harrison, J., & Baron-Cohen, S. (1997). Synaesthesia: An introduction. In S. Baron-Cohen & J. Harrison (Eds.), *Synaesthesia: Classic and contemporary readings* (pp. 3–16). Oxford: Blackwell.

Hoffman, R. (1978). Developmental changes in human evoked potentials to patterned stimuli recorded at different scalp locations. *Child Development, 49,* 110–118.

Howells, T.H. (1944). The experimental development of color-tone synesthesia. *Journal of Experimental Psychology, 34,* 87–103.

Jacobs, L., Karpik, A., Bozian, D., & Gothgen, S. (1981). Auditory-visual synesthesia. *Archives of Neurology, 38,* 211–216.

Jacome, D.E. (1999). Volitional monocular Lilliputian visual hallucinations and synesthesia. *European Neurology, 41,* 54–56.

Kelly, E.K. (1934). An experimental attempt to produce artificial chromaesthesia by the technique of conditioned response. *Journal of Experimental Psychology, 17,* 315–341.

Leuba, C. (1940). Images as conditioned sensations. *Journal of Experimental Psychology, 26,* 345–351.

Leuba, C., & Dunlap, R. (1951). Conditioning imagery. *Journal of Experimental Psychology, 41*, 352–355.

Lewkowicz, D.J., & Turkewitz, G. (1980). Cross-modal equivalence in early infancy: Auditory-visual intensity matching. *Developmental Psychology, 16*, 597–607.

Luria, A. (1968). *The mind of a mnemonist.* New York: Basic Books.

Marks, L.E. (1975). On colored-hearing synesthesia: Cross-modal translations of sensory dimensions. *Psychological Bulletin, 82*, 303–331.

Marks, L.E. (2000). Synesthesia. In E. Cardena, S.J. Lynn, & S.C. Krippner (Eds.), *Varieties of anomalous experience: Phenomenological and scientific foundations.* Washington, DC: American Psychological Association.

Marks, L.E., Hammeal, R.J., & Bornstein, M.H. (1987). Perceiving similarity and comprehending metaphor. *Monographs of the Society for Research in Child Development, 52*, 1–100.

Martino, G., & Marks, L.E. (2001). Synesthesia: Strong and weak. *Current Directions in Psychological Science, 10*, 61–65.

Mattingley, J.B., Rich, A.N., Yelland, G., & Bradshaw, J.L. (2001). Unconscious priming eliminates automatic binding of colour and alphanumeric form in synaesthesia. *Nature, 410*, 580–582.

Maurer, D. (1993). Neonatal synaesthesia: Implications for the processing of speech and faces. In B. de Boysson-Bardies et al. (Eds.), *Developmental neurocognition: Speech and face processing in the first year of life.* Dordrecht: Kluwer.

McGurk, H., & MacDonald, J. (1976). Hearing lips and seeing voices. *Nature, 264*, 746–748.

Morgan, G.A., Goodson, F.E., & Jones, T. (1975). Age differences in the associations between felt temperatures and color choices. *American Journal of Psychology, 88*, 125–130.

Nunn, J.A., Gregory, L.J., Brammer, M., Williams, S.C.R., Parslow, D.M., Morgan, M.J., Morris, R.G., Bullmore, E.T., Baron-Cohen, S., & Gray, J.A. (2002). Functional magnetic resonance imaging of synesthesia: Activation of V4/V8 by spoken words. *Nature Reviews Neuroscience, 5*, 371–375.

Odgaard, E.C., Flowers, J.H., & Bradman, H.L. (1999). An investigation of the cognitive and perceptual dynamics of a colour-digit synaesthete. *Perception, 28*, 651–664.

Palmeri, T.J., Blake, R., Marois, R., Flanery, M., & Whetsell, W. (2002). The perceptual reality of synesthetic colors. *Proceedings of the National Academy of Sciences, USA, 99*, 4127–4131.

Paulesu, E., Harrison, J., Baron-Cohen, S., Watson, J.D., Goldstein, L., Heather, J., Frackowiak, R.S., & Frith, C.D. (1995). The physiology of coloured hearing: A PET activation study of colour-word synaesthesia. *Brain, 118*, 661–676.

Podoll, K., & Robinson, D. (2002). Auditory-visual synaesthesia in a patient with basilar migraine. *Journal of Neurology, 249*, 476–477.

Ramachandran, V., & Hubbard, E. (2001). Psychophysical investigations into the neural basis of synaesthesia. *Proceedings of the Royal Society of London, B, 268*, 979–983.

Ramachandran, V., & Hubbard, E. (2003). Hearing colors, tasting shapes. *Scientific American, 233(5)*, 52–59.

Share, D.L., & Gur, T. (1999). How reading begins: A study of preschoolers' print identification strategies. *Cognition and Instruction, 17*, 177–213.

Stevenson, R.J., Boakes, R.A., & Prescott, J. (1998). Changes in odor sweetness resulting from implicit learning of a simultaneous odor-sweetness association: An example of learned synesthesia. *Learning and Motivation, 29*, 113–132.

Vike, J., Jabbari, B., & Maitland, C.G. (1984). Auditory-visual synesthesia: Report of a case with intact visual pathways. *Archives of Neurology, 41*, 680–681.

Werner, H. (1940). *Comparative psychology of mental development.* New York: Harper.

Wolff, P., Matsumiya, Y., Abrohms, I.F., van Velzer, C., & Lombroso, C.T. (1974). The effect of white noise on the somatosensory evoked responses in sleeping newborn infants. *Electroencephalography and Clinical Neurophysiology, 37*, 269–274.

Part V

Commentary

12

Synesthesia: Implications for Attention, Binding, and Consciousness—A Commentary

Anne Treisman

S ynesthesia invites us to imagine a world of experience different from that in which most of us live. It fascinates us because it offers a case where qualia—those essentially private, subjective experiences—can be shown to differ substantially between individuals, or at least to differ in the conditions in which they arise. Despite the strangeness, it seems fairly easy to imagine synesthesia without directly experiencing it, because it usually involves a familiar set of sensations. The strangeness (for most people) is in the context that elicits them. By far the most common form generates illusory colors from spoken or written words or characters, but a variety of other pairings can also occur. Researchers have looked for possible functional accounts of the origin of synesthesia and speculated about its developmental history. In addition, both psychologists and philosophers have used synesthesia as a window through which to gain insight into more specific questions, including the nature of feature binding, the role played by attention, and, more ambitiously, the nature of consciousness. The chapters in this book offer grist to these mills.

Speculations on the Origins of Synesthesia

In looking for an evolutionary story to predict the mapping of qualia to external stimuli, we might expect some pressure for qualia to correlate with those distinctions that are most relevant for survival. What might they be? One could imagine having one kind of qualitative experience for friends, another for various kinds of danger, perhaps separating those requiring flight from those requiring fight. For example, good things to be approached (ice cream, comfortable pillows, or potential mates), might elicit qualia of type x (say, colors), and things to avoid might all elicit qualia of type y or z (say, varying brightness or pitch). On this view the qualia would arise at a late stage, well beyond the level of perceptual processing. It is possible that simpler organisms, if they have qualia at all, show this kind of organization. In fact, humans also embody this evolutionary pressure through the qualia that accompany emotions—fear of snakes, guns, thunder and lightning, pleasure for food, friends, comfort, and so on. Synesthesia, if it occurred in the domain of emotions, would presumably take the form of unusual and arbitrary pairings, such as amusement on seeing a snake or an enemy.

There are, however, countervailing pressures to discriminate the nature of the information on which we base our responses and to learn to represent the world. This maximizes the flexibility of behavior, leaving us free to choose appropriate responses in particular contexts rather than hard wiring them all. Sensory receptors, by their nature, must be segregated by the type of physical stimulus to which they respond—for example, wavelengths, sound frequencies, or chemical composition. At more central stages of perceptual coding, we modify the sensory distinctions and segregate the data by their sources, using the variations in reflectance, shape, texture, pitch, and loudness that characterize real world objects and events. It is at this intermediate level that qualia typically arise. We experience the compromises between physical distance and retinal size, viewing angle and frontal plane, illumination and reflectance, that we call the visual constancies and that reflect both the objects in the world and the viewing conditions under which they appear. Still more centrally, we classify and label objects or events, whether with words or with nonverbal "mentalese." Synesthesia is often triggered in a top-down direction from this higher level, influenced by meaning. For example, Smilek, Dixon, and Merikle (this volme) changed the synesthetic color experienced by their observer by embedding it in either a letter or a digit context. But the effect was on perceptual qualia, generated from an earlier level in the process through some form of reentry—not categories but sensations.

So far, nothing suggests that synesthesia, as actually experienced, would be advantageous to the goals of fitness and survival. Perhaps the redundancy of representation creates some benefit—two sets of qualia for one set of stimuli. Could this redundancy as such conceivably convey some advantage in speed and salience? Or might it compensate in cases of sensory or brain damage to specialized areas? I would argue against this; that there is, in fact, no real redundancy at the perceptual level because the dependencies are one way; colors are evoked by physical letters, but letters are not evoked by physical colors. If letter discrimination fails, the color too will disappear.[1] The redundancy is only in the qualia, not in the sensory coding. However this could be useful in memory retention if patterns of color are better retained than patterns of letters or number. Some synesthetes have claimed that the additional qualia help them remember better by providing distinctive codes for alphanumeric symbols or words. One synesthete was tested on recall of digits and showed superior immediate recall, no forgetting over a 48-hr delay, and a large decrement when the digits were presented in colors incongruent with her synesthetic colors (Smilek, Dixon, Cudahy & Merikle, 2002). The remarkable mnemonist described by Luria (1968) also had extensive synesthesia, a fact that may or may not be a coincidence. However, any advantage to his memory was at least partly offset by the intrusiveness of the synesthetic qualia, which blocked his ability to form conceptual abstractions. Altogether these pressures do not seem to have been strong enough for the majority of us to evolve more than one type of qualia per type of sensory input.

So far I have considered only the literal form of synesthesia, in which qualia are directly evoked by the stimuli. There is also a much more widespread phenomenon that may be related: the widely shared propensity for metaphorical mapping. For example, most people associate high tones with light colors, small objects, and spatial height, and low tones with dark colors, large objects, and low spatial positions; "hot" tempers are associated with "seeing red" and calm with "a green thought in a green shade" (Marvell, 1681). The metaphorical mappings reflect a fundamental aspect of our use and understanding of language, particularly in literary contexts and poetry (Ramachandran & Hubbard, 2001b).

Many researchers (including Maurer & Mondloch, this volume) have proposed that synesthesia is an earlier or more extreme form of this universal propensity to create analogies. However, it seems difficult to reconcile the idiosyncracy of the synesthetic mappings and their limited range for any individual synesthete (often only alphanumeric characters with colors) with the more systematic metaphorical links expressed in our use of language and in our conceptual or emotional associations across different sense modalities. Synesthetes do not generally experience in a more concrete form the most widely shared metaphorical associations. They show little or no agreement among themselves on the particular word–color mapping selected. There are exceptions: in color–taste synesthesia, some tastes are mediated through sound similarities; for example, Ward and Simner (2003) reported that "the phonemes that trigger a given taste tend also to appear in the name of the corresponding foodstuff (e.g. /I/, /n/ and /s/ can trigger a taste of mince /mIns/) and there is often a semantic association between the triggering word and taste (e.g. the word blue tastes 'inky')." But in general, synesthetic mappings are arbitrary.

If the two phenomena are indeed distinct, then a further question arises: whether the sensory convergence that seems to be experienced by infants (Mark & Odgaard's "monesthesia," this volume) provides the roots for synesthesia, as proposed by Maurer and Mondloch (this volume), or for metaphor, or for both along two separate developmental paths, or, indeed, for neither.

Given the difficulty of finding a plausible evolutionary advantage conferred by synesthesia, we need some alternative story. It may appear in occasional individuals as a byproduct of some other adaptation. The proposal that it reflects incomplete pruning of neural connections between different specialized modules in the course of neural maturation seems currently the most likely possibility (Ramachandran & Hubbard, 2001b). However, the fact that in speech–color synesthesia it seems to take over the visual color areas in the left hemisphere (Nunn et al., 2002) suggests that, once present, it may confer some advantages. It certainly appears to give pleasure and to be highly valued by most synesthetes, although exceptions do occur (see Day, this volume).

Is Attention Necessary for Synesthesia to Occur?

I turn next to consider what synesthesia can teach us about psychological mechanisms on the one hand and philosophical puzzles on the other. One important debate concerns the role of attention. This is an interesting issue because it may throw some light both on the level at which synesthesia arises and on the mechanisms of attention. The question is discussed in a number of the chapters in this book, and authors divide into two different camps.

In trying to make sense of the findings, it may be helpful first to distinguish several senses in which processing can be said to be automatic or free of attentional demands. Processing may be described as automatic: (1) if it occurs involuntarily and cannot be voluntarily controlled; (2) if it can be applied in parallel across different elements within a single task, as in visual search for pop-out targets; (3) if it can be done concurrently with some other task without suffering interference; or (4) if it takes place without awareness of the evoking stimuli. Not all these criteria always coexist. Indeed, research on synesthesia illustrates a number of possible dissociations. Table 12.1 summarizes the results from a variety of different paradigms (most of them described in other chapters in this book).

Voluntary control

Synesthesia does seem to be involuntary. It can give rise to McCollough aftereffects, even in observers who do not know what to expect (Blake et al., this volume). It causes interference or facilitation in the Stroop-like task of naming actual colors that are either incongruent or congruent with the synesthetic colors of letters that immediately preceded them (Blake et al., this volume; Rich & Mattingley, this volume). This interference can, however, be indirectly modulated, for example, when attention is directed to one or the other level of a global–local stimulus (Ramachandran & Hubbard, 2001a). The other criteria for automaticity are more controversial, as shown by the debates in this book.

Parallel Processing

Parallel processing is typically tested in search tasks and in tests of the salience of grouping. Smilek, Dixon, and Merikle (this volume) and Blake et al. (this volume) reported that a target letter in a background of other letters can be found much faster by synesthetes for whom its color is distinctive than by nonsynesthetes, suggesting to Smilek et al. that synesthetic colors are bound to graphemes before the graphemes are explicitly recognized. If the target had to be consciously recognized before generating its synesthetic color, the search would already be over, leaving no scope for any benefit to accrue. However, as Sagiv and Robertson (this volume) point out, the result is ambiguous: It could be due to the synesthetic colors of the distractors only, allowing them to be more easily discarded as nontargets, or it could also mediate pop out of the target's synesthetic color. Sagiv & Robertson tested which of these alternatives occurs in synesthesia and obtained a clear answer (see table 12.1).

Search is fast or parallel only when the distractors generate synesthetic colors, implying that the performance of synesthetes differs from that of normals only when distractor colors are available to benefit search through grouping and guidance effects. If the distractors produce no colors (because they are nonsense shapes), the target no longer pops out. There is no evidence from the search task, then, that the target identity is preattentively or unconsciously available.

The same argument may not apply, however, to the camouflage variant of search, also used by Smilek, Dixon, and Merikle (this volume) in which the search elements are placed on a colored background that either matches or does not match the target's synesthetic color. They found faster search when the target's synesthetic color contrasted with the background than when it roughly matched the background color. According to Sagiv and Robertson's (this volume) argument, what should matter here is whether the distractors match or mismatch the background rather than whether the target does. These have not, to my knowledge, been separated in the camouflage paradigm. Smilek et al. (2002) used a similar camouflage paradigm in a classification task with a single item that either matched the background color or contrasted with it. They found faster responses when there was a contrast. However, Blake et al. (this volume) found no interactions between synesthetic color and background color in a vowel/consonant classification

Table 12.1. Is synesthesia automatic?

| | | Criteria | | |
Experimental Paradigm	Involuntary	Parallel	No impairment in dual task	No Awareness
Stroop	Y (Blake, Rich)	N (Sagiv, Spatial effects)	N (Rich: Gap in frame)	N (Rich)
Search		Y for distractors, N for target (Sagiv, Blake) Y (Smilek)		Y (Smilek) N (Sagiv)
Attentional masking		Y (Smilek)		
Background camouflage		Y (Smilek, Search (Smilek, RT) N (Sagiv, RT; Blake, RT)		
Crowding				Y (Ramachandran)
McCollough effect	Y (Blake)			
Salient grouping		Y (Blake, Smilek, Ramachandran)		
Global/Local	N (Ramachandran)		N (Rich) N (Blake)	
Attentional Blink			N (Rich)	

Y = yes; N= no. Authors' names refer to chapters in this volume.

task. Sagiv and Robertson attribute the synesthetic benefit of contrast to possible artifacts in the strategies participants could use. When they controlled the strategies, they found no evidence that the synesthetic color contrast from the background helped the target emerge preattentively.

Using a grouping paradigm, both Ramachandran and Hubbard (2001a) and Smilek et al. (this volume) found that the shape of a group of elements can be made salient by their synesthetic color, giving apparently parallel access to each element of the embedded shape without requiring a serial scan. The synesthetic color in this demonstration does seem to be available in parallel across a number of elements. Observers were given plenty of time for the group to emerge, so the synesthetic color may help maintain the grouping once it is formed rather than mediating its initial emergence.

Sagiv and Robertson (this volume) devised a different test of parallel processing in which they varied the spatial layout to place synesthetic distractors either inside or outside the window of attention. They showed that naming the colors of target dots was slowed more when the competing letters were within the window of attention than when they were not. Their result shows that spatially deployed attention results in parallel processing, at least within the window of attention.

Dual-task paradigms

Dual-task paradigms test whether attention, in the sense of resources from a limited pool, can make a difference to the degree of synesthesia generated. Rich and Mattingley (this volume) varied the difficulty of a concurrent gap discrimination task and found less effect of congruity or incongruity between synesthetic and objective colors in color naming when the task was more demanding. Rich and Mattingley, Blake et al. (this volume), and Ramachandran and Hubbard (2001a) showed reduced synesthetic interference from the letters at the unattended level when the stimuli were global letters made of local letters. Mattingley, Rich, Yelland, and Bradshaw (2001) tested the Stroop congruency effect on color naming in an attentional blink paradigm and found that synesthetic interference and facilitation were eliminated not only when the inducing letter was invisible because it occurred during the attentional blink, but also throughout the task, whenever participants were required to do the competing task. It seems clear that by the dual task criterion, attention to the inducing letters can modulate the strength of the synesthetic color, or at least the degree to which it interferes with the primary task.

Absence of awareness

Can synesthetic colors be generated by letters that are not consciously seen? Here again, there is some apparent disagreement in the results. Strong evidence for implicit generation of synesthetic colors comes from Ramachandran and Hubbard's (2001b) demonstration that colors can be seen even when the letter itself is invisible because of crowding in peripheral vision. In contrast, Rich et al. (this volume) found no evidence that briefly presented masked letters could interfere with color naming in their Stroop-like paradigm, even though the same masked letters did prime letter-naming. Proving the null hypothesis is always tricky; it could be that letter naming is more susceptible to priming and interference than color naming is, or that there is simply higher variance in color-naming times (Blake et al., this volume).

More generally, we may be able to resolve the disagreements by considering why the letters (or other evoking stimuli) fail to reach awareness. It is quite possible that they are blocked from consciousness for different reasons and at different levels of processing, depending on the paradigm used, and that the same cause will affect their ability to generate synesthesia. For example, if the exposure is too brief to generate a conscious experience, it may also be too brief to generate synesthetic qualia. There may be some minimal duration of activation that is needed to fire cross-cortical connections to generate synesthetic sensations, and this level of activation may also be sufficient to ensure conscious awareness. Below that level, the activation may still be sufficient to prime perception within the same module (a briefly exposed letter priming a subsequent presentation of the same letter). Alternatively, the letters could fail to be seen even with an extended exposure duration if there is interference from adjacent or subsequent contours or if attention is directed elsewhere. In this case the letter may be identified within its module and generate its synesthetic color but may be actively suppressed from conscious awareness because it is competing at the output of the module with other stimuli. Binocular rivalry may offer a further test of the role of conscious awareness in synesthesia. Suppose G is red and X is blue for a particular synesthete. If we show her an array of Gs to one eye and an array of Xs to the other, she would probably see the two fields alternating, or perhaps a patchwork of areas containing the two letters. The question is whether the colors rival as well as the letters and, if so, whether they can get out of step with the letters. This would offer further evidence that letters need not be conscious to generate their synesthetic color. An analogous dissociation of real color from shape and location can be found when the color of a stimulus is suppressed in rivalry, but its shape and location are able nevertheless to generate stereoscopic depth (Treisman, 1962).

The results presented in this book cast further doubt on the concept of automaticity, confirming that the different criteria need not cohere. Is there any way of reconciling the disparate results to reach some conclusions about synesthesia? On the issue of unconscious processing, the paradigms that fail to show it all use time pressure to prevent awareness, whereas the best demonstration of unconscious synesthesia is its emergence in the crowding paradigm, where time is not an issue. Among the parallel processing paradigms, the salient grouping induced by synesthetic contrasts is, again, not a time-limited process but rather one in which parallel access to the synesthetic colors is maintained once they have been generated. In the search tasks, the account given by Sagiv and Robertson seems convincing, the distractors group by color once they have been processed, and this facilitates their rejection. In dual-task tests, there is unanimity that synesthesia is reduced when attention must be shared with or devoted to some other task. Finally, in tasks testing voluntary control, there is again unanimity that synesthesia is involuntary and can only be indirectly modulated—for example, by attending to stimuli at a different scale. A reasonably coherent story can be told if we assume that it takes a little time for synesthesia to emerge and that it emerges more strongly when attention is directed to the evoking stimuli. Consciousness of their identity may not always be necessary if sufficient time is available. However, this last issue is still controversial.

Synesthesia and Binding

Can synesthesia throw any light on the binding problem—the question how we integrate the different features of an object to form a correct unified whole? Synesthesia by definition links two normally independent qualia, so it seems a promising domain to explore in relation to binding. There are three possible ways of solving the binding problem: (1) through conjunction detectors that directly sense the co-occurrence of particular features such as a rectangular red horizontal object moving left; (2) by serial attention to each filled location to determine which features share the same origin (the feature integration theory account; Treisman & Gelade, 1980); and (3) through synchronized neural firing to label the features that belong to the same object (Singer & Gray, 1995). All three are almost certainly correct to some degree. Single units that act as conjunction detectors for certain properties have been described by many neuroscientists (e.g., Gross, Rocha-Miranda & Bender, 1972; Tanaka, 1996). However, the combinatorial explosion makes it unlikely that this could be a universal solution. We can see any of millions of arbitrary combinations the first time they appear. There is considerable evidence for the second, attention-based account (see Treisman, 1996, 1999, for reviews) and also for the third (Singer & Gray, 1995; but see also Shadlen & Movshon, 1999). These two accounts answer different versions of the binding problem and are therefore perfectly compatible. Focused attention could solve the problem of specifying which features should be conjoined, and synchrony could be a way of coding the conjunctions once they have been identified.

Kahneman, Treisman, and Gibbs (1992) distinguished object identification (by matching to stored types in a recognition network) from object perception, equated with the activation of temporary object files or tokens. They proposed that the perceptual experience of seeing a particular instance of an object depends on forming an integrated representation, binding its current features in an "object file" addressed primarily by its temporo-spatial coordinates. When a particular word is heard or seen, the theory predicts that it will form a token representation to mediate conscious experience of the sound or sight. Perhaps a synesthetic experience is evoked when the relevant letter or word imports its associated color into the object file that mediates experience of the word.

Prima facie, synesthesia seems to offer an unusual form of binding against which these accounts might be tested. However, it differs from the normal cases in several ways. First, one of the relevant features is internally generated. The color comes not from the senses but indirectly, from the identity of the associated shape. So a single sensory feature gives rise to two different qualia. Second, the color is bound to the letter or word in the sense that they are permanently linked, but it need not always be perceptually bound in the sense that the shape and color form a single integrated percept. In some synesthetes, the color is seen as located in the letter, although the actual color of the ink can also, in some mysterious way, be clearly seen. Other synesthetes do not experience the colors as perceptually bound to the letters. One synesthete (Rich & Mattingley, 2002) describes his experiences as clearly not bound: "Tuesday is yellow. I don't see it anywhere in particular; rather I have a general awareness of yellowness in relation to the word" (p. 44). Tyler (this volume) writes "I do not see the synesthetic image at the same time as the visual array from the outside world, but I can switch voluntarily between seeing and thinking of the image of something. It is almost as though I can look through the page or the wall to see the dark field of the imagination behind it" (p. 35). In the case of cross-modal synesthesia (e.g., speech–color), the sound and the color cannot be bound to form an integral object in the same way that features can be bound within a single modality. Perhaps the color is bound to a visual image of the letters generated from the auditory letter or word.

Synesthetic binding also differs from regular binding in that there is actually no binding problem, in the sense of no uncertainty about which features belong together. They are permanently linked, perhaps hard wired. All that happens in a synesthetic experience is that the physical stimulus reliably evokes an illusory feature on a different dimension. Thus it seems more likely that the association to the evoked feature is stored with the permanent word types than with particular tokens. This would also explain why synesthesia is asymmetric: Words evoke colors but colors do not usually evoke the corresponding word.

Feature integration theory would predict that if binding is involved in synesthesia, then attention should also be needed. Its role is controversial. However, the role envisaged for attention is assumed to suppress illusory bindings and to determine the correct ones by narrowing the focus to one item at a time. These roles seem not to be relevant to synesthetic binding. Perhaps if several synesthetic stimuli were simultaneously presented and attention were diverted, the colors might migrate between the letters or words producing illusory synesthetic conjunctions. This seems unlikely. The usual report is that when attention is diverted from a shape, no color is experienced, not that the color is seen attached to the wrong object. Moreover, the integrated percept of synesthetic feature with stimulus features occurs only in some synesthetes who "project" the color onto the shape, so attentional binding is unlikely to be the whole answer. It would be interesting to test whether these projective synesthetes are the only ones who depend on attention for their synesthetic experiences, whereas those who see colors in the mind's eye, or floating above the object, do not. This would strengthen both feature integration theory and the hypothesis that attention is essential for the occurrence of synesthesia, as would the occurrence in the same individuals of illusory conjunctions when their attention is diverted elsewhere.

A simple demonstration that attention is necessary to synesthesia would be weaker evidence for its role in binding because there are two other reasons that attention might be needed in synesthesia: (1) to identify the shape and meaning of the eliciting shape, and/or to bring it above a threshold at which it elicits color qualia; and (2) to retrieve the "correct" synesthetic binding from memory. All in all, much as I would like feature integration theory to be relevant, it seems most likely that attention plays one or both of these additional roles, ensuring that the eliciting stimulus is coded to a sufficiently high or conscious level to elicit synesthetic qualia.

On the other hand, it is intriguing that PET or fMRI activation in left parieto-temporal areas is reported to be present during synesthesia. Parietal damage leads to large deficits in binding in Balint's syndrome patients (Humphreys, Cinel, Wolfe, Olson & Klempen, 2000; Robertson, Treisman, Friedman-Hill & Grabowecky, 1997). These are the same areas that seem to be active in perceptual binding in normal participants (Corbetta, Shulman, Miezin & Petersen, 1995). Whether this coincidence reflects some kind of binding in synesthesia as well is still an open question.

Could the synchronized firing account of binding be relevant in synesthesia? Synchrony in the theory maintains the binding of the preselected features, rather than selecting which features should be bound. It could therefore be the neural code underlying the temporary conscious experiences of synesthesia. For example, a sensorily activated word could be represented by firing at a particular rate in one set of neurons, which in turn might generate synchronized firing in the neurons representing the synesthetic color. Permanently synchronized firing does not seem a plausible way of maintaining the long-term associations. Some structural connections would be needed to ensure that synchronous firing in one module automatically evokes it in another.

Synesthesia and Qualia: Implications for Functionalist Accounts of Consciousness

What implications does synesthesia have for the philosophical analysis of consciousness? Gray (this volume) uses the existence of synesthesia to disprove functionalist accounts of consciousness. Like him, I am quite uneasy with the functionalist account of consciousness, which seems to leave out something essential. However, Gray's use of synesthesia to attack functionalism seems problematic. He defines functionalism as follows:

> A full function for a given difference between qualia then consists in a detailed account of the corresponding differences in inputs, outputs, and the mechanisms that mediate between input and output. If such a full functional account is given, then, according to functionalism, there is no further answer to the original question, what is the difference between the subjective experiences (the qualia) of red and green? (p. 130)

Gray then draws two inferences: (1) "for any discriminable difference between qualia there must be an equivalent discriminable difference in function; (2) "for any discriminable functional difference, there must be a discriminable difference between qualia" (p. 130). The first inference seems fine, but I am less sure about the second. It does not follow from "all dogs are animals" that "all animals are dogs." Gray is well aware of this. But then he describes the claim as reasonable for domains in which qualia normally accompany functions. This seems odd to me. If the input-mechanism-output functions have more than one component, then they could differ in one component but share another. Qualia that arise in the shared component might well be indistinguishable, even though the earlier components (and any qualia associated with those) are different. In the case of synesthesia, the inputs are obviously different and go to different sensory processing mechanisms, but the outputs from these mechanisms could end up activating the same area and producing the same qualia. I can press a switch and turn a light on with my finger or with my thumb or by reaching with a stick. The effect on the light is the same even though the muscles used are different. Sensory psychologists have shown that we hear a change in the direction of a sound both when the intensity ratio at the two ears changes and when the time of arrival of the sound at the two ears changes. Is the case of synesthesia logically different from this? Or is it different from the existence of multiple cues to visual depth? Or, for that matter, is synesthesia different from the parallel experiences of color from an after-image and from a real object that Gray cites later in his chapter?

In colored–hearing synesthesia, functional magnetic resonance imaging (fMRI) results suggest that the same brain area is activated both by visual colors and by the sounds of words (Nunn et al., 2002). Because different pathways to this area activate it in color vision and in auditory word synesthesia and yet the qualia are the same (assuming for the moment that this is the case), Gray suggests that functionalism must be wrong. But, if anything, I would think that the finding supports the functionalist view. It locates a single area of activation that gives rise to the same qualia, despite very different origins. There is no claim that the color qualia arise within either set of separate pathways leading to the jointly activated area. Either these pathways perform functions that remain unconscious, or they may give rise to different qualia (for instance, the sounds of the words in the case of speech–color synesthesia and the shapes and brightnesses in the case of visual letters).

A more serious challenge to the functionalist view might be the occurrence of qualia that are identical arising from activations that share nothing in common. The fMRI results of Nunn et al. (2002) might be cited as examples in this context, too, if we take corresponding areas in the two hemispheres as being functionally distinct. The synesthetic colors in this study were associated with activation in area V4/V8 in the left hemisphere, whereas visually detected colors activated the corresponding areas in the right hemisphere. Of course, these areas do have a considerable amount in common—the symmetry and correspondence in function between the two hemispheres. But if we accepted the argument that corresponding areas in the two hemispheres are sufficiently different for their shared qualia to pose a problem for the functionalist account, it would not be necessary to appeal to synesthesia to disprove functionalism. It would be sufficient that nonsynesthetes see identical colors (and experience many other identical qualia) whether the corresponding areas of the right or of the left hemisphere are active.

In another argument against functionalism, Gray (this volume) suggests that it depends on an associative learning account of synesthesia. He and his colleagues collected data to refute this claim, finding no evidence that synesthesia could be induced by extensive pairing of colors and words (see Nunn et al., 2002). The data are interesting, but the parallel with functionalism seems somewhat arbitrary. "Function" in relation to functionalism need not imply a purpose or goal; it is used rather in the sense of "operation"—what is done rather than why. Sparking over is a function in this sense, even though, as Gray (this volume) states, "the occurrence of the synesthetic color experience in colored-hearing synesthesia plays no functional role in relation either to speech or language perception or to color vision" (p. 141).

The hypothesis that Gray (this volume) proposes as an alternative to functionalism the "tissue" hypothesis: "A contrary view, however, holds that there is something special about the actual components out of which brains are made and that this something provides a necessary condition for consciousness" (p. 134). Gray's analysis of synesthesia in terms of sparking over due to hard-wired connections between areas that are not usually connected seems plausible and is also favored by other researchers (e.g., Grossenbacher & Lovelace, 2001; Ramachandran & Hubbard, 2001b). But it is less clear to me that it conflicts with the functionalist claim that the hardware is irrelevant and that all that matters is the function being implemented. I would argue that the two hypotheses are incompatible only if no other physical instantiations of sparking over can exist, which is certainly not the case. The words "sparking over," in fact, originate with electrical circuits rather than with neuroscience.

The controversy will be difficult to resolve because a lot depends on how we determine whether two functions are the same across different physical instantiations. Whether they are judged the same must depend on the level of abstraction being considered. Those supporting the tissue hypothesis could always argue that there are differences in function at a level below that selected level and that these are differences that mediate the presence or absence of qualia. The difference between the tissue view and the functionalist view then becomes quite elusive. But unless functionalism can offer a reasoned account of which functions are identical to qualia and which are not, it still faces the problem of accounting for consciousness. The hope is presumably that functionalism will be able to do that with further research. This is what the search for the neural correlates of consciousness is about. The goal is to find a difference in the functions that will predict when there should be qualia and when there should not. Even then, I am not certain that Chalmers' (1995) "hard problem" of consciousness will dissolve away. But I see that as a problem for functionalists, and not for the existence of synesthesia.

Clearly, we have a great deal left to learn about synesthesia and the issues to which it relates: attention, binding, and consciousness. This book offers a progress report and some important signposts of the directions for future research. Explorations of the neural basis of the experience are likely to play a central role.

Acknowledgments This research was supported by National Institutes of Health (NIH) grant number 1 RO1 MH58383, "Visual coding and the deployment of attention," and by NIH grant number 1RO1MH062331, "Spatial representations and attention," held jointly with Lynn Robertson.

Note

1. Unless the discrimination remains unconsciously present, which may perhaps leave synesthetic experiences intact.

References

Chalmers, D.J. (1995). The puzzle of conscious experience. *Scientific American, 273*, 80–86.

Corbetta, M., Shulman, G.L., Miezin, F.M., & Petersen, S.E. (1995). Superior parietal cortex activation during spatial attention shifts and visual feature conjunction. *Science, 270*, 802–805.

Gross, C., Rocha-Miranda, C.E., & Bender, D.B. (1972). Visual properties of neurons in inferotemporal cortex of the macaque. *Journal of Neurophysiology, 35*, 96–111, 802–805.

Grossenbacher, P.,G., & Lovelace, C.T. (2001). Mechanisms of synesthesia: Cognitive and physiological constraints. *Trends in Cognitive Sciences, 5*, 36–41.

Humphreys, G.W., Cinel, C., Wolfe, J., Olson, A., & Klempen, N. (2000). Fractionating the binding process: Neuropsychological evidence distinguishing binding of form from binding of surface features. *Vision Research, 40*, 1569–1596.

Kahneman, D., Treisman, A., & Gibbs, B. (1992). The reviewing of object files: Object-specific integration of information. *Cognitive Psychology, 24*, 175–219.

Luria, A. (1968). *The mind of a mnemonist.* New York: Basic Books.

Marvell, Andrew. (1681). The garden. In M. Marvell (Ed.), *Miscellaneous poems.* (Reprinted 1969). Menston, UK: Scolar Press.

Mattingley, J.B., Rich, A.N., Yelland, G., & Bradshaw, J.L. (2001). Unconscious priming eliminates automatic binding of color and alphanumeric form in synaesthesia. *Nature, 410*, 580–582.

Nunn, J.A., Gregory, L.J., Brammer, M., Williams, S.C.R., Parslow, D.M., Morgan, M.J., Morris, R.G., Bullmore, E.T., Baron-Cohen, S., & Gray, J.A. (2002). Functional magnetic resonance inaging of synesthesia: Activation of V4/V8 by spoken words. *Nature Neuroscience, 5*, 371–375.

Ramachandran, V.S., & Hubbard, E.M. (2001a). Psychophysical investigations into the neural basis of synaesthesia. *Proceedings of the Royal Society London, B, 268*, 979–983.

Ramachandran, V.S., & Hubbard, E.M. (2001b). Synaesthesia—a window into perception, thought and language. *Journal of Consciousness Studies, 8*, 3–34.

Rich, A.N., & Mattingley, J.B. (2002). Anomalous perception in synaesthesia: A cognitive neuroscience perspective. *Nature Reviews Neuroscience, 3*, 43–52.

Robertson, L. Treisman, A., Friedman-Hill, S., & Grabowecky, M. (1997). The interaction of spatial and object pathways: Evidence from Balint's syndrome. *Journal of Cognitive Neuroscience, 9*, 295–317.

Shadlen, M.N., & Movshon, J.A. (1999). Synchrony unbound: A critical evaluation of the binding hypothesis. *Neuron, 24*, 67–77.

Singer, W., & Gray, C.M. (1995). Visual feature integration and the temporal correlation hypothesis. *Annual Review of Neuroscience, 18,* 555–586.

Smilek, D., Dixon, M.J., Cudahy, C., & Merikle, P.M. (2002). Synesthetic color experiences influence memory. *Psychological Science, 13,* 548–552.

Tanaka, K. (1996). Inferotemporal cortex and object vision: Stimulus selectivity and columnar organization. *Annual Review of Neuroscience, 19,* 109–139.

Treisman, A., (1962). Binocular rivalry and stereoscopic depth perception. *Quarterly Journal of Experimental Psychology, 14,* 23–37.

Treisman, A. (1996). The binding problem. *Current Opinion in Neurobiology, 6,* 171–178.

Treisman, A. (1999). Solutions to the binding problem: Progress through controversy and convergence. *Neuron, 24,* 105–110.

Treisman, A., & Gelade, G. (1980). A feature integration theory of attention. *Cognitive Psychology, 12,* 97–136.

Ward, J. & Simner, J. (2003). Lexical gustatory synesthesia: Linguistic and conceptual factors. *Cognition, 89,* 237–261.

Author Index

Subject Index

focusing on one level, ignoring another, 115–116

limited capacity, 111–112

modified standard Navon-type local-global stimuli, 113

parallel processing, 243–245

rapid serial visual presentation, 117–119

restricting, for prime processing, 112

switching between local and global levels, 113–114

voluntary control, 242–243

Attentional blink paradigm, 117–120

Attention/awareness. *See also* Spatial attention; Visual awareness

achromatic figure inducing synesthetic experience, 57

digits embedded in colors, 76–79

four-dot masking, 79–80

modulating synesthesia, 97–98

perceptual grouping, 80–82

role in binding, 76, 84–85

Stroop task, 58

support for binding after, 82–84

support for binding before, 76–82

Auditory color experiences

absolute pitch, 37–38

Beethoven, 39–40

chromatic quality of chords, 39

color associations with chord types, 38–39

color-sound associations, 37–40

major and minor chords, 39

perceived colors of chords, 39

pitch synesthesia, 38

Wagner, 40

Auditory cortical areas, activation in deaf adults, 200

Auditory presentation, grapheme-color synesthete, 162

Auditory replay, epileptic auras, 40–41

Auditory-visual interactions, McGurk effect, 163

Autism, connections to synesthesia, 11

Autobiography, synesthesia, 30

Automaticity

doubt on concept, 246–247

synesthesia, 244

synesthetic colors, 75

Awareness. *See also* Attention/ awareness; Visual awareness

absence, 245–247

making inducing stimuli from, 110–111

Babies. *See also* Neonatal synesthesia

cross-modal correspondences, 196–197

Balint's syndrome

functional imaging study, 102

illusory conjunctions, 92

Beach, Amy

colored hearing, 23

synesthete, 20, 21

Beethoven, color associations, 39–40

Bilingual synesthetes, colored graphemes, 162

Binding. *See also* Preattentive binding

after attention and awareness, 82–84

before attention and awareness, 76–82

behavioral evidence of, as problem, 91–92

digits embedded in colors, 76–79

feature integration theory, 91, 92, 249

four-dot masking, 79–80

perceptual grouping, 80–82

preattentive, 92

role of meaning in, 85–87

synesthesia and, 247–250

Binocular rivalry, consciousness, 246

Biography, synesthesia, 30

Birds. *See* Neonatal synesthesia

Birth. *See also* Neonatal synesthesia

adult like synesthesia at, 194–196

Blessing, synesthesia, 26

Blind adults

neuroimaging studies, 198

synesthetes seeing color, 17

visual cortical activity, 198–200

Blind sight effect, synesthetes, 168

Blood oxygen level dependent (BOLD) activity

behavior of synesthete and signal change, 156

colored-hearing synesthesia, 133

neural basis of synesthesia, 61–64

neural locus of experience, 64–68

object-substitution masking, 60

perpetual grouping, 80–82

photisms, 75

pop-out effect, 59–61

positron-emission tomography (PET), 65, 67

primes and targets, 58

projective vs. associative synes-thetes, 48–49

reaction times to name video colors, 86

reasons for studying, 69–70

recognition of inducing stimulus, 57

response times, 52–53

role of attention, 57

role of attention and awareness in binding, 76, 84–85

role of meaning in binding, 85–87

schematic of possible pathways for form to evoke synesthetic color, 62

semantic context modulating perceived color, 50

spatial attention, 93

Stroop effect, 51–52, 58

support for binding after attention and awareness, 82–84

support for binding before attention and awareness, 76–82

synesthetic colors interacting with real colors, 55–57

synesthetic colors vs. real colors, 51–55

target digit search, 59–60

target-distractor pairing, 59

targets and distractors, 52

unusual conscious experiences, 74–76

varying across individuals, 92–93

Color localization, higher and lower synesthetes, 161

Color matching experiments, synes-thetic vs. real colors, 56

Color-phonemic synesthesia
functional magnetic resonance imaging (fMRI), 65–66

positron-emission tomography (PET), 65

Colors. *See also* Auditory color experiences; Color-graphemic synesthesia; Synesthetic colors
coexistence, 99–101
Crayola Crayons, 13
criteria for selection, 13
number associations, 35–36
synesthetic vs. real, 51–55

Color synesthesia
neural contributions, 101–102
types, 15

"Coming out to my family", synesthe-sia, 18

Competition, synesthetic Stroop task, 109–110

Concurrents, synesthetic experience, 4

Congruency effect
color-naming times, 111, 112–113, 119–120
inducing synesthetic colors by ignoring stimuli, 116–117
magnitude, 113, 116
manipulating, 113
synesthetic colors and color naming, 109–110

Consciousness
alien color effect, 139–141
awareness of red, 166–167
behavior and, 165–166
binocular rivalry, 246
blindside effect, 168
causal mechanism, 128–129
crowding effect, 167–168
functionalism, 129–130, 250
functionalism and hard problem of, 127–130
functionalism vs. tissue approach, 133–136
hard wiring and colored-hearing synesthesia, 136–138
implications for functionalist accounts of, 250–252
neural correlates of, 128
philosophy, 127, 250
primary and secondary inferences, 130
qualia and function, 130
top-down imagery, 168

inferences, 130

vs. tissue approach, 133–136, 252

Functional magnetic resonance imaging (fMRI)

absence of overlap of activations, 67

activation in visual cortex of blind adults, 198–200

auditory cortical area activation in deaf adults, 200

colored-hearing synesthesia, 133, 138, 143, 251

color-phonemic synesthesia, 65–66

synesthesia, 29

Gap-discrimination task, restricting attention for prime processing, 112

Gerstmann's syndrome, components, 182

Gift, synesthesia, 26–30

Global stimuli. See Local-global stimuli

Graphemes. See also Color-graphemic synesthesia

second language, 162–163

tactile, 162

Graphemes within words, synesthetes, 162

Guided search, visual search, 94–96

Hallucinations, Charles Bonnet syndrome, 137

Hard wiring hypothesis, colored-hearing synesthesia, 136–138

Higher synesthetes

color localization, 161

lower and, 154–158

psychophysical properties of induced colors, 156

Hockney, David, synesthetic colors to musical stimuli, 26

Hominid brain organization, 175

Hyperconnectivity gene, emotions, 164

Imagery, synesthetes, 162

Inducer identification, influence of synesthetic color, 59

Inducers

effect of attention on, 97–98

synesthetic stimuli, 4

Inducing stimuli, masking, from awareness, 110–111

Infants. See also Neonatal synesthesia

behavioral evidence for cross-modal correspondences, 201–202

evidence for transient connections, 197–202

linking auditory and visual information, 193–194

neuroimaging studies, 200–201

Institutionalization, pressure on synesthetes, 19–20

Interference effects, letter naming, 58–59

Intermodal vs. intramodal synesthesia, 230–231

Intramodal vs. intermodal synesthesia, 230–231

Investigation, personal, synesthesia, 11–12

Language

adaptationist hypothesis, 176–177

"anatomy is destiny", 173

children, 206

comparative linguistics, 179

cross-modal correspondences, 204–206

evolution, 176–183

Gerstmann's syndrome, 182

manual gesturing, 180–181

metaphorical associations, 172

mirror neurons, 179–180

proto-language theory, 179, 182–183

reading, 232

spandrel hypothesis, 176–177

synergistic boot-strapping of three effects, 181–182

synesthetic boot-strapping theory, 177, 178

synkinesia, 180

thinking, 183

word sound and object appearance, 177–178

Learned associations vs. genuine sensory events, 68

Learning, role in synesthesia, 231–232

Reaction times
  background color congruent or
    incongruent, 99
  color naming, 75
  judging color of target dots, 97–98
  judging color patch, 94
  naming central target, 96
  naming video colors, 86–87
Reader information, synesthesia, 30
Reading, learning, 232
Real colors, synesthetic colors
  interacting with, 55–57
Response times
  number lines, 158–159
  shape of distribution, 159
  target-present trials, 52–53
Rimsky-Korsakov, Nikolai, colored
  musical keys, 22–23

Scientific background, consciousness,
  127
Scientific phenomenon, criteria to
  gain acceptance, 147–148
Search. *See* Visual search
Secrecy, synesthetes, 18
Seizures, auditory replay, 40–41
Self-hypnosis, visual consequences, 41
Sensory brain maps, cross-activation,
  152–154
Sensory cross-talk. *See* Cross-talk
  theory
Sensory matching, children and
  adults, 202–204
Sensory perceptions, synesthesia,
  27–28
Sensory phenomenon, synesthesia,
  149–151
Shape definition, color-graphemic
  synesthetes, 53
Sibelius, Jean, synesthete composer
  and musician, 23, 24
Sixth sense, synesthesia, 26
Size, sensory matching, 202–204
Smell synesthesia, types, 15
Sound synesthesia, types, 15
Spatial attention. *See also* Attention;
  Attention/awareness
  color-graphemic synesthesia, 93
  modulating synesthesia, 97–98,
    103–104

Spatial interactions, double-digit
  number, 162
Special gift, synesthesia, 26–30
Speculations, origins of synesthesia,
  239–242
"Still mostly in the closet," synesthesia,
  18
Stimulus, coexistence of, and synesthetic color, 99–101
Stroop effect
  alien color effect, 140–141
  attentional manipulations, 116
  inducer letter, 58
  naming colors, 51–52, 139–140
Stroop experiment
  evaluating color naming, 93–94
  role of meaning in binding, 85–87
  top-down influences on synesthesia,
    160
Stroop interference, synesthetes, 157
Stroop task
  automaticity of synesthetic colors,
    75
  measures of competition, 109–110
  modified version, 58
Surface lightness, sensory matching,
  202–204
Synesthesia. *See also* Color-graphemic
  synesthesia; Neonatal synesthesia; Theories of synesthesia
  attention modulating, 97–98
  benefits, 20–26
  binding, 247–250
  cases with multiple, 14–15
  category synesthesia, 12
  causes, 152–154
  challenges in study, 7–8
  cognitive, 12
  colored-hearing, 131–133
  color selection criteria, 13
  colors for alphabet letters and
    numbers, 13–14
  concurrents, 4
  constraints on future theories,
    227–228
  cross-activation of sensory maps,
    152–154
  description and terms, 6
  developmental, 3
  diagnosing, 4–5

Tissue approach, functionalism vs., 133–136, 252
Top-down influences
    ambiguous stimuli demonstrating, 160
    synesthesia, 159–160
Torke, Michael, contemporary composer, 25
Touch synesthesia, types, 15
Trigger factor, neurological aspects, 12

Video colors, reaction times for naming, 86–87
Vision synesthesia, types, 15
Visual awareness. *See also* Attention/awareness
    synesthesia and, 98–99
Visual color experiences. *See also* Experiences
    associating colors with alphabet and numbers, 36–37
    color associations of others, 36
    color of numbers, 35–36

colors with numbers, 34–37
cross-modal sensory experience, 36
obligate synesthesia, 35
printed color and synesthetic color, 35
Visual cortex, blind adults, 198–200
Visual imagery, cross-activation of sensory maps, 159–160
Visual processing, synesthesia, 61
Visual search
    design experiments, 93–94
    guided search, 94–96
    pop out, 94, 96
    reaction time to judge color patch, 94
    sample search displays, 94, 95
    synesthesia facilitating, 93–97
Visual selective attention, color-graphemic synesthesia, 108
Visual synesthesia, brain injury or seizures, 16–17

Yoga, visual consequences, 41